Cases and e

Personnel

Cases and exercises in

Personnel

William F. Glueck
The University of Georgia

1978   Revised Edition

BUSINESS PUBLICATIONS, INC.   Dallas, Texas   75243

Irwin-Dorsey Limited   Georgetown, Ontario   L7G 4B3

© BUSINESS PUBLICATIONS, INC., 1974 and 1978

ISBN 0-256-01952-5
Library of Congress Catalog Card No. 77–91323
Printed in the United States of America

1 2 3 4 5 6 7 8 9 0 ML 5 4 3 2 1 0 9 8

*To my parents
and
my brothers and sisters*

PREFACE

The purpose of the book is to provide materials to apply the theories and research findings in personnel. It is designed to be used simultaneously with personnel texts or by itself.

The book contains the following types of materials.

Cases. The cases take place in a variety of settings. They are of varying lengths. The cases describe conditions which are sometimes troubled, sometimes good, and frequently a mixture of both. All the cases are based on real situations. But the situations are frequently disguised. In the first edition, fifty-nine cases were included. In this revised edition, fifty-four cases are given. Seventeen cases were included from the first edition. The others are new to the book.

Incident cases. These casettes are designed to determine if the user can ask the right questions from preliminary data to adequately analyze the problem situation. Eleven incident cases are provided in the revised edition.

Role playing exercises. Role playing exercises allow participants to experience a different kind of learning by placing themselves in the focal persons' positions. Ten role playing exercises are included in this edition.

Cost benefit exercises. Exercises that focus on assessing the value of a personnel activity are included in this edition. One of these is new.

Field experience exercises. Fourteen field exercises require the student to do field research to understand a problem or analyze a personnel activity. Most of these popular exercises are new.

In-basket exercises. Three in-basket exercises are included in this edition. One is new. The two from the first edition are revised.

Bibliography. A new bibliography has been written for the text.

Index. An alphabetical index of the items used is included in this edition.

A very thorough *Instructor's Manual* is available for the revised edition of this book.

A number of persons have graciously granted permission to reprint their items for this book. They include Joseph Towle; James A. Lee; K. Mark Weaver and John T. Wholihan; P. D. Jimerson and D. L. Ford;

James C. Hodgetts; R. Tagiuri and B. Rundlett; Kurt E. Chaloupecky; Lynda Diane Baydin and Alan P. Sheldon; Howard R. Smith; Jerry L. Wall; Ronald M. Zigli and Daniel W. Rountree; Sam Daudy and Bill Burnett; Dev S. Pathak and Gene E. Burton; Leo Rachmel; Claude I. Shell; I. B. Helburn and Darold Barnum; Richard M. Ayres and Thomas L. Wheelen; Robert H. Finn; Sherman Tingey; Curtis E. Tate, Jr.; Richard B. Chase; Michael Jay Jedel and Thomas M. Kennedy; Cary Thorp; and Fremont Shull.

I wish to thank Dean William Flewellen; Richard Huseman, Head, Department of Management; and my colleagues in the department at the University of Georgia for their help and encouragement for this revision.

I also wish to thank Cynthia Martin, my graduate research assistant during this year, and Jean Miller, my administrative assistant, for their help on the revision.

I hope the book will provide you with materials that will enable you to become a more effective manager or personnel manager.

February 1978   *William F. Glueck*

CONTENTS

PART TWO
INCIDENT CASES AND ROLE-PLAYING
EXERCISES IN PERSONNEL

INTRODUCTION

This book provides a series of experiences designed to help you understand better the management of people at work. The media used include cases, incident cases, role-playing exercises, cost-benefit, field, and in-basket exercises. The section of the book which introduces each medium will explain what it is, why it was chosen, and how to use it. A variety of experiences is provided to involve you in real-world problems and thus help you gain an understanding of people at work. Some of you will be introduced to personnel work through these media. Most already will have been exposed to the literature and research of personnel. Many of you have had experiences at work that will help you deal with the exercises.

Most of the topics that usually are considered as part of personnel or managing people at work are treated herein. Cases or exercises are included about such topics as employment (manpower), planning, recruiting people, and selecting applicants. Experiences also are given about orienting and assigning people to jobs, developing careers, and evaluating employees' performance. Some cases or exercises deal with developing managers, compensating people for their work, training, providing safe working conditions, and dealing with unions. Other cases and exercises deal with difficult employees, minority employment, leadership and supervision, and evaluation of the effectiveness of the personnel program.

People work for many different kinds of organizations; therefore, many different kinds of examples are given. The settings include small, medium, and large organizations from many places in the United States and Canada. The settings are in business, government, hospitals, universities, and symphony orchestras. Some cases depict good personnel practices; others depict poor personnel practices. Rarely is there just one factor to be considered. Most often there is one or more major factors and some secondary factors.

In doing these exercises, which simulate real life, you may often feel you don't have all the information you'd like to have before making a decision. Actually, there are many real-life situations where there isn't sufficient time or money to acquire enough information. Sometimes the information isn't available. You may often wish to state what additional information you would *like* to have; however, based on what you know now and what you can reasonably infer, you can make your decisions accordingly.

Most of the situations presented here are disguised; nevertheless, they are all based on real situations. Few organizations like to reveal real situations. Cases are not designed to illustrate optimum conditions but to serve as learning mechanisms which will allow you to distill your experience, the theories you have learned, and the research you have carried out and to apply them to a given situation.

Cases in personnel

PART ONE

A case is a description of an administrative situation and usually includes information about the setting of the situation. This information includes such things as geographic location, organization size, and business or sector. Often the case describes the background of the key factors involved in the experience. Finally, the case describes the happenings in the administrative situation.

PURPOSES OF CASES

The purposes or objectives of analyzing cases in personnel include the following:

1. To improve the decision-making ability of managers or potential managers. Decision making is a skill which can be improved with practice. This is especially true when the individual first analyzes a case on his or her own and then discusses it in a group. Each member of the group benefits from the insights and solutions offered by others in the group. Many management experts believe that decision making is at the core of effective management. The cases treated herein are centered on the person at work. The role to be played by the analyst can be that of a supervisor of persons or a personnel specialist.

2. In addition to developing managerial abilities such as more effective decision making, the case method is designed to expose management students to the environment of managerial decision making and to develop facilitative attitudes useful for effective decision making. Thus, cases present to the analysts situations which require them to make decisions and thus take risks under time pressure and with uncertainty surrounding the decision. The student must make a choice by discussion time. He or she often may feel that there is inadequate information provided in a case for making an optimal decision. This

is also true in much managerial decision making. There is information the decision maker would like to have, but it is not available, or there is no time to get it, or it would be too costly to acquire. The decision maker must make a decision based on the limited information available. Because cases are necessarily short and lack some information, they help to provide students with the situations for developing facilitative attitudes.

3. Another major purpose in using cases is to provide the opportunity to apply research findings and theoretical explanations to real situations and test their applicability. Frequently, one may have learned cognitively what a research study found or have understood what a theorist said about why people behave the way they do. But the ultimate purpose of managerial training is to improve managerial behavior and thus, hopefully, improve the satisfaction and development of the employees, the organization's performance, and the manager's satisfaction and success. If management students cannot apply these findings to real situations, they may have been taught a body of knowledge which is interesting and intellectually challenging, such as a study of optics might be a clergyman or chemistry to a social worker, but this knowledge is not likely to contribute significantly to the students' successful careers. Unless students can apply the research and theory accurately and insightfully to simulations of reality such as cases and exercises, it is not likely they will be able to do so in the real problem situation.

STRUCTURING CASE ANALYSES

There are many ways of analyzing cases and discussing them. To be most effective, all members of the class or discussion group must contribute something. This moves the learning situation away from the one-way communication method, or lecture. Lectures, no matter how brilliantly done, involve only a few human faculties. If care is not taken, the lecturing process degenerates into the sounds being emitted from the lecturer's mouth, traveling through the air, and scarcely pausing in the receiver's brain, before passing into the pencil taking notes. In case discussions, each discussant delivers his or her thoughts, reacts to others' thoughts, and defends his or her own. The discussant thus is using brain, mouth, eyes, ears, and probably hands to convey the message. This is how learning is accelerated and/or enriched.

One useful technique is to structure the discussion, at least to some extent. If the discussion jumps from point to point, it may be difficult for many discussants to follow. One model for structuring these cases is the following:

Step one: Clearly define the major and secondary problems involved in the case. These problems can be classified by such topics as personnel activity—for example, selection, evaluation, and compensation. Stating and agreeing upon the topics and rank ordering of them sets the agenda of the discussion. This is not always easy to do. Because of differences in the discussants' backgrounds, there will be varying interpretations of the data. Moreover, not all the information in the case is essential or even useful in understanding the situation. In a real work situation, the supervisor (manager, administrator, and so forth) is flooded with clues and information. The effective supervisor must separate the relevant from the irrelevant and focus on the former.

Step two: Develop a model of the cause of the problem (or success). There are many possible relations that influence the results. These factors include:

A. Individual factors.

The cause might be in the perception, motivation, abilities, or attitudes of the persons in the case.

B. Dyadic factors.

The significant factor can be the relationship between two crucial actors in the case, such as superior-subordinate.

C. Small group factors.

The work-group interrelationships might be the paramount factor influencing such problems as restriction of output or success of the football team.

D. Intergroup relations.

The cause of the problem can be systematic differences in several groups who must interact: salespersons and production managers, doctors and nurses, unions and managements.

E. Environmental factors.

There may be factors in the work environment which are crucial—time pressures, economic factors, governmental pressures, and so forth—that lead to the results described. So too in a case, you must arrange the data, the variables, and so forth into a model of the situation. In some cases, the ages of the people may be vital information, for example, when evaluating future pension costs or management succession. In other situations, it may be interesting, but not crucial, to know ages. The race of an applicant may be important information in a firm under affirmative action pressure. On the other hand, it may be totally irrelevant to the analysis of a health and safety case.

Step three: Consider alternative solutions to the problem or explain the successful experience.

Once you have defined your problem and modeled the relationships, the next step is to consider a reasonable number of solutions—the more the better. However, one usually cannot consider a large number because of time pressures and the limited ability of most people to compare a large number of alternatives. Most of us eliminate from serious consideration those solutions which seem least likely to solve the problem quickly and expeditiously. Three or four alternatives are systematically compared factor by factor.

Step four: Choose and implement a solution.

The analyst chooses a solution and is prepared to defend that choice. The analyst also plans how she or he would make it work. Thus, if the solution is to fire a person, several things must be considered to make sure the choice was the right one and one which is workable. For example, when the firing should be done, how it should be done, and by whom it should be done must be considered, as well as clearing the matter with superiors.

There are many analytical structures to which cases can be fitted. The structure just described has proved to be a useful one.

STUDENT PREPARATION FOR CASES

A few hints may help you prepare good case analyses. First, read the case, underlining important points and making some rough notes of what you think are the key problems and their causes. Do some preliminary thinking about solutions. If you have the opportunity, discuss your ideas with others in the class. Then lay the case aside for a while.

Second, return to the case later and reread it. Make added notes. Where there is not enough information, make reasonable assumptions and state them. Remember, in your proposed solutions, that what you suggest being done might affect others. Make sure you don't solve a problem in one department and cause one in another. Write up your first draft report now. Put the case down again.

Third, return to the case later and make sure it says all you want to say and the way you want to say it.

This approach will help you begin to develop your analytical abilities. First, you will learn to separate the important information from the less important. Next, you will begin to apply the research and theories you have learned to the problems. Then you will begin to increase your repertoire of solutions and analyze them rationally and logically, computing the trade-offs. Finally, you will remember to anticipate the implementation problems.

CATEGORIZING CASES

The cases are given in the next section of this book. It has been customary to classify cases by topics, and this has been done here. If a case is classified under "Orientation," you can be sure that this is a major focus of the case. However, it may not be the only focus of the case. The cases are realistic; rarely are they single problems or singly-caused problems. Look for all the personnel and human aspects that seem relevant.

A. INTRODUCTION TO PERSONNEL MANAGEMENT

---

1. Genevieve Chemicals, Ltd.—I

Genevieve Chemicals, Ltd., (GCL) is a large chemical company located in Montreal, Canada. The firm now employs approximately 2,500 persons.

Much of its growth has come about since 1945. Most of the growth took place because of mergers and acquisitions. GCL's basic business grew from about 100 employees in 1930 to 750. The rest of this growth came from the corporate strategy of acquiring smaller, often family-run firms in businesses allied to GCL. Thus, it is now a rather well-developed chemical firm covering much of the chemical industry. However, it is not nearly so large as giants like Imperial Chemicals, Dupont, or Monsanto.

As the company has grown, so has its personnel activity. In the beginning, the individual managers were responsible for their own personnel activities. The departments hired their own people, paid them what was necessary, and gave them on-the-job training. No special recruiting was necessary. Walk-ins and employee recruitment took care of that. The managers interviewed the applicants and hired the best ones. No formal evaluations were done on employees or managers. Few employee benefits were provided. Safety was a minor function—the responsibility of the industrial engineers. The plants were not unionized, and supervisors handled their own discipline problems.

As GCL grew, especially by the mergers, the managers could no longer handle all the personnel functions. A formal personnel department developed at company headquarters, with personnel specialists at each location to advise the managers on personnel matters. They also performed those functions which managers delegated to them. But personnel was viewed as a staff function, really an extension of the manager's will.

The first personnel executive was Arthur Mathis, a McGill University graduate. He had been with GCL in the accounting and payroll functions. He was appointed to the office by the president, Etienne Jonquiere.

Under Mathis, Phase I of the personnel development took place. Because of his training in payroll, Mathis tried to develop a systematic compensation system for all employees. He established a series of job grades with maximum and minimum pay for each grade. He then tried to place all jobs of similar skill within a grade. A primitive form of job evaluation using a point scale was developed.

Next, his assistant, Pierre Joliette—a graduate of Laval University—was asked to prepare a merit-rating system for assessing raises systematically. He did this and set up an individual incentive, piecework system for some employees.

The next project was to develop a benefits package. This concentrated on a small pension system. But Joliette also developed policies about vacations, rest periods, tea breaks, accident compensation, cafeterias, and recreation programs at the plants.

About this time, health and safety was transferred to personnel, and John Mazze was hired to supervise that program. He developed safety policies and made safety inspections.

Finally, the department began to professionalize training. A training director, Basil Akula, was hired. He scheduled classes, mostly technical in nature, and taught them at the various plant locations.

Mathis retired in 1957 when the company had 1,000 employees. As his final act prior to retiring, he developed a personnel manual for the company and distributed it to the plant managers, top management, and all personnel specialists. The personnel manual was 25 pages in length.

Requirement. For a firm of this size and considering the period, how well-developed was the personnel function at GCL? What additional functions should the company have performed?

Genevieve Chemicals, Ltd.—II

After Mathis retired, the president of Genevieve Chemicals, Ltd., (GCL) Etienne Jonquiere, considered the matter of who should continue the personnel function. Several candidates were recruited and interviewed. In the end, Pierre Joliette was appointed. But he was not sure that the president was entirely satisfied with him. Joliette knew that he must win Jonquiere's confidence. One way to do that was to move slowly and to build a success record as soon as he could.

Joliette prepared a list of projects that he felt needed attention, which included:

1. Development of good job descriptions for multiple uses in personnel.

2.   Improvement of recruiting at GCL.
3.   Development of a formal orientation program for the company.
4.   Improvement of selection methods.
5.   Involvement of the personnel department in counseling and discipline functions.
6.   Preparation of contingency plans in case the unions tried to organize GCL.

Joliette felt that he should take the functions one at a time and proceed from the least controversial to the most controversial, building confidence along the way. So he developed the job descriptions first. These he felt would help in recruitment, selection, promotion, and compensation. Jonquiere did not respond to Joliette's cover letter attaching the job descriptions.

Next Joliette developed better recruiting methods for GCL, systematizing the advertising, preparing literature for college recruiting, and training the recruiters and employment interviewers in the latest techniques. He sent President Jonquiere a report on this. The president acknowledged receipt of the report and thanked him for it.

At this point, Joliette developed a set of plans regarding possible unionization. He recommended that GCL improve its compensation and benefits plan now to avoid possible unionization. The president sent Joliette a warm letter of congratulations and approval of the project.

Now, Joliette felt he was getting someplace. So he moved ahead on the selection project. He began to develop weighted application blanks for some jobs. He also suggested the use of a test battery. The president sent a cool letter accepting the weighted application blanks but disapproving of the use of tests because they were so costly.

Joliette was disturbed but proceeded with his new orientation program for all newly hired employees. He prepared printed material that described the company rules, company pay, and benefit plans. The plan also involved a session on "how to get along at GCL." The new employees were told about the idiosyncrasies of the company and their particular supervisor. This helped cut turnover drastically. The president was quite happy with the new program, and he often spoke a brief word of welcome to some of the groups of new employees.

Joliette had almost exhausted his project list. Next, he prepared a Phase III list. On it were several projects:

1.   Involving personnel in counseling and discipline (unfinished from Phase II).
2.   Arranging for a management development program.
3.   Formal auditing of personnel through turnover and absenteeism analysis.
4.   Developing employment planning procedures.

Joliette was thinking about these projects when he received a call from a large firm in Toronto. They made him an excellent offer. Since he had never felt that he had the full confidence of the president of GCL, Joliette accepted the offer.

At the time he left in 1963, GCL had 2,000 employees. The personnel manual Joliette had prepared for the company was 72 pages.

Requirements. For a company of this size and considering the period, evaluate the development of personnel at GCL. How could it be improved?

Genevieve Chemicals, Ltd.—III

President Jonquiere was somewhat shaken when Joliette left. In their final interview, Joliette told the president that he had not felt that Jonquiere had supported him adequately. Actually, Jonquiere had thought very well of Joliette, and now realized he had not communicated this to him. Jonquiere resolved not to make that mistake again.

In the interim, while GCL was looking for a new personnel manager, the company was unionized. This disturbed the president even more; he realized how much he had lost in losing Joliette.

Jonquiere hired Leo Beaupre to replace Joliette. Beaupre was almost as experienced as Joliette, but to get him, GCL had to pay a 15-percent higher salary. He had been the personnel director of a shipbuilding company. Beaupre communicated with Joliette, and essentially he picked up where Joliette left off. Beaupre developed a personnel audit, set up a skills inventory, and projected employee demands. He began a formal management development program, and he interjected personnel in the counseling and discipline function. The president strongly supported Beaupre in these projects.

But one day Issac Athanassiades, one of GCL's best division managers, came to see Jonquiere. He said, "Etienne, I am getting a lot of complaints from my supervisors and department heads. They feel that personnel has castrated them. Whenever they want to fire or discipline a man, he is sent first to personnel for counseling. Too often, we get a letter back saying in effect to give him another chance. You made it quite clear that personnel was an important function here. So up until now, I've tried to avoid this issue. But personnel is just a staff function. We are the line. This would have never happened if Joliette were still running personnel. Beaupre has gone wild. Look at this personnel manual. It's 125 pages long with lots of rules and regulations. We only have 2,500 employees, not 250,000. You've got to do something!"

Jonquiere was shocked. GCL had never had a case of line-staff conflict before. He felt he had to support Beaupre. Beaupre had doubled the size of the personnel department to do the job.

Requirement. How could the president handle this case? Who really should decide discipline cases?

2. Selecting a Personnel Manager

Stephen Comish is president of Heraclius Toy Company (HTC), Evanston, Illinois. Heraclius is a large manufacturer of toys. It has been in business for 100 years.

HTC manufactures toys and allied products for all age groups. It sells them direct to large retailer-wholesalers, such as department store chains and variety store chains. The company also markets its products to wholesale toy distributors who deliver them to toy retailers of various kinds. For young children, HTC produces items such as blocks, stuffed animals, pull toys, and others. For adults, the company assembles games, both floor and board varieties.

HTC has been very successful. It has been managed primarily by the Comish family until now. But Comish's sons, Justin and Alexander, show no interest in the firm. Justin is in medical school. Alexander worked for the firm for five years and then quit. He is pursuing a Ph.D. in geology and plans to work for a large oil company. Comish's brothers' sons— Theodosius, Zeno, and Manuel—tried the firm but have long since left it. Theo joined a stock brokerage firm. Zeno is an architect, and Manuel is a drifter, living off the HTC dividends.

So Comish realizes he must begin to build a management team which can help him run HTC now and see that it survives when he is gone. Comish has filled the finance vice president's job. He chose Phillip Folts, a 38-year-old banker, who had also worked for the Federal Reserve Bank.

The production manager is Robert Midani, who is 58. He came up the hard way. He's been with HTC in production for as long as Comish can remember. Midani is a good man.

Comish himself likes to dabble in the marketing side, but he's bringing along an executive there, too, Curtis Szilagi. Szilagi graduated from Northern Illinois University in marketing five years ago, after working as a toy salesman for ten years.

Comish feels his greatest need is for a strong personnel executive. He is wondering if Joe Kavran, his old friend at a consulting firm he has used, can give him advice on this issue. He has sent Kavran the vitae of four persons he's considering for the job (Exhibits 1, 2, 3, 4). Comish constructed the curriculum vitae of Rommy Andrisani whom he liked very much.

Georgina McCarthy received rave reference letters. Follow-up calls confirmed that she was an outstanding girl, a real "comer." T. Charles Bishop is one of the best blacks Comish ever interviewed. Bishop's mother lives

EXHIBIT 1
CURRICULUM VITAE—ROMANUS ANDRISANI

Personnel data:	Age, 47 years
	Married to former Theodora Alexandrides, 27 years
Children:	John, age 25
	Alex, age 21
	Matthew, age 17
	Anna, age 14
Education:	Graduate, Evanston High School
	Dale Carnegie Course
	LaSalle Extension University Course
Experience:	2 years, toy clerk, variety store
	5 years, production of toys, HTC
	17 years, salesman, HTC
	3 years, HTC sales supervisor, eastern half of United States
General:	Character excellent
	Hard worker
	Well liked by co-workers

EXHIBIT 2
CURRICULUM VITAE—GEORGINA McCARTHY

Personnel data:	Age, 29 years
	Single
Education:	Graduate, with honors, Bronx School of Science
	B.S.B.A., Personnel Administration, City University of New York
Experience:	Two years, employment recruiter, Macy's
	Two years, selection interviewer, Schaeffer Beer, Inc.
	Three years, wage and salary administrator, Wrigley's, Inc.
	At present, benefits program supervisor, Sears, Inc. (for one year)
References:	Adolph Mathis, supervisor at Macy's
	Helen Nordson, supervisor at Schaeffer
	Maurice Soslow, supervisor at Wrigley
	Justinian Gillis, supervisor at Sears

EXHIBIT 3
CURRICULUM VITAE—T. CHARLES BISHOP

Personnel data:	Age, 36 years
	Divorced
	Two children, Susan, age 12, and Buddy, age 7
Education:	Graduate, Tuskegee High School
	Bachelor of Education, Tuskegee Institute
Experience:	Five years, grade school teacher in the southern United States
	Four years, officer in the U.S. Army
	Four years, guidance counselor, secondary schools, Chicago
	Three years, personnel department, City of Chicago
Reference:	Hartley Binks, supervisor of personnel, City of Chicago

EXHIBIT 4
CURRICULUM VITAE—CASIMIR CZARNEKI

Personnel data: Age, 55 years
                Widower
                Two children, age 32 and 28
    Education: South Chicago High School
                Two years at DePaul University
                Night school in business administration and personnel
    Experience: Five years, military
                Five years, Bethlehem Steel Company (production)
                Lewandoski Manufacturing in production, and last five years in
                personnel
    Reference: Constantine Lewandoski, former president of Lewandoski
                Manufacturing.

with him and takes care of his children. His reference letter was satisfactory.

Cas Czarneki was an interesting case. His employer of many years had
gone bankrupt. A small pen and pencil manufacturer, it had not been too
competitive, and when the founder had a stroke, the firm closed. Czarneki
had been a jack-of-all-trades, but he had a fair amount of personnel
experience.

Comish said he was looking for a person who would run a good ship,
be creative but not rock the boat, one who would keep the costs down but
keep the employees happy.

Requirement. You are Joe Kavran. Design a program to select the best
personnel manager for HTC. What additional information would you
acquire? Based on what you know, who would you hire and why? What
criteria should be used to select a personnel manager?

3. Ajax Electronics Company, Inc. (A)*

In 1965 Art Johnson was hired as personnel manager of the radio
division of the Ajax Electronics Company. This was a new division to be
established in Salt Lake City, Utah, and would require the hiring of
some 2,000 engineers, technicians, and assemblers over the next 18
months.

The new management of this division, transferred from the headquarters plant in Chicago, was very concerned that careful selection

---

* This case has been disguised. It was prepared by Professor James A. Lee, Ohio
University, Athens, O., as a basis for class discussion.

procedures be used in the appointment of supervisors. They were aware that Mr. Johnson was trained, qualified, and licensed as a psychologist and urged him to use his professional knowledge and techniques to improve the selection of supervisors and managers for this new division.

At this time there were a number of psychology consultants operating throughout the United States assisting in the selection of managers and executives. Most of them were using a variety of the psychology tests at that time to assist them in their evaluation of candidates sent to them by various of their clients. Prominent among these tests were the two most popularly used projective tests—the Rorschach Ink Blot Test and the Thematic Apperception Test. Mr. Johnson refused to administer these tests on ethical grounds to the considerable disappointment and irritation of his superiors. The Chicago headquarters had been using psychology consultants for several years to assist them in executive selection. When they heard of this refusal through the general manager of the new radio division, they recommended to the general manager that one of the consulting firms which they had used be called in. This particular consulting firm had a small office in Salt Lake City staffed by a Ph.D. psychologist who was qualified to administer these various tests.

Mr. Johnson protested the use of this agency on the grounds that various aspects of candidates' personalities would be revealed by the tests, yet no serious effort was planned to explain the findings to the candidates. He argued that since some of these test results might reveal serious personality problems or neuroses the communication of the findings to the candidates could be extremely disturbing and/or require far more counseling time than the company was willing to provide.

The company decided to proceed with the engagement of the consulting firm anyway, and Mr. Johnson was trying to decide whether to acquiesce or jeopardize his job by pursuing his position further.

Ajax Electronics Company, Inc. (B)*

In 1967 after Art Johnson had been personnel manager of the radio division of Ajax Electronics Company for two years, the International Workers began to attempt organization of the work force. They used the usual approaches. Leaflets were distributed at the gate, and employees were invited to attend organization meetings. This attempt was still in progress seven months later but appeared to be unsuccessful. The largest

---

* This case was prepared by Professor James A. Lee, Ohio University, Athens, O., as a basis for class discussion.

turnout at one of their organization meetings, at which the women assemblers were offered free orchids and men employees free beer, was 37 employees. Two of the group were really voluntary spies unknown to the management of the division. They came in the next day to tell Johnson of all the promises made by the union organizers and of other general topics discussed at the meeting.

In his monthly report for October 1967, Mr. Johnson included a paragraph describing the efforts to date. This portion of his report was forwarded to the Chicago headquarters as part of the general manager's report. The Chicago headquarters personnel people became concerned that the union might succeed and decided to send a team to assist Mr. Johnson in resisting the organization attempt.

A part of the Ajax decentralization plan was to move to areas that were not heavily unionized, and they were concerned over each attempt to organize any new division.

Three people from corporate headquarters including the vice president for industrial relations met with Mr. Johnson on the morning after their arrival to offer some suggestions. The first suggestion came as a result of inquiring about the hiring policies. It appeared to them that Art Johnson was not aware of what they felt were certain ethnic groups' propensity to unionization. More specifically, one of these headquarters' managers, Mr. Romanov, suggested to Mr. Johnson that he should not hire people of Polish extraction on the grounds that they are well known to have been engaged in early communist organizations in Chicago and tended to join unions more than others.

Mr. Johnson flatly refused to consider this advice in spite of the persistant urgings and couched threats by the headquarters people. An on-the-spot analysis of the performance appraisals of all employees whose last name appeared Polish revealed that, if anything, the Polish employees were slightly better than average for the division. These results were countered by the headquarters' official by saying that their work performance was not the issue.

The argument continued at luncheon to a point at which Mr. Johnson refused to discuss it further and walked out of the restaurant.

In discussing the incident with his wife that evening, Mr. Johnson was wondering if he should blow the whistle on this company by reporting these happenings to the National Labor Relations Board. He was certain that this would result in the end of the careers of the three headquarters men because the NLRB or the IUB would be delighted to hear of such behavior. (The labor laws of both the United States and the state of Utah prohibit discrimination in employment on the basis of race, religion, national origin, etc. These laws also prohibit this kind of management activity designed to thwart the organization of unions.) As he went to work the next morning, he was pondering the consequences of this course of action and was yet undecided of what course he would take. He knew too that his own career with this company and likely with others would be either finished or seriously jeopardized if he went to the NLRB.

Discussion questions

1. If you were in Art Johnson's shoes, what action, if any, would you take? Why?
2. How should the company resist the union organization attempts?
3. What ethical and legal problems could the company encounter by using the tests as a selection device?

4. World International Airlines, Inc.*

BACKGROUND

World International Airlines is a foreign-based multinational commercial air carrier. The corporate offices for its Western Hemisphere operations are located in New York City, New York. The company employs many hundreds of multilingual and multicultural employees since its operations maintain World International terminals in South America, Central America, Mexico, the United States, and Canada, all of which comprise the Western Hemisphere territory. In all of the continents the district managers, whose territory may involve several countries or, in the case of the United States, several states, are usually multilingual Europeans. The assistant managers are usually multilingual nationals of the country. The general manager of the Western Hemisphere is a native Spaniard while the personnel manager is a Spanish-American. Both the general manager and personnel manager are multilingual and multicultural. While many air carriers in the Western Hemisphere have experienced strikes and work stoppages in the past, there is no history of strikes having ever occurred at World International Airlines.

The present general manager is a man in his mid-50s. He has worked his way up to the top of the Western Hemisphere's organization. He has handpicked all of the men who are district managers in each of the aforementioned countries. He knows over 90 percent of the company's employees in the New York offices on a personal basis and is well liked by

---

* This case was prepared by Professors P. D. Jimerson of Iowa State University and D. L. Ford of the Herman C. Krannert Graduate School of Industrial Administration, Purdue University. It is intended for classroom discussion only, and is not an illustration of good or bad management practices.

all of his subordinates. On one occasion when he was away attending a NTL-sponsored workshop in California, the employees from the New York offices surprised him with a huge birthday cake, complete with decorations and even champagne. His job performance has earned him influence and power in Spain. In addition, the present general manager's educational background is more along the classical line typical of many Spaniards in his socioeconomic class (that is, law, engineering, etc.) as opposed to a more applied business and management education background.

CHANGE IN SENIOR PERSONNEL CREATES PROBLEMS

The company is in a state of flux. The present general manager, John Nepia, is scheduled to be transferred to Barcelona, Spain, and a new man, Stephen Esterant, has been sent to replace him. The present general manager has had little or no input into the selection of the new general manager. However, the incoming general manager has an outstanding record in the Eastern Hemisphere, and it is rumored that he is being groomed for something big. Coupled with this impending change in senior personnel is the fact that international flights are currently in a state of flux since a review committee is currently deliberating on a new rate structure.

John Nepia was scheduled to depart New York on April 30, 1972. Stephen Esterant arrived March 20, 1972. There was to be at least a 30-day transition period before the departure of Mr. Nepia. Problems on the setting of the international rate structure became acute on or about April 20, 1972, and Mr. Nepia's departure was delayed and termed indefinite since he was actively participating in the rate-setting negotiations with the FAA.

During the transition period Stephen was to make himself acquainted with all of the district general managers as well as the rank and file employees. Stephen visited all of the district offices; he met and talked with district managers, sales personnel, and operations personnel, and he made comments wherever he felt that company policy was not being followed. He seldom found anything worthy of praise if it did not comply with established company policy.

The first sign of difficulty came when the corporate chauffeur in New York asked to speak to John Nepia, the outgoing general manager. The outgoing general manager has maintained a policy of being accessible to any of the company's employees. The driver explains the following.

I've been with this company for five years now. I like my work and I like my job. But I don't believe that I should get less respect because I'm a driver. I don't like the idea of having to drive Mr. Esterant's wife and her friends around on a shopping trip in downtown New York. I don't think it's part of my responsibility to walk his dog or carry his wife's packages. I realize that I *work* for him, but I refuse to be treated as though I were his *servant*. I decided that if this treatment continues on his part I will have to find out what grievance procedure is available and file an official complaint.

John Nepia was quick to assure the driver that the matter would be looked into and he would get in touch with him as soon as he knew more about the situation.

Other rumblings came from the operations employees. They contended that Stephen Esterant was thoughtless, unappreciative, and distant in his interactions with them. They further believed that he felt and acted "too damned superior." For example, one of the operative employees related the following story. "Once Stephen visited the baggage-handling area at Chicago where a new computerized routing system was being tested. He had worked with a similar system before and immediately spotted some procedures which would increase the efficiency of operation. He proceeded to tell the employees that they didn't know what they were doing and questioned their intelligence."

The most recent sign of major discord came when the district managers sent a plea to John Nepia begging him to implore Spain to recall the new general manager. In their opinion, morale had suffered greatly, and Stephen was the direct cause.

The outgoing general manager and Jason DuBryne, the director of personnel, were good and long-time friends. They had survived many crises together. Therefore, John called in his trusted friend to seek advice and ponder their problem and their possible courses of action.

Jason was considered by many of the employees to be a firm, but fair, administrator. He often prided himself of the fact that he was always available to talk to and help his people. He was often consulted by members of the firm concerning interpersonal matters. These consultations often concerned private as well as corporate issues.

During their meeting, the personnel manager acknowledged to John that the situation was indeed grave; however, at no point in the conversation did he indicate what his personal beliefs were concerning the problem. He stated that he did not believe that the heir apparent was technically incompetent. He also suggested the possibility that the heir apparent just did not understand the way of doing business in the Western Hemisphere. The meeting ended with John Nepia deciding that a conversation with Stephen Esterant was needed.

THE NEW GENERAL MANAGER'S VIEWPOINT

Stephen Esterant was named to head the Western Hemispheric operations of World International Airlines, Inc., as a reward for his outstanding service as a district manager in Spain. He was told that he was selected because he had been able to bring district offices into compliance with company operations policy and to maintain or increase sales volume at the same time.

Stephen had served in five other district posts prior to receiving this promotion. He was 32 years old and married to a woman who was a member of a wealthy and influential family in Spain. In fact, Stephen's wife's family was one of a few wealthy families owning a substantial portion of World International Airlines stock. Stephen was a man who knew what he wanted, and he knew how to get it. He moved briskly about his affairs asking no favors *from* anyone and giving no favors *to* anyone. He appeared to be the coming star in the organization.

Stephen Esterant received a memo from John Nepia requesting that he meet with him and Jason DuBryne, the personnel director, about a matter of apparent great importance. Enroute to the meeting he pondered over what would possibly be discussed. He, of course, had a few items on his own agenda. Since coming to New York, Stephen had become aware of several problems involved in his becoming the new general manager. He was displeased by the apparent lack of respect given to him by his subordinates as well as the "cocky" attitude of the hourly employees. He was sure that John and Jason were aware of the attitude problems, and yet he could not understand why they had not dealt with these matters sooner and in a stronger manner. From Stephen's point of view, he felt there was a need to run a tight ship, as he had done in the Eastern Hemisphere. He obviously had a distaste for the hourly employees' practice of calling managers by their first names and a lack of deference to those in authority, as was often done not only in the New York offices, but also throughout the rest of the Western Hemisphere operations. He also wanted to tell John and Jason that he needed to have them run less interference for him. Since he was soon to be general manager, he believed that he should start to handle intergroup conflict and decide about policy disputes so that the organization could easily recognize its new boss and leader. He resolved that if the opportunity arose in the meeting he would raise these issues with John and Jason.

As he reached the door to John's office, Stephen turned the knob and jauntily entered the office to meet with John Nepia and Jason DuBryne, not really knowing what to expect.

Discussion questions

1.   What do you think took place during the meeting? How would you confront Stephen? How would you expect Stephen to react?
2.   Was the problem simply a matter of leadership style or were cultural differences involved?
3.   Do you think the 30-day transition period for Stephen was necessary? Did any problems arise from John's delayed departure?

B. EMPLOYMENT PLANNING

1. The WESTLABS Plan*

Western Laboratories, Inc. (WESTLABS) is a Portland, Oregon, firm, which specializes in manufacturing contact lenses and selling them directly to the prescribing practitioner. At Portland there are approximately 30 production employees paid on an hourly basis and a supporting staff of 6 office employees paid on an hourly basis. Except for some of the supervisors and managers of the firm, all the employees are female. Additional laboratory and supervisory personnel at branches in other cities bring the company payroll to over 60 employees.

In 1971 management of the WESTLABS became quite concerned about the high rate of absenteeism that it was experiencing in Portland and at its branch operations. After considering several possible courses of action, the company decided to experiment with a novel work week that featured a four-day, 36-hour work schedule with an opportunity for the employees to receive 40 hours of pay. The plan was to be introduced at the firm's Santa Fe branch and, if successful, was to be implemented at the Portland lab and at the other branches.

WESTLABS has traditionally paid wages and provided benefits that were considered to be competitive in the communities in which they have laboratories. The fringe-benefit package included seven paid holidays, earned vacations based on time with the company, a 15-minute break in the morning and in the afternoon, a sick-pay plan providing partial pay for the time missed due to illness, life insurance paid by the company, health insurance with employee contributions coupled with a matching company contribution, and a profit-sharing plan.

The primary purpose of introducing a four-day work week was to combat the absenteeism problem, but other reasons supported the change. These reasons included:

---

* By Professor Cary D. Thorp, Jr., University of Nebraska.

1. Recruitment—It was felt that the company would enjoy a recruiting advantage over other companies by offering 40 hours of pay in four instead of five days.
2. Production—It was felt that the company could achieve an increase in production by using this system.
3. Work rules—The institution of a new working system would make it possible to tighten up certain work rules.
4. Overtime—The plan provides an excellent opportunity for scheduling overtime as one day each week is available for extra time.
5. Fringe benefits—It was felt that some of the fringe benefits had grown out of 14 years in business as expedients rather than as desirable benefits. Sick leave was a particularly difficult benefit. The company had experimented with several systems with little satisfaction to the company.

Because it was important to the firm to remain open to fill orders five days a week, the plan called for splitting the employees into two sections. Both sections would work a nine-hour day, 7:30 A.M.–5:00 P.M., Monday, Tuesday, and Wednesday and would alternate working a nine-hour day on Thursdays and Fridays. One section would work on Thursday and be off on Friday while the other section would have Thursday off and work on Friday. The following week the two sections would reverse the order of work and time off. Thus, every employee had a regular weekday off each week.

An important part of the new plan was bonus pay for perfect attendance. If the employee was at his or her station on time in the morning and at lunch breaks, he or she would receive four hours of bonus pay each week. That is, if the 36 hours were actually worked with not as much as one minute of tardiness, the employee would be paid for 40 hours. The four bonus hours pay would be lost for tardiness or absence regardless of whether or not the absence or tardiness was excusable. Therefore, one missed day of work cost the employee 13 hours of pay (9 hours for the missed day plus the four-hour bonus).

WESTLABS would no longer pay sick leave or holiday pay. There are always four days to work in every week so there would be no need for paid holidays; the entire work force would have the holiday off but would work the other four workdays during the holiday week.

Sick leave would be surrendered by the employees in order to have the extra day off. From a management standpoint sick leave had been one of the most troublesome problems; it would be a relief to do without it. The day off provided time to do some of the chores that some sick leave in the past had presumably been used for.

Breaks would also be abolished. The two daily 15-minute breaks were typically stretched into something greater than that so considerable time would be saved. Coffee would be allowed at each work station at all times. The work process was such that this concession would not be disruptive to production.

Insurance benefits, vacations, and profit-sharing plans were to be retained.

Requirement. Having determined the details of the plan, what should the president next consider in order to implement the plan successfully? Will this plan work with these employees?

2. Johnston Industrial Products*

The Johnston Industrial Products Company, a multiplant corporation headquarted in Kansas City, is considering locating a new manufacturing plant in the Midwest to produce its line of electrical switches. The production process for the new plant is a relatively simple one, involving the fabrication and assembly of lightweight parts into finished units. For most production jobs, the training period will be less than three days, and new employees can generally "make standard" in less than two weeks. The average plant employee will be paid "the going community rate" for work of this type. In most of the communities being considered by Johnston, that rate would be in the neighborhood of $2.60 per hour. Plans call for the new plant to be operated on a two-shift basis with 200 production employees scheduled for each shift. At the time the management of the company was considering this plant in September 1973, the national unemployment rate was approximately 4.5 percent.

Henry Wilhelm, chairman of the board, received the following proposal from an executive committee charged with selecting a plant location:

After considering a number of midwestern cities as plant sites, the committee has unanimously agreed that the best location would be Lincoln, Nebraska, provided that the board will consider a modification in the nature of the work force of 200 employees for the second shift would result in substantially in- of the caliber that we need for efficient production on the first shift. However, as is true of all of the other cities that we considered, to recruit a full-time work force of 200 employees for the second shift would result in substantially in- creased recruitment expenses and a work force of lower quality.

However, by splitting the second shift into half-shifts we would have more than an adequate supply of labor. We could utilize townspeople for the first shift (7:30 A.M.–4:00 P.M.) and university students for the evening shift (4:00 P.M.–12:00 P.M.). The evening shift could be operated on a split-shift basis with 200 students working from 4:00 P.M.–8:00 P.M. and a second group of 200

---

* By Professor Cary D. Thorp, Jr., University of Nebraska.

students working from 8:00 P.M.–midnight. In that way, students would have a 20-hour work week, leaving them sufficient time for their academic studies. During the summer, when many students are not in school, we could operate the second shift on a normal basis, offering employment on a second shift to those student-employees who are looking for a full-time summer job. We should have little difficulty recruiting 400 students, since the total college enrollment in Lincoln (University of Nebraska, Nebraska Wesleyan, and Union College) is over 25,000.

Requirement. As board chairman, how would you:
1. Evaluate the proposal? What advantages and disadvantages do you see in this plan?
2. What additional information would you like before making a final decision, and how would you go about getting it?

3. Walker Space, Inc.

Walker Space (WSI) is a medium-sized firm, located in Connecticut. The firm essentially has been a subcontractor on many large space contracts which have been acquired by firms such as North American Rockwell and others.

With the cutback in many of the National Aeronautics and Space Administration programs, Walker has an excess of employees. Stuart Tartaro, the head of one of the sections, has been told by his superior that he must reduce his section of engineers from nine to six. He is looking at the following summaries of their vitaes and pondering how he will make this decision.

1. Roger Allison, age 26, married, two children. Allison has been with WSI for a year and a half. He is a very good engineer, with a degree from Rensselaer Polytech. He's held two prior jobs and lost both of them because of cutbacks in the space program. He moved to Connecticut from California to take this job. Allison is well liked by his co-workers.
2. LeRoy Jones, age 24, single. Jones is black and the company looked hard to get Jones because of affirmative action pressure. He is not very popular with his co-workers. Since he has been employed less than a year, not too much is known about his work. On his one evaluation (which was average) Jones accused his supervisor of bias against blacks. He is a graduate of Detroit Institute of Technology.
3. William Foster, age 53, married, three children. Foster is a graduate of "the school of hard knocks." After getting out of World War II, he started to go to school. But his family expenses were too much, so he dropped out. Foster has worked at the company for 20 years. His

ratings were excellent for 15 years. The last five years they have been average. Foster feels his supervisor grades him down because he doesn't "have sheepskins covering his office walls."

4. Donald Boyer, age 32, married, no children. Boyer is well liked by his co-workers. He has been at WSI five years, and he has a B.S. and M.S. in engineering from Purdue University. Boyer's ratings have been mixed. Some supervisors rated him high, some average. Boyer's wife is an M.D.

5. Mel Shuster, age 29, single. Shuster is a real worker, but a loner. He has a B.S. in engineering from University of California. He is working on his M.S. at night; always trying to improve his technical skills. His performance ratings were above average for the three years he has been employed at WSI.

6. Sherman Soltis, age 37, divorced, two children. He has a B.S. in engineering from Ohio State University. Soltis is very active in community affairs: Scouts, Little League, United Appeal. He is a friend of the vice president through church work. His ratings have been average, although some recent ones indicate that he is out of date. He is well liked and has been employed at WSI for 14 years.

7. Warren Fortuna, age 44, married, five children. He has a B.S. in engineering from Georgia Tech. Fortuna headed this section at one time. He worked so hard that he had a heart attack. Under doctor's orders, he resigned from the supervisory position. Since then he has done good work, though because of his health he is a bit slower than the others. Now and then, he must spend extra time on a project because he did get out of date during the eight years he headed the section. His performance evaluations for the last two years have been above average. He has been employed at WSI for 14 years.

8. Robert Treharne, age 47, single. He began an engineering degree at M.I.T. but had to drop out for financial reasons. He tries hard to stay current by regular reading of engineering journals and taking all the short courses the company and nearby colleges offer. His performance evaluations have varied, but they tend to be average to slightly above average. He is a loner and Tartaro thinks this has negatively affected his performance evaluations. He has been employed at WSI 16 years.

9. Sandra Rosen, age 22, single. She has a B.S. in engineering technology from Rochester Institute of Technology. Rosen has been employed less than a year. She is enthusiastic, a very good worker, and is well liked by her co-workers. She is well regarded by Tartaro.

Tartaro doesn't quite know what to do. He sees the good points of each of his section members. Most have been good employees. They all can pretty much do each other's work. No one has special training.

He is fearful that the section will hear about this and morale will drop. Work would fall off. He doesn't even want to talk to his wife about it, in case she'd let something slip. Tartaro has come to you, Edmund Graves, personnel manager at WSI, for some guidelines on this decision—legal, moral, and best personnel practice.

Requirement. You are Edmund Graves. Write a report with your recommendations for termination and a careful analysis of the criteria for the decision. You should also carefully explain to Tartaro how you would go about the terminations and reasonable termination pay. You should also advise him about the pension implications of this decision. Generally 15 years' service entitles you at least to partial pension.

4. The Corporate Policy*

Sands Manufacturing Company, a 50-year-old company, has grown from a small manufacturing concern to a leader in its industry with a complete line of material handling equipment. Over the years some engineers have become product experts of unquestioned caliber. The company finds, however, that these experts are not able to adapt easily when transferred to a new job situation. This has hurt the company in the last ten years because of the tremendous growth and resulting need for older, experienced engineers to take over supervisory roles in new product areas. To give these personnel a broader background and experience in new job situations, the vice president of engineering has instituted a policy to encourage engineering personnel to be more mobile within the company's various branches of engineering.

John Turner, three years out of college, has been working as a design engineer under Lawrence Conner, supervisor of new products in the product design division. John has done moderately well but really doesn't enjoy design work as much as he thought he would. Instead he feels he would prefer to "get my hands dirty" in one of the test division labs.

Don Sutter, a project engineer in the test division, has been in the same department since he graduated from college 12 years ago. He has worked his way up from test engineer to his present position and would be next in line for promotion to supervisor. The current supervisors, however, don't show any sign of either moving to another area of being promoted to another job. For this reason Don sees his chance of being promoted to

---

* This case was prepared by Professors John Wholihan of Bradley University and K. Mark Weaver of the University of Alabama based on work by Charles Laitner, Jr. The case was prepared as a basis for class discussion rather than to illustrate either effective or ineffective handling of an administrative situation.

supervisor in this department as very limited now. Don feels he should take advantage of the new policy encouraging mobility so he requests a transfer to a design area. The request is given considerable attention, and a trade is negotiated between the managers of the test division and the product design division. Now Don, a project engineer with only test experience, is assigned to work for Lawrence Conner. John Turner, formerly a design engineer, is assigned to work as a test engineer in the group Don came out of.

John begins work in his new capacity and in a few months is quite satisfied with the move. Don, on the other hand, has encountered some problems which he hadn't anticipated. Don's new supervisor, Lawrence Conner, is less than happy with the trade since he had spent nearly three years developing John Turner as a design engineer and now finds he has lost him and gained a highly paid project engineer who has no design experience or knowledge of the design process.

Don also finds that his co-workers are not pleased to see another project engineer added to the group. Lee Jones, a project engineer himself, has felt that he would be the next candidate for promotion to supervisor within the design division. Will Round, senior design engineer, felt that he would soon be promoted to project engineer. He now feels that this will not occur while there are two project engineers in the group. Both Lee and Will see Don as a threat to their anticipated promotions and privately vow to give Don as little help as possible. The other design engineers and draftsmen also realize Don's design background is limited. They are not overly anxious to have to work with a weak project engineer and casually let it be known.

Lawrence, not knowing how else to use Don, assigns him to concept a new material-handling product modeled after one currently on the market. This includes contacting the company's marketing and manufacturing groups to solicit their input, doing an extensive review of advertisements and sales brochures of the products currently on the market, and traveling extensively to talk with potential customers. (Contact within the design department is minimized during the concept phase of a design.)

After nearly a year Don concludes that this new product has great potential and reports this to his supervisor, Mr. Connor. The marketing and manufacturing groups deliver similar reports to their respective divisions, and the company product committee decides that a prototype machine should be built.

At this point Conner would normally have assigned the project engineer who had worked on the original concept to lead the prototype design effort. In this case, however, he decides that Don really wouldn't be able to handle it. Instead he assigns Lee Jones as the project engineer to lead the prototype design effort and has Don report directly to Lee. Lee, not wanting the project to be slowed down, assigns a menial job to

Don and proportions the rest of the work to the others in the group. In the following months Don finds it harder and harder to accept his situation. He is responsible for an insignificant part of the project which he had originally concepted. Lee somehow never has time to listen to Don's suggestions regarding the overall development of the project. Will Round, the senior design engineer, has not only kept back information from Don,

EXHIBIT 1
JOB DESCRIPTIONS

Engineering supervisor: Has first-level line responsibility in the engineering department. Reports to general supervisor.

Project engineer: Has responsibility to set up and direct work on engineering projects. No line responsibility. Reports to the engineering supervisor.

Senior design engineer: Has responsibility for major portions of projects. Provides technical assistance to younger engineers. Reports to the engineering supervisor.

Design engineer or test engineer: Has responsibility for specific parts or components of a design or for specific tests. Reports to the engineering supervisor.

Draftsman or technician: Has responsibility to assist design or test engineers. Reports to the engineering supervisor.

EXHIBIT 2
ORGANIZATION CHART FOR ENGINEERING DEPARTMENT (DESIGN DIVISION PERSONNEL—new products department)

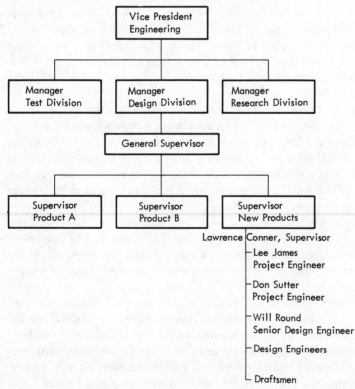

EXHIBIT 3
KEY PEOPLE IN THE CASE

Supervisor Lawrence Conner, 55-year-old man, started in shop at the age of 16, somewhat a theory X type supervisor, has little chance for advancement himself.

Project Engineer Lee James, 37 years old, worked his way up from draftsman, distrustful of college graduates, and seldom gives help to anyone.

Project Engineer Don Sutter, 34 years old, college graduate, an upward mobile, has experience in test division only.

Senior Design Engineer Will Round, 38 years old, got his degree at night school, rapidly becoming aware of diminishing chances for promotion.

Design Engineer John Turner, 25 years old, college graduate, worked in design department three years, and would like a chance at test work.

but has gone out of his way to make Don's job harder and to discredit Don's design efforts. The design engineers and draftsmen don't make things any easier for Don either.

After two years in the design division Don feels completely out of place and defeated. He can't seem to get any cooperation from the rest of the group, only an occasional joke about the quality of his work. He has learned practically nothing as a designer, he feels, and has been frustrated in his attempts to participate as a project engineer this past year. At the same time he sees the test division where he was once highly regarded, being rearranged. With this he feels that he has no doubt lost any chance of returning to his former position.

Discussion questions

1. What should be done with Don Sutter?
2. What is wrong with the company policy regarding transfers?
3. What types of guidelines should be established to prevent similar circumstances from taking place in the future?

C. ATTRACTING, SELECTING, ASSIGNING, AND ORIENTING

1. International Airlines

International Airlines is a medium-sized firm in its industry. Headquarters is in New York City. It is not well known to the general public because its business is charter passenger flights and freight, not scheduled passenger service.

Charter flights are reduced-price flights, normally contracted for by persons belonging to affinity groups. The Elks from St. Paul, Minnesota, plan a trip to Norway for a vacation. Or XYZ Encyclopedia Company offers a trip to Spain as an incentive to its salesmen.

The airlines have been a glamour business. Many went to work for the industry because world travel promises adventure and excitement, especially to persons from small towns. The industry has not had to pay high wages to attract good people, though turnover in some jobs is high.

Recently, the airline industry has become less glamorous to some potential employees. One factor has been many well-publicized plane crashes; another has been hijackings and bomb scares. These ordeals have been dramatized on television. The industry is also attacked because of noise and air pollution. Disclosure of illegal contributions to President Nixon's campaign has damaged the industry's image, as have kickback scandals.

International Airlines has been having trouble hiring quality stewardesses, baggage handlers, and mechanics. Even accountants are difficult to hire. In the past, IA relied on walk-ins and those referred by employment agencies.

The IA personnel department has been asked to prepare a personnel recruitment campaign. It should prepare a budget and determine the number of man-hours required to hire 25 stewardesses (usually college graduates), 5 accountants, 10 baggage handlers, and 15 mechanics for expected increases in business three months from now.

Discussion questions

1.   Develop a personnel recruitment campaign for the company.
2.   What costs should be included in the budget?

2. Hargrove Pipeline Company—I

Hargrove Pipeline Company is a large firm with locations in the Southwest and Midwest. The company had the need for some persons with business experience. Many of its current personnel had engineering backgrounds.

The company recruiters had gone to a number of colleges. One of them went to the University of Texas. The recruiters made a special point of interviewing logistics majors and petroleum land management majors. The recruiters had done a thorough job of screening resumes and looking for persons with the best grades and extracurricular activities leadership. Finally, the top candidates were asked to take a battery of tests at the University of Texas.

From all this information, five of the best choices were offered a chance to visit one of Hargrove's locations. One candidate refused, for she had already taken a job. Two seemed rather enthusiastic. One was out of town looking at another job, and the last one was ill and put off the decision.

The recruiters invited the two most willing candidates, who had been rated as first and fourth choices, to come in. The first choice, Joseph Trump, was invited to come in the next Monday.

Trump had outstanding qualifications. He had a B + to A − average. He had taken all solid courses, no "gut" courses. Trump had been president of the Society for Advancement of Management and vice president of the Student Council. He was attending the University of Texas on a partial scholastic scholarship. He earned the rest of his expenses working in evenings and weekends.

Trump had some problems in his personal life. His wife was unable to work as a result of complications from the birth of their child, who had severe birth defects. Trump's widowed mother called on him for help from time to time.

Trump was not subject to military call because of previous football injuries.

Trump's personality was just what Hargrove wanted—sincere, determined, and mature, with the proper mix of extrovert and introvert. The candidate wanted to work for Hargrove because the location that was offered was in Texas and because he liked the work. He had worked two summers for a pipeline company and enjoyed it. His father had also been a pipeline man.

The usual procedure at Hargrove was to give a candidate a site tour, followed by a series of interviews with various officials, including potential supervisors. This was the procedure followed for Trump. Most of the interviews went well. Then Trump was to be interviewed by Harland Rappaport, whom the recruiter, Al Laufer, had identified as a key decision maker and a possible future supervisor. Trump was a bit uneasy when he entered Rappaport's office.

After the pleasantries, the interview went like this:

Rappaport: Well, I'm a believer in getting right down to business. Time is money, you know. You are a logistics and transportation major, I see. Tell me, what do you think the major provision is of Section II, *Transportation Act of 1940?*

Trump thought quickly. He remembered they had covered a lot of points about that law last year in class. He just couldn't think of it now, when he really needed to know. He realized that Rappaport was looking at him intently.

Trump: You know, I know that, but I can't remember the exact details section by section right now. Would you like to know the gist of the law overall? I could give you that.

At this, Rappaport stood up. He had been taking notes in a three-ring binder. He snapped it shut as he stood up.

Rappaport: I think you're wasting my time. Here I've been given a big buildup about how great you are. You are a logistics major, and you don't know a simple thing like that! I never went to college, and yet I know things like that; I think you're wasting my time! I believe I'll call Al Laufer in to take you onto your next interview. We're finished here, aren't we?

Rappaport paused as his hand rested on the phone.

Trump was very upset. He didn't know what to say. He could only mumble: "If you say so."

Rappaport called Laufer, who came and took Trump for coffee. Then Laufer rushed back to Rappaport.

Laufer: What did you do to that kid? He's all upset.

Rappaport: I've been reading some articles about selection. Some experts feel that the best way to select someone is to put him or her in a stressful situation that comes close to the conditions on the job. So I put Trump under stress. He flunked, if you ask me.

Laufer: That's just great! We need someone badly for a job like this and here you are playing amateur games. He's really a good kid. Now you've jinxed us for sure.

Rappaport: Just because they went to college doesn't mean they can cut the mustard. I don't want any kid who cracks under a little pressure like that to work for me!

Requirement. You are Al Laufer. How do you handle this situation with Trump? With Rappaport? Is the stress interview a good predictor of future performance?

Hargrove Pipeline Company—II

Laufer rushed from Rappaport's office. He got to the coffee-break area. Trump seemed himself again. Laufer was very solicitous and tried to give the best possible impression to Trump.

As Trump was about to leave to return to Austin, the men had a final conversation.

Laufer: Joe, I've talked to most of the people at the office and the impression is very favorable. Would you be interested in receiving an offer, if I should be in a position to make one?

Trump: Yes, Al, I think so. I've always loved the pipeline business and this part of the country.

Laufer's job now was to gather opinions from those at the office. They all were very impressed with Trump, except Rappaport. So Laufer bucked Rappaport and went to his boss, Ziggie Nicholson, and the operations manager, Daryle Mills, for a decision. They decided to make an offer to Trump. They also decided that Trump should work for Stan Reddick. Reddick was delighted.

Laufer called Trump at once. The conversation went like this:

Laufer: Joe, this is Al Laufer at Hargrove. We'd like to make you an offer of a job. We'll meet all your conditions of starting time, transportation costs, and we can offer you $50 a month more than you asked. What do you say?

Trump: My wife Nicola and I have discussed it, and we think we'll take the offer from Panhandle instead.

Laufer: Joe, was it money? Perhaps I could go back to the boss on that one?

Trump: No, it wasn't money. In fact, you are offering more money.

Laufer: Well, if it's supervisor, you'd be working for Stan Reddick.

Trump: No, it's just that I think the Panhandle offer is a better opportunity. But thanks anyway.

Laufer is convinced that the real reason Trump turned down Hargrove's offer was Rappaport. Now Laufer must call up their fourth choice candidate, George Zimar. Laufer wonders if he'll run into the same game all over again. Should he try to talk to Rappaport and his boss? Should he try to warn Zimar that Rappaport likes to play games and that he should be ready to roll with the punches? Laufer wonders.

Requirement.   You are Al Laufer. How do you proceed now so that you can hire a logistics specialist? What can be done to change Rappaport's behavior in the future?

3. Carol's Interview

Carol Williams is 21, married, and a graduating senior at a good state university in the eastern United States. Carol is majoring in personnel. She works 15 hours per week for a government agency to pay her school and living expenses. Her grade point average is 3.5 (maximum is 4.0), and she took a rigorous program.

Since she is close to graduating, Carol has begun to look for a job. She likes the government agency, but her job there is secretarial and she wants a management job. None is available at the agency due to a recent budget cutback.

Carol's boss, Martha Sembrick, recommended that Carol contact a firm in the area. Her brother is a vice president there, and Martha has met one of the personnel executives, Vance Takovo. Martha suggested she call Vance.

Carol has had several experiences in which she called people like Vance, and they had a series of excuses (out of town, in a meeting). So she decided to go right to the company and ask to talk to Vance.

The company is a medium-sized financial concern employing about 3,000 persons and about 500 managers.

Carol arrived at the corporate headquarters. She asked the receptionist to see Vance. The receptionist called personnel. Vance didn't come out. But Karen did. Karen introduced herself as from personnel and asked Carol to follow her. Karen was about 35 years old. Carol assumed Karen was Vance's secretary. When Carol entered the office, Karen closed the door and sat down with her.

Carol: I asked to see Vance Takovo.

Karen: I know, but I am a personnel interviewer, and I'll be handling your case.

Carol: But I specifically asked to see Vance.

Karen: I'm sorry, but we have a policy here: Women interview women, men interview men. How fast can you type and do you take shorthand?

Carol: I'm not here to interview for a clerical job. I'm finishing a college degree in business and want to get a part-time management trainee job leading to full time when I graduate.

Karen: I interview for clerical jobs, but there are no management trainee jobs available. Now complete this application blank (Exhibit 1).

Carol: Two guys that I know—John Lerbinger and Bill Grahan—have part-time trainee jobs here.

Karen: I don't know about them. Complete the application blank.

Carol completed some of the blank as shown in Exhibit I but did not fully complete it since she found some of the information requested uncalled for.

Carol: Again, I won't take secretarial work. I want to talk to Vance.

Karen: Now you'll take this clerical test.

Carol: I guess you didn't hear me. I'm not interested in clerical work.

Karen: Everyone who applies for a job here must complete this test.

Carol took the test (it took 20 minutes), but she was getting angrier by the minute.

Carol: You mean to tell me that everyone—men applying for jobs as accountants and salesmen—must take this test too?

Karen: Yes. Well, thank you for applying, and if we have anything, we'll call you.

Carol left very angry. She told the incident to Martha who called Vance and her brother and denounced the whole incident, telling them both what a good candidate Carol would make.

Carol also described the incident to her personnel professor who called the vice president personnel to express his concern about the application blank and general procedure. The executive, Art Lindauer, said:

Lindauer: Most of what she told Carol was not true. Women don't just interview women, for example. And not everyone has to take the clerical test. The whole incident is embarrassing, and we've been meaning to look at that application blank. We'll do that soon.

Casewriter: Frankly, Art, Carol's ready to file an EEOC complaint. I'm doubtful she'd work for you now under any circumstances and your place will get a bad name here at State.

Lindauer: We'll reinterview her and hope she'll be satisfied.

That day, Carol was reinterviewed by three persons (Vance and two other male personnel executives). Vance explained what the standard interview should be. He also explained that the company had just cut 100 people from the payroll by attrition because of poor business and profit. Vance, in effect, apologized and said he'd call Carol back if any job turned up. At this writing three months later, Carol was graduating and had never heard from Vance.

EXHIBIT 1

APPLICATION FOR EMPLOYMENT

Name _____ Telephone _____
        Print last name   First   Middle   Area code

Present
address _____
        Street and number   City   State   Zip code

Last
address _____
        Street and number   City   State   Zip code

Date of
birth _____ Age_____ Sex_____ Height_____ Weight_____

Are you a citizen of the
United States of America?_____ Soc. Security No._____

ALL QUESTION MUST BE ANSWERED

I. FAMILY STATUS

☐ Single

☐ Married—date of marriage _____ ☐ Engaged—wedding date_____

☐ Separated—
   date of separation_____ ☐ Divorced—date _____

☐ Widowed—date
   of spouse's death _____ Number of children _____

Name and age of children_____

Name of spouse_____ Age_____

Spouse working ☐ permanently ☐ temporarily ☐ part time.

Occupation _____

Father's occupation (present or former)_____ Age_____

Number of brothers_____ Number of sisters_____

II. EDUCATION

Give an outline of your education by completing the table below:

Type of school	Name and location of school	Main field of study	Dates attended From	To	Graduate Yes	No	Average grades earned
High school							
Trade or technical							
College							
Other							

If you left school without graduating, what were the reasons?_____

What were your best liked subjects_____ Least liked subjects_____

AN EQUAL OPPORTUNITY EMPLOYER

EXHIBIT 1 (*continued*)

III. EMPLOYMENT RECORD

1. Name and address of employers (begin with most recent and work backward)	2. Nature of employer's business	3. Kind of work you did
Name		
Address		
City State		
Name		
Address		
City State		

4. Person under whom you worked	5. Length of service (month and year)	6. Salary or commission earnings	7. Why did you leave this employment?
Name	From	First month	
Title			
Telephone	To	Last month	
Name	From	First month	
Title			
Telephone	To	Last month	

(Note: List additional employers on back of form if necessary. Be sure to answer all 7 questions for each employer listed.)

Please indicate any employer you do not wish contacted at this time and why.

IV. SUPPLEMENTARY INFORMATION

Position applied for _____ Salary expected _____

Date available _____ Length of time you plan to work _____

Have you any friends or relatives employed here? _____

If so give names and relationship _____

Who recommended you apply here? _____

V. DRIVING STATUS

Do you have a valid driver's license? ☐ Yes   ☐ No

What state? _____ Operator's number _____ Have you, or any member of your household, ever had your driver's license revoked? ☐ Yes   ☐ No.

If yes, what date? _____ Which member and why? _____

Do you have automobile insurance? ☐ Yes   ☐ No   Have you ever been cancelled or refused? ☐ Yes   ☐ No   If yes, when and why? _____

Have you ever been convicted for any offense? ☐ Yes   ☐ No   If yes, explain.

EXHIBIT 1 (continued)

VI. PHYSICAL CONDITION

How many days have you lost by reason of illness or injury during the past two years? _____

For what cause? _____

Give reasons and cause for any time you have spent in a hospital, sanitarium, or rest home as a patient _____

Give reasons if you have ever been rejected for life or health insurance _____

Are the members of your immediate family in good health? _____

If not, give age and condition _____

To what extent do you use intoxicating liquor? _____

VII. MILITARY SERVICE RECORD

Have you served in the U.S. Armed Forces? _____ (If yes) Date active duty started _____

Which branch of the service? _____ Starting rank/rate _____

Duties while in service _____

Date of discharge _____ Reasons for discharge (Honorable, Disabled, etc.) _____

Rank/rate at discharge _____ Were you hospitalized while in service? ☐ Yes ☐ No

If yes, from _____ to _____ For what reason? _____

How much pension or disability compensation are you receiving? _____

For what reason? _____

What special training did you receive, or other usable skills did you acquire, while in the service that should be considered? _____

Present military classification _____

VIII. FINANCIAL

	Value	Amount owed	Monthly payments
Property owned			
Home	$	$	$
Other real estate or property	$	$	$
Home furnishings (exclude personal effects)	$	$	$
Automobile(s)	$	$	$

Other obligations

If renting, what rent do you pay? _____ $_____

Do you pay alimony or child support? _____ $_____

Amount of outstanding obligations due banks, credit unions, or finance companies not shown in amounts owed above $_____ $_____

Amount of outstanding medical bills, time payments, or charge accounts not shown in amounts owed above _____ $_____ $_____

EXHIBIT 1 (*concluded*)

General information
Spouse's earnings ————————————— Amount $————
Any independent source of income?————————— Amount $————
Do you have a savings account?————Approximate Amount $————

IX. MEMBERSHIPS AND ACTIVITIES

Note: Omit the names of organizations which indicate the race, creed, color, or national origin of members.

Name of organization or type of activity	*To what extent do you partcipate?*	*Hours spent per week*	*Offices held during past five years*
Religious	Omit name here		
Business, honorary, or social			
Sports and hobbies			

X. REFERENCES Do not include relatives, former employers, or employees of this company.

Name	*Street and number*	*City*	*Occupation*

I hereby certify that my answers to all questions herein are true and complete. ——————————— Companies has my permission to communicate with my present and past employers (except as indicated on page 2), and the schools I have attended, in determining my qualifications for employment.

I understand that ——————————— Companies may, as part of their normal employment procedure, request an investigative consumer report which may be prepared through personal interviews with my friends, neighbors, and associates, which will provide information as to my character, general reputation, personal characteristics, and mode of living; and that upon written request within a reasonable time, additional detailed information as to the nature and scope of the investigation, if one is made, will be furnished to me.

Date——————————— APPLICANT'S SIGNATURE———————————————

Discussion questions

1. How would you instruct the receptionist to handle walk-in applicants?
2. How should personnel organize its interviewing: men interview men, etc.? Should the walk-ins be randomly assigned? Part time, one person; full time for another? How?
3. How would you redesign the application blank?
4. How would you retrain Karen to handle future applicants?
5. Should Carol have filed a complaint? What would have happened on it?
6. If Vance called tomorrow offering Carol another interview for a management trainee job, should she take the interview?

4. Who Should Do the Hiring?*

The Hackney Paper Box Company operates 46 corrugated box factories from California to Maine. On June 18, Hackney started hiring personnel for a new plant in Cincinnati, Ohio. The plant was to hire approximately 130 persons with all higher management and other key personnel to be transferred from other plants. Twelve potential front-line supervisors were to be hired locally and sent to other Hackney plants for four to six months training. The projected management structure at the new plant is shown in Exhibit 1. Hackney was a highly centralized company, except for production, sales, and employment; all other functions were performed by personnel from the Chicago corporate office.

Mr. James Gulfstead, corporate employment manager, arrived in Cincinnati on June 16 and went through the mechanics of setting up an employment office in the yet-to-be completed Hackney plant. On June 18, he hired a secretary to help him in his work and to be the secretary to the plant manager when he arrived on the scene. On June 19, he started recruiting the 12 potential supervisors to be sent to other plants to be trained for Hackney's Cincinnati plant. This task was completed by July 22 with all 12 potential supervisors scheduled to report to work between July 20 and September 1.

Mr. Gulfstead returned to Chicago on July 22 and scheduled a July 27 meeting with the corporate director of manpower planning and the assistant vice president of manufacturing—midwest. At this meeting they reviewed possible promotions and transfers for the jobs of sales manager, assistant plant manager, and employment manager. During

---

* This case was prepared by Professor James C. Hodgetts of Memphis State University and is intended to be used as a teaching device rather than to show correct or incorrect methods of operations.

EXHIBIT 1
CINCINNATI PLANT—HACKNEY BOX COMPANY

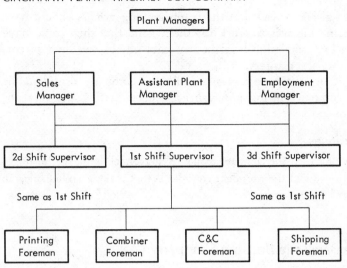

the two months that followed, various prospects were contacted and selections were made.

On January 2, Mr. Gulfstead returned to Cincinnati and proceeded to hire the remaining 130 employees for the plant. On February 1, the foreman trainees all returned to Cincinnati, and the plant started production on February 7. Also on February 1, Mr. Jack Oneran was promoted to plant manager at Cincinnati from his position as assistant plant manager at the Hackney plant in Buffalo, New York.

Although the plant was to have started production on February 7, it was April before the first quality box was shipped, and a year later the plant was only producing at 42 percent of capacity. At this point in time, Mr. Jack Oneran, plant manager, was asked by his boss, the assistant vice president—midwest, to justify this low production record.

Mr. Oneran had been waiting for this for a long time. He felt that the company policy of permitting the personnel department to do the hiring was wrong and that one of the major production problems in the plant stemmed from the way people had been acquired. He had fired the secretary hired by Mr. Gulfstead soon after he arrived. She was quite popular with the office staff but just not willing to put forth the effort necessary to hold down the top secretarial job in the plant. This had caused considerable dissatisfaction and insecurity in the office. Also, the assistant plant manager and Mr. Oneran had worked together before and never had gotten along. The assistant plant manager said he would never have accepted the job if he knew Mr. Oneran was going to be plant manager. Also, he felt that he should have been in on the hiring of the front-line supervisors.

Mr. Oneran also believed that the front-line supervisors should have had some say in who was to work for them—and that they could have been valuable in hiring high-level hourly paid employees such as corrugator operators and printers.

When Mr. Oneran's report was read by the company president, he decided that company hiring policy needed investigating but was uncertain of what course to take.

Dicussion questions

1. What is wrong with the company policy of personnel doing the hiring?
2. What factors should the president consider before making any changes in the hiring policy?

5. Midville Beverage Bottling Company (A)*

Jim Jackson is manager of the Midville Beverage Bottling Company. The city of Midville is a growing and progressive community of almost 225,000 people. Besides Midville, this soft drink bottling company owns and operates three small branch plants in Riverdale, Elmgrove, and Lake City. The combined population of the entire territory is close to 350,000. Last year the company sold nearly 2.5 million cases of all products.

The manager, Jim Jackson, started out before World War II as a route salesman, worked his way up through the ranks, and has been general manager now for eight years. Midville is a family-owned business. Mr. Smith was owner-manager when Jim joined the company in 1937. When Mr. Smith passed on in 1959, the widow and Dr. Smith, the only son, promoted Jim from sales manager to general manager.

Soon after he took over, Jackson appointed Harry Jones as general sales manager. Harry started on the routes and worked his way up. Harry is well liked in the organization and by the trade. Under Harry's direction, sales have increased every year; so has share of market. In fact, last year was by far the best in the plant's 57-year history. Sales of the plant's major soft drink were up 14 percent and the rapid growth of the new products and one-way packages added extra volume on top of that.

Even so, Jim is worried. He's due to retire in six years and has given a lot of though to the problem of who will be his successor. The general

---

sales manager would normally be the logical man; but Jim is not at all sure that Harry is capable of assuming top management responsibilities. As Jim put it to Mrs. Smith, "There isn't a better sales manager in the business. But as general manager, I just don't think Harry would be successful. He's very good at handling people, but when it comes to budgets and other administrative jobs, Harry's lost." Mrs. Smith asked Jim what he planned to do.

Midville Beverage Bottling Plant (B)*

Jim's first step was to hire a young man, Bill Shelby, as his staff assistant. Bill had a good background in marketing consumer products and was well known by supermarket operators and buyers throughout the entire area. Bill had graduated from the state university six years before. Bill was very personable in manner and dress and had all the latent attributes of an up-to-date, fast-thinking, forward-minded manager. For the first time, the company developed sales forecasts, case sales, budgets, operating budgets, and so on. Organization charts were instituted and a continuing educational program was started throughout the entire organization.

As Jim Jackson said, however, "It was all great, but I guess it was too much, too soon. This, I presume, was faulty timing on my part. But I felt we had so much to do and so little time to do it. Small but telling non-compliance began to show up in every department. The 'old-timers' just wouldn't accept Bill. One of the route supervisors, for example, told Harry to keep that 'smart-aleck out of my territory before he gets it all messed up. If he thinks he can change everything around after I've had it running smoothly for 15 years, he's got another think coming.' The older supervisors especially seemed to resent the 'young upstart.' So finally I figured it would be best to find Bill another job before the fire burst into flames."

Shortly before Bill Shelby left, Jim hired another staff assistant, Frank Farnsworth. Frank, too, was well educated and, what was more important to Jim, had experience in the soft drink business.

"Maybe the reason the others wouldn't accept Bill Shelby was because he hadn't grown up in the business." said Jim to Mrs. Smith. "Frank Farnsworth, on the other hand, has worked for a progessive competitive bottling plant in another section of the country and has risen to assistant sales manager. He should work out just fine."

---

* This material was prepared by R. Tagiuri and B. Rundlett, as a basis for class discussion. It is not designed to illustrate either correct or incorrect handling of administrative problems.

Frank Farnsworth proved to be an "eager beaver" and would work with his hands and heart, as well as his head. Sales contests were initiated and advertising beefed up for the first time in years. New products and new packages were added to the line. Beverage department studies were undertaken, and the company's products received more shelf space, greater dominance, and increased sales in almost all larger supermarkets and other food stores as a result.

But as Jim reported to Mrs. Smith several months later, "While sales are up and business is humming, these new activities seem to focus attention on our previous inadequacies, and opposition to Frank Farnsworth has begun to grow just as it did against Bill Shelby."

"I don't quite understand," said Mrs. Smith.

"Well," said Jim, "just the other day one of our best route managers went over Harry's head to tell me that, 'These new-fangled ideas about rearranging beverage departments just won't work. My stores are different. Tell that guy to keep out of my territory.'"

"What are you going to do now?" said Mrs. Smith. "If you let Frank Farnsworth go, you'll be right back where you started." Jim agreed. But the resistance and antagonism to Frank Farnsworth continued to grow. Jim finally found him a good job in another soft drink bottling plant in the part of the country from which he had come originally.

After these unfortunate experiences with the first two young men, Jim hired a third "trainee." But, as Jim said, "He was the most over-recommended man I ever knew. So when after a few months he did not work out, I let him find another job.

"We still need a bright young man not steeped in the one-product, one-package, one-price philosophy, well-grounded in the general refreshment business, who will look *forward* to developing our sales, profits, and people. But I have great doubts that the old-timers will accept anyone of this caliber. They seem to be resisting any change for the better and regard all outsiders as a threat. Frankly, I just don't know what steps to take next."

Midville Beverage Bottling Plant (C)*

After the third young "trainee" left, Jim talked with several other bottlers and found many with somewhat similar problems. Briefly, he found that most of today's plant managers had come up through the

* This material was prepared by R. Tagiuri and B. Rundlett, as a basis for class discussion. It is not designed to illustrate either correct or incorrect handling of administrative problems.

ranks, from route salesman to route manager to sales manager to plant manager. And, like Jim, many plant managers were concerned about the whole problem of management succession.

The first bottler Jim talked to pointed out that it's almost impossible to find talented, well-educated young men today who are willing to start at the bottom and work up. Also, starting salaries for college men are too high by comparison with current wage structures in most bottling plants.

The second plant manager with whom Jim talked felt that present middle management in most bottling plants, his own included, are generally not qualified by education to take over top jobs. Yet, if a top man is brought in from outside, the rest of the organization rebels. They resent the outsider, the man who "leap frogs" over them. What's more, morale of the route managers suffers when outsiders are brought in over them. They see no future for themselves.

The third bottle told Jim that he had hired a sales manager away from a used-car dealer to take over as assistant sales manager. One of his route managers had asked, "Why wasn't I considered for the job?" This plant manager had offered various training courses and night school programs to his route managers, but none of them had shown much aptitude or interest. He therefore felt that he had made the only move possible. "You can't expect cream to rise to the top if all you pour in is skim milk. So I just felt obliged to bring in a top-flight man from the outside," he told Jim.

The fourth bottler asked Jim why Harry couldn't be groomed to take over. Jim answered by saying, "As I told Mrs. Smith, Harry Jones is the best sales manager in the business. His record proves that. But he's never had much experience with fiscal matters, production schedules, taxes, purchasing, and all the 101 other administrative jobs required of a general manager."

"Has Harry ever shown an interest in general management? Have you ever given him the opportunity to learn?" this bottler asked. "Well, some maybe," replied Jim. "But I figure a man ought to stick to what he does best. And for Harry, that's selling, sales promotion, advertising, sales training, and trade relations; not fiscal and administrative activities."

The last plant manager Jim talked to said, "Jim, as you know, we don't want to 'raid' or 'pirate' from other bottlers. There has always been an unwritten agreement among us bottlers not to hire top men away from another plant. But maybe the time has come when we ought to join together in some way to find an answer to this problem." Jim agreed but didn't quite know how this might be done.

Jim Jackson thought over carefully what his fellow bottlers had said. "It still boils down to the fact that there's no one in my plant capable of taking over," he reflected. "Suppose I had a bad accident or became seriously ill, who'd run Midville? Hindsight says I should have been developing my replacement over the last five or ten years. But I haven't. So, what do I do next?"

Discussion questions

1. What should Jim Jackson do now to find a capable replacement for his position? For future positions?
2. Why did the employees at Midville resent Bill Shelby and Frank Farnsworth?
3. What could be done now and in the future by the bottlers if they did join together?

6. The Agency

Martha Conklin is the personnel specialist responsible for a large government department in Washington D.C. Her agency, like many others, hires large numbers of clerical employees. Typically, most of these are young, single girls just leaving high school, or they have finished two years of high school and taken clerical programs in local proprietary "business colleges."

Martha has studied the turnover records of her agency. She has also seen the data on other agencies for similar jobs. It does not make good reading.

	Turnover records		
Agency	This year	Last year	2 years ago
Martha's	42%	38%	31%
Agency 1	26	32	34
Agency 2	24	27	29
Agency 3	30	24	26
Agency 4	28	25	23

Martha realizes that some of the turnover is due to normal attrition. The girls get married and move away. Or they decide to get more schooling, or they do not like the boss or the work.

The girls work mostly on their own, but their supervisor is there to help them. The job consists of routine typing and filing of client's requests for assistance. The typists transcribe interviewer's notes and file the results for action later.

Martha has noted that little is done in terms of a formal orientation program. The girls receive booklets from personnel on fringe benefits and so forth. They are introduced to their supervisor, who takes over from there. Many supervisors are busy and give the girls a "lick and a promise" introduction.

Martha is wondering if she should do something about orientation and see if this would help with the turnover. Typically, there are about 100 girls working in this job at any one time. They are supervised by five fairly senior supervisors.

Discussion questions

1. You are Martha. How would you convince your superior that a formalized orientation program is needed?
2. How could Martha obtain specific information on the reasons why the turnover rate is so high in her agency?

7. Frazer's Department Store—A College Senior Views the Employment Process

Frazer's Department Store has approximately 800 employees and about 325 of them are sales people. The personnel department consists of Mr. Stone, the personnel manager; Mrs. Willoughby, the training supervisor; and four or five others whom I have not met. Mr. Stone is a very busy man. I was employed as a salesman in the men's furnishings department.

First, it is important to tell you of my attitude and my opinion of a job at Frazer's before my interview for employment. I had a very high regard for the store's merchandise, employee relations, and customer contacts. I also had the idea that as a college senior I was going to be treated on a higher level than other employees. I believed this, not because I thought myself superior to the other employees, but because of my college education and my previous retail training. I also believed that my store service would not only be a job, but something of an educational program in merchandising, publicity, personnel, and organization.

I had two interviews before I actually started my selling job. My first interview was with Mr. Stone. (Before the interview, I filled out an application blank which asked for details about my work experience and personal information.) I sat in the personnel office a few minutes waiting for Mr. Stone. When he walked in, he introduced himself to me in an

---

Note: Many colleges and universities are integrating work experiences and educational programs for certain students. Some of these programs, called "cooperative courses," provide that students work in industry for one term and then attend school the next. Other programs require students to work in business or industry for shorter periods of time. This case is a student report pertaining to his experience in a department store. The case was written by the late Carl Dauten.

uninterested and indifferent manner. (I hope I do not sound overcritical, but it is the truth.) We then proceeded to his office. He did not ask me to be seated, but after a few moments of hesitation I sat down. I expected him to start the conversation, so I remained silent while he looked over my application blank. After two or three minutes of silence he asked me a few questions about my previous employment. He then read my application blank again. Up to this time I had felt confident and relaxed, but because of the silence and Mr. Stone's seemingly indifferent attitude, I began to feel slightly nervous. He then interrupted the silence by saying, "At the present time there are no openings, but we will call you when we want you to start. You'd better wear a necktie when we call you back." I then said good-bye and left.

After being notified two weeks later that Frazer's had an opening for me, I received my second interview. I was interviewed by Mrs. Willoughby, who is an assistant to Mr. Stone. She is a charming, tactful, and courteous woman. Throughout the entire interview she seemed interested in my problems and questions, and she made me feel important and comfortable.

At the beginning of the interview, she told me of the different positions that were open and asked me which job I would prefer. It was this consideration which gave me a feeling of importance. We then agreed on the job best suited for me, and she courteously said good-bye. Because of Mrs. Willoughby, my attitude toward Frazer's again changed (for the better). Mrs. Willoughby made me a friend of the store.

The day after my final interview, Mrs. Willoughby, who is also in charge of training new employees, took me and two others into a conference room and started our training. The room was very comfortable; it was equipped with a round table, ash trays, and fairly comfortable chairs. We were allowed to smoke. She handed us a pamphlet on store rules and regulations which she explained, clarifying the policies and explaining why the rules were important.

After acquainting us with store regulations, she taught us how to write the different types of sales checks (charges, deliveries, cash sales, will-call, and C.O.D.). She used a good procedure in teaching us different transactions. Each of us was handed a sales book; she then took each kind of purchase, told us how to write it up, and then she wrote out an example and showed it to us. She then described another transaction, and we wrote it up independently, and she checked the final results. After going through each type of sale, she gave us a review and stressed the important points to remember. Before closing the session, Mrs. Willoughby told us that if we had any problems, we should "come up and see her" and she "would try to straighten them out."

During the entire session, Mrs. Willoughby appeared to be an excellent teacher and a charming individual. There is only one criticism I had about my centralized training, and that is I was not informed about the exact duties of my job. Apparently, Mrs. Willoughby did not give us much information about our jobs, because she expected our supervisors to do that.

After my training in the personnel department, Mrs. Willoughby took me to the men's furnishings department and introduced me to the floor-walker who seemed to be a courteous and respected person. He, in turn, introduced me to a salesman in my department, who showed me the stock and introduced me to some "tricks-of-the-trade." This initial introduction was brief and quite inadequate.

I wasn't introduced to the head of my department, and, therefore, I did not know who my boss was. Besides not being introduced to my boss, I also wasn't introduced to any of the other salesmen. From the way some salesmen acted, I thought they resented my presence in the department.

Another inadequacy of my job introduction was the failure to inform me of the proper techniques of selling including wrapping packages and making change. I wasn't told exactly what was expected of me.

Numerous problems arose from these shortcomings. Before I learned who was my boss, a salesman told me to go eat lunch, which I did. When I came back, the boss of the department met me and was angry. Our relationship was complicated and disagreeable from the start.

Another problem arose from the improper introduction to my job. My boss saw me wrapping a package in what he thought was an incorrect way; nobody had told me the proper method. He reprimanded me and then took his own time to teach me what he considered to be the proper method. Other salesmen wrap packages differently. This could have been avoided, if I had been taught correctly in the first place.

Since I wasn't told exactly what duties I was to perform, I had only a general idea of what was expected of me. During the period I worked in this specific department, I thought that the work I performed was adequate. After a few weeks on the job, however, I was notified that I was only doing an average amount of work and that they expected much more from me. I am positive that this episode could have been avoided if I had known exactly what was expected of me.

Discussion questions

1. You are Ralph Smith, a consultant hired by Frazer's to recommend improvements for the personnel department. What do you suggest?
2. What is the significance of the impressions received by the individual in the case?

D. CAREER DEVELOPMENT, EVALUATION, AND TRAINING

1. San Jose Plastics

San Jose Plastics likes to think of itself as a good corporate citizen. The firm is a large manufacturer of plastic goods, publicly held but still under strong influence of the family that founded it some time ago. The founder, Harvey Filley, was the son of a Christian minister. Harvey was always more interested in the people who worked for him and his customers than the production or financial sides of his business. As a result, SJP was a good corporate citizen long before that became fashionable or expected.

An expression of the importance that is placed on these areas at SJP is the large size and relatively great power of the personnel and public relations department. The public relations area deals with the press and with both family and company gifts to the community. These gifts have been extensive. A wing of the art museum was given in memory of Harvey's wife. The hospital has received buildings and equipment. Nearly every organization, from Little League to local schools, has received gifts from the company at some time or another.

This philanthropy has extended to individuals, too. Management tries to help out employees in financial need. Needy persons in the community have received financial assistance, too, and this is done without fanfare or excitement. The firm and its management long ago adopted the view that these activities were simply good business, and that long-run rewards would balance out the short-run costs.

SJP has an extensive benefits program for its employees, down to and including distribution of Christmas turkeys. Wages are outstanding for the area. The payoff has been an excellent record of very low turnover, little or no absenteeism, high quality, and excellent productivity. One of the benefits provided by SJP is the availability of counseling on the full range of career, financial, and personal and psychiatric problems. This is provided by the counseling section, part of the personnel department. The section consists of three professionals and one clerk. The professionals are:

Joyce Riggs, age 31. Joyce does career and financial counseling. She has a B.S. in personnel management and an M.A. in organizational psychology.

Walter Kaup, Ph.D., age 39. Walt is a psychologist. He also does some career counseling, and works with personal problems such as alcoholism and drug abuse, and works with motivation problems.

Jenny Manion, M.D., Ph.D., age 45. Jenny is a psychiatrist. She works with the more serious problems referred to the counseling section.

Recently one of the firm's supervisors mentioned a problem with one of his employees to Dr. Manion. He is considering referring the employee, Frances Courtney, for counseling.

Frances is 43 and fairly recently divorced. The divorce occurred after her three children were grown and left home, but the marriage had been in trouble for some time before that. Frances was a graduate of a good liberal arts college with a degree in English Literature. She felt that she had given up her career to raise her family. As her children grew older, she began taking courses in literature and creative writing, hoping to re-establish her identity as separate from her husband and children. Frances' hopes for a writing career ran into problems, however, as she began to receive criticism on her work in the courses. Her grades were generally "Bs" rather than "As", and her professors were often negatively critical. Few of them had much positive to say about her work. Eventually, she decided that it "wasn't worth it," and dropped the idea of a writing career.

As the children left home, Frances' ability to tolerate her unhappy marriage began to decline, culminating in the divorce. At about this time she applied to SJP for a job, both for financial support and to provide some purpose to her life. She has held a number of clerical and assistant-to jobs. Presently she is assigned to the market research section of the firm, assisting on projects intended to evaluate possible new products. Her supervisor feels she is capable of doing good work, but is not performing at that capacity.

Discussion questions

1. As Dr. Manion, how would you proceed with Frances' case?
2. To whom would you assign her?
3. What is the likelihood of success with her?

2. Kehoe Publishing

Kehoe Publishing is a medium-sized firm located in Cheyenne, Wyoming. It is a family-owned firm, having been founded by Bernard Kehoe in 1940.

Kehoe publishes a variety of material. Its major enterprise is the publishing of books, such as textbooks, for well-known book companies. Many of these firms, whose names are well known to the public, don't actually publish many books. They are essentially marketing organizations which contract with companies like Kehoe to publish their books. They are shipped then to regional warehouses where the "publisher" fills orders from bookstores, schools, and other customers.

At present, Bernard Kehoe is 65 years old. He is wondering about his management team, especially since he is not in the best of health.

His team consists of the following:

1. Thomas Mautner, age 47. He was employed by Kehoe after 20 years' experience with a book publisher to which Kehoe sells many of its books. The customer had no objections to Mautner's move.
2. Warren Kehoe, age 31. He is Bernard Kehoe's son and has been with the firm for six years, after completing college and two years in the service.
3. Wayne Taylor, age 36. He joined the firm 14 years ago. He has had a variety of experiences with the firm.
4. Melvin Zollitsch, age 59. He has been with the firm since it was founded. He is experienced primarily in production of books.
5. Norman Littlefield, age 54. He joined the firm in 1942. He is experienced primarily in production of books.

Up until now, whenever Kehoe has gone on vacation, he has divided up his responsibilities. But he wonder what would happen if he died or followed his wife's idea that they retire to Arizona but didn't sell out.

Really Littlefield and Zollitsch couldn't handle the business. They are almost as old as Kehoe and do not have the breadth of experience necessary. But he has a real dilemma over the other three. Taylor has been there longest of the three but has less experience overall than Mautner. Yet Taylor feels he's the senior man and should have serious consideration. Kehoe leans towards Mautner. His age is one desirable factor. He also succeeded with another company. And maybe if Kehoe would admit the truth, he'd have to say he knows more about his son and Taylor and thus more of their faults than about Mautner since he's only been with Kehoe Publishing three years.

Part of Kehoe's dilemma is over his son Warren. Kehoe can't really forget when Warren was a kid and all the mistakes he made then. Kehoe doesn't like the way Warren's wife is always pushing him to take over his father's job. Kehoe really resents that! He's not ready to quit yet! Besides, Warren still needs a lot of "seasoning."

Another part of his problem is his oldest son Benjamin. Kehoe had groomed this son to take over the firm. However, after almost eight years with the firm, Benjamin, Jr., left Cheyenne and the business to become a professional photographer. Photography had been his hobby. Kehoe had always assumed that Ben, Jr., would take over. When he left, Kehoe had put off the decision of who would succeed him.

What if he gave Warren more authority? How would Mautner and Taylor react? Their wives would like it, but what would it do to the business? Although he loved Warren, Kehoe had trouble imagining Warren succeeding him.

Once Kehoe had considered selling out, but his wife pointed out that probably would mean Warren would lose out. The prospective buyer would not guarantee present management their jobs.

Requirement.   You are Joe Rimler, Kehoe's friend at the country club. You are personnel manager at a large agribusiness firm in the area, but you have known Kehoe and his family for years. You and Kehoe went to school together. He's come to you for advice. How do you suggest he resolve his dilemma? Could Bernard organize the firm so it could be managed jointly? How? Is Bernard really ready to retire?

3. Farace Recreation, Inc.

Farace Recreation (FRI) is a medium-sized manufacturer of recreation equipment. Their major products are pleasure boats and boating equipment for middle-class buyers. Farace seeks the family recreation market, not the rich yacht trade. The major plant and home office is located in Asheville, North Carolina. The company also has a branch plant at Redlands, California. The firm employs approximately 1,275 persons.

Farace has been in business since the mid-1920s, but most of its growth has come since 1950. With the increase in leisure time and as more families have achieved middle-class status—often with two persons working to achieve it—boating and similar recreational products have increased in sales tremendously. Farace does not produce the motors. It mainly produces the boats themselves and allied equipment for safety and pleasure. The organization chart describing some of the relations at Farace is given in Exhibit 1. The two plants are organized identically. The staff support units, such as personnel and accounting, report to the plant managers. But the home office vice presidents have functional advisory authority over these units as well.

Vice President—Personnel John Papgeorge is 54 years old. He is a

EXHIBIT 1
ORGANIZATION CHART OF FARACE RECREATION, INC.

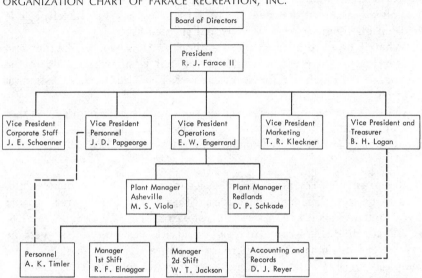

graduate of the University of North Carolina's business school. In the last ten years he has taken short courses in personnel offered by the university, the University of Florida, and Virginia Tech.

Art Timler is 31 years old. He was a personnel major at Wake Forest University where he received his B.S.B.A. He had six years personnel experience with a large textile firm in North Carolina before joining FRI two years ago. He likes his job at Asheville. He gets along well with Mitch Viola and Reggie Elnaggar. His relations with Wilbur Jackson are correct and a bit distant, but he has tried to improve them ever since he's been there. Early in his tenure there, he didn't hire Jackson's cousin for a job because he didn't appear qualified. Ever since then, there have been strained relations between Jackson and Timler.

Papgeorge has been trying to improve the quality of employee evaluation at FRI. Timler has cooperated. In his recent classes for supervisors, Timler has discussed effective use of performance evaluation. The firm uses a graphic-rating scale. Timler has emphasized the importance of the evaluation interview. He has stressed the discussion of positive points first, then negative points. He suggested that the supervisors not dwell on the negative points too much. Rather, they should be mentioned in reference to how the supervisor could help the employee improve in the future. To determine if his training was taking, he secretly taped some of the evaluation meetings of some of the supervisors. A summary of the data on these tapes is given in Table 1. An excerpt from Frank Jones' interview with Claude Kelly follows:

TABLE 1
DISTRIBUTION OF TIME IN A SAMPLE OF EMPLOYEE EVALUATIONS

			Evaluation score (100 = perfect)	Supervisor's comments		Employee responses	
				Positive (%)	Negative (%)	Positive (%)	Negative (%)
Supervisor	1	Joe Kishkoones					
Employee	# 2	Bill Morey	85	20	60	5	15
	# 7	Hank Sheffieck ...	90	30	60	5	5
	# 9	Carl Burns	70	10	65	5	20
Supervisor	3	Dick Camealy					
Employee	# 4	Pete Smith	68	10	80	0	10
	# 6	Jake Collons	92	15	70	5	10
	# 8	Stan Osterhaus ...	87	12	80	3	5
Supervisor	5	Frank Jones					
Employee	# 5	Ken Ipade	74	5	80	0	15
	# 6	Claude Kelly	78	10	70	0	20
	#10	Sherwin Chew	76	5	85	0	10
Supervisor	8	Paul Justis					
Employee		Vern Swanda	88	50	20	20	10
		Curt Graybard	90	60	10	25	5
		Mario Carrabino ..	93	70	7	20	3

Jones: Well, Kelly, you've seen the sheet I turned in on you. You do a good job about three-and-a-half to four days out of five. I guess I'm real thankful for that. But just about every week I have a Friday or Monday problem with you.

Kelly: What do you mean a problem?

Jones: Well, you goof off a lot. I tell you to do something one way and you go your own way.

Kelly: I've been here about as long as you. Isn't a guy supposed to have anything to say about his work?

Jones: I didn't say that. Besides, I'm the supervisor here. I don't care if you've been here a hundred years, you'll take your orders from me. So if you want to get your ratings up, you'll watch it on Mondays and Fridays from now on. But as I said, you do a pretty good job.

Later, Jones was heard to say that Kelly was driving him crazy. "He won't do anything on his own before asking me what to do. I can't get my work done."

Requirement. You are Art Timler. Evaluate the status of performance evaluation at Asheville. Design a program to improve the shortcomings you've detected.

4. Problems in Evaluation—I

In a large electric power plant in Saskatoon, Saskatchewan, Canada, they have been having difficulty with their performance evaluation program. The organization has an evaluation program by which all operating employees and clerical employees are evaluated semiannually by their supervisors. The form which they have been using is given in Exhibit 1. It has been in use for ten years. The form is scored as follows: Excellent = 5, above average = 4, average = 3, below average = 2, and poor = 1. The scores for each question are centered in the right-hand column and are totaled for an overall evaluation score.

The procedure used has been as follows: Each supervisor rates each employee on July 30 and January 30. The supervisor discusses the rating with the employee. The supervisor sends the rating to the personnel

EXHIBIT 1
PERFORMANCE EVALUATION FORM OF ELECTRIC POWER PLANT

PERFORMANCE EVALUATION

Supervisors: When you are asked to do so by the personnel department, please complete this form on each of your employees. The supervisor who is responsible for 75 percent or more of an employee's work should complete this form on him or her. Please evaluate each facet of the employee separately.

Quantity of work	Excellent	Above average	Average	Below average	Poor	Score
Quality of work	Poor	Below average	Average	Above average	Excellent	
Dependability at work	Excellent	Above average	Average	Below average	Poor	
Initiative at work	Poor	Below average	Average	Above average	Excellent	
Cooperativeness	Excellent	Above average	Average	Below average	Poor	
Getting along with co-workers	Poor	Below average	Average	Above average	Excellent	

Total _____

Supervisor's signature _____

Employee name _____

Employee number _____

department. Each rating is placed in the employee's personnel file. If promotions come up, the cumulative ratings are considered at that time. The ratings are also supposed to be used as a check when raises are given.

The system was designed by the personnel manager who retired two years ago, Joanna Kyle. Her replacement was Eugene Meyer. Meyer is a graduate in commerce from the University of Alberta at Edmonton. He graduated 15 years ago. Since then, he's had a variety of experiences, mostly in utilities like the power company. About five of these years he did personnel work.

Meyer has been reviewing the evaluation system. Employees have a mixture of indifferent and negative feelings about it. An informal survey has shown that about 60 percent of the supervisors fill the forms out, give about three minutes to each form, and send them to personnel without discussing them with the employees. Another 30 percent do a little better. They spend more time completing the forms but communicate about them only briefly and superficially with their employees. Only about 10 percent of the supervisors seriously try to do what was intended.

Meyer found out that the forms were rarely retrieved for promotion or pay-raise analyses. Because of this, most supervisors may have felt the evaluation program was a useless ritual.

Where he had been previously employed, Meyer had seen performance evaluation as a much more useful experience, which included giving positive feedback to employees, improving future employee performance, developing employee capabilities, and providing data for promotion and compensation.

Meyer has not had much experience with design of performance evaluation systems. He feels he should seek advice on the topic.

Requirement. Write a report summarizing your evaluation of the strengths and weaknesses of the present evaluation system. Recommend some specific improvements or data-gathering exercises to develop a better system for Meyer.

Problems in Evaluation—II

Maurice Botswick, a consultant specializing in personnel administration, has come to Saskatoon from his office in Calgary to examine the power plant's evaluation system. It is expected that he will propose an alternative system to Eugene Meyer for approval by his superiors. Normally, Ross Flamholtz, the top manager of the power plant goes along with Meyer's suggestions.

Flamholtz is 59 years old, an engineer by training. His interest has always been in direct operations of the plant. He has shown little interest in the people or money side of the utility. He pays more attention to equipment maintenance and replacement and the purchase of materials used to produce the electricity. Flamholtz is a conservative person, always addressing everyone as Mr. or Mrs. or Miss. He is quiet, retiring, and an introvert. In his period of top management (the last two years), he has introduced no major changes in policy. His health is not good, and he has made it known that he would like to retire in three years and go to live with his daughter in Victoria, British Columbia.

After examining Meyer's data and interviewing persons around the plant, Botswick is sitting in Meyer's office. Botswick said:

Gene, before I go any further, I thought I might bounce my present thinking off you. Your program lacks employee involvement. It involves one way communication—supervisor to subordinate, or no communication at all.

Many of your supervisors have many persons to supervise. Typically, they have 15–20 to oversee. They can't possibly observe this many people and evaluate them well. What would you think of this three-pronged improvement program?

1. Improve your supervisory rating program by getting a better form, training the supervisors in the importance of its use and how to use it, and increasing the number of reviews from two to four annually.
2. Institute a peer evaluation system to give the supervisors more data. That is, the people in each section rate each other (except for themselves) 1–15 best to worst. There is evidence that this is a good addition to the supervisor's information.
3. Introduce a "rate your supervisor" program. When the supervisor rates the employees, they rate him or her. This gets dialogue going and improves performance of both employees and supervisors.

Requirement. You are Meyer. Evaluate these suggestions for your power plant and decide how to proceed before giving Botswick the go ahead. How do you think Flamholtz will react to these suggestions? If you were Meyer, how would you convince Flamholtz to implement some or all of them?

5. Gobdel, Lee, and Page*

This incident and case takes place in Honolulu, Hawaii. Gobdel, Lee, and Page (GLP) is an international public accounting firm and, as such, has offices and affiliates located throughout the world. Larger firms such

---

* By Kurt E. Chaloupecky, department of accounting, Southwest Missouri State University, and William F. Glueck.

as GLP audit 80 percent or more of the firms listed with the U.S. Securities and Exchange Commission.

Certified public accounting firms have a number of functions. Usually, 60 percent of their business is auditing; that is, the firm independently examines the records and other supporting documents which companies have used to prepare their financial statements. As a result of their investigation, they offer an opinion of the financial statements, that is, on their preparation in accordance with generally accepted accounting principles applied on a consistent basis. The remaining 40 percent of the business involves accounting services such as the installation of computerized accounting system and preparation of tax returns. The Honolulu office has its personnel divided into three areas: audit (60 percent), administrative services (accounting systems) (15 percent), and tax (25 percent). One third of the audit division specializes in small business auditing and managerial advice.

While GLP has offices worldwide, its home office is located in New York. It has about 50 offices in the United States (one of which is in Honolulu) and 50 outside the United States. All offices operate similarly, offering the same services and the same quality. The firm has a standardized set of operating procedures and rules which are set by the home office. GLP is a partnership. There are about 500 partners around the world.

Most public accounting firms have four professional levels: partners, managers, seniors, and juniors. The Honolulu office has the following number of professionals: 4 partners (one of whom is designated managing partner), 8 managers, 10 seniors, and 14 juniors. Each partner has absolute authority and responsibility over "his" clients. Every partner of the firm is a general partner and participates in the firm's managerial decisions. The more responsibility and seniority, the more influence individual partners tend to have.

Although there are exceptions, public accounting firms do not normally grow in size by merger of CPA firms, as often happens in industry. In contrast, they grow as their clients grow. Many clients "outgrow" their local CPA firm's services and switch to larger regional or international firms such as GLP.

Firms such as GLP are compensated by their clients based on a fixed fee; that is, the firm estimates the number of hours it will take to perform the audit and charges a fee based on these hours times a billing rate per hour. To reduce the fee, clients put pressure on the firm to perform the audit in shorter periods of time. Lurking in the background is the possible loss of the account. However, few major clients do, in fact, switch CPA firms.

This client pressure plus the desire of the partnership for greater profitability translates into a general awareness and concern for time in CPA firms. Time pressure becomes a pressure to reduce the time officially spent on the job by juniors and seniors who do most of the field work. Time budgets expressed in terms of hours per step are set for each step of the audit. Often, these budgets are "ideal" times and leave no margin for unexpected problems. Because of career pressures, no one admits that the time budgets are "challenging." When an accountant gets behind, he often works overtime without charging for it. Charging for it would be an admission that one could not meet the goals. Unofficially, some seniors expect juniors, while charging a normal eight-hour day, to work from eight until six o'clock, with as little time off for lunch as possible.

The time pressure becomes most serious during the first four months of the calendar year because of audit report and tax return deadlines. It is not atypical for a senior to accumulate (over and above overtime not charged) 600 hours of overtime per year. The majority of these hours are accumulated during the busy season. It is not uncommon for seniors and juniors to work 80 hours per week to complete audit and tax reports on time. Twelve-hour days, seven days a week, become burdensome by April 1. Overtime expectation is reinforced by values associated with being a "professional accountant." This takes professional dedication indeed.

GLP's concept of professionalism includes total dedication to the profession and the firm. Hours of work are not to be questioned because such questions are considered unprofessional. Preparation for training meetings is expected to be done by the employee on his own time. He is also expected to prepare for the CPA examination on his own time. Overtime or out-of-town assignments are made with little or no advance notice. Personal inconvenience is not important to a truly professional individual.

GLP'S PROMOTION ARRANGEMENT

Professional accountants are recruited by GLP at college campuses. All except a few lawyers and computer specialists have degrees in accounting. International firms such as GLP pay handsome salaries. Indeed, GLP considers a portion of the salary paid during the first three years of employment to be an investment which hopefully will provide future dividends. Smaller local or regional firms cannot afford to make such an investment.

To assure that only the best accountants are promoted to partner, an "up or out" system has been developed. It is expected that anyone who is to remain with GLP must pass the CPA examination. Roughly 25 percent of the candidates sitting for the exam pass. Secondly, a time frame for each level is set. Unless you make partner by age 35, or shortly thereafter, you will basically never make it. Thus the upwardly mobile accountant must pass through all four levels in about 13 years. Although all promotions come from within, GLP prides itself on not being tied to seniority. Merit alone is rewarded. Typically 25 percent of newly hired juniors are weeded out within two years. Salaries generally reflect the evaluation of the accountant. If one does not get a good raise, one is being told something. Over an eight-year period, less than 20 percent of those hired are retained by the firm.

Professional development continues at all levels as all experiences are considered to be learning experiences. Juniors are assigned to a variety of seniors to aid in the audit. This allows the junior to receive wide experience and to be widely evaluated. His or her work is reviewed by the senior, then the senior's manager, and finally by the partner in charge of the client. At each level a point sheet is prepared indicating additions or corrections needed, as seen by each level of the hierarchy. These corrections or additional comments are returned to the lower levels of the hierarchy to be cleared and thus become a learning experience. Corrections and additions are reviewed and approved through the same chain of command.

After each assignment, the supervising senior and manager writes a written evaluation of the work of the junior or senior under his or her immediate supervision. This evaluation covers not only technical competence, but also subjective factors such as judgment, imagination, leadership, and resourcefulness. Thus the firm creates multiple evaluations of each person. However, part of these evaluations are indeed subjective.

The subjectivity may be reinforced by the social system at GLP. Juniors and seniors work primarily in the field at the client's office. They go to lunch together, and when on out-of-town assignments, it is expected that one take dinner with the group and afterwards to have a few drinks with the others. Partners and, to a lesser extent, managers work primarily in the firm's office. They, therefore, spend more time together go to lunch together, and so forth.

HARRISON HAMILL

The case of Harrison Hamill who experienced such a promotion system is worth considering. Harrison Hamill graduated from a mainland private college in accounting with an A — average. Wishing to specialize in tax accounting, he took his first job with the Internal Revenue Service for two years. He visited at GLP whenever home in Honolulu, and it became clear that he would like to work with them. They offered him a position. At age 23, he was hired by GLP.

Hamill worked very hard. At age 25 he was made a senior. He helped bring in a fair amount of tax business, but most of it was small business, not the prestigious accounts the partners usually seek. He moved ahead reasonably well and passed his CPA exam at age 26. He was concerned that he might not make partner. For tax accounting is off the mainstream of auditing. However, he socialized with others in the firm as much as he could, worked hard, and minded his own business.

Hamill kept his options open, however. He went to many events—

alumni and others—to broaden his circle of friends. But at age 34 he knew he wasn't going to make it. Little signs were given: office size, raises, invitations not extended. Quietly, he visited smaller firms and eventually joined one that made him a partner. There were two other partners and a few juniors. Hamill actually took a compensation cut to do this, but he felt he had no real choice. At best he could have stayed on as a "lesser being," a manager with only cost of living raises. However, even this position could not be considered permanent.

Hamill wondered where he had gone wrong. Was it when he turned down a transfer opportunity to Los Angeles? Did he unintentionally send a signal that he wasn't willing to pay the price? Should he have transferred to the auditing division? Was tax accounting too far off the mainstream? He wondered why there had to be an up-or-out system and why at age 35. To his nonaccountant friends, he explained that he wanted to strike off on his own and stop being an organization man. But his accountant friends knew what really happened.

Hamill was told, when he asked, that he was pleasant, competent, and a good tax man. But that his evaluations indicated he lacked complete dedication to GLP.

Requirement. Comment on the effectiveness of promotion policies at GLP. Does GLP consider its cost of turnover in this example?

6. Burlington Furniture

Burlington Furniture Company is a medium-sized manufacturer of quality furniture, located in Burlington, Vermont.

The furniture market generally can be categorized as lower-priced mass market goods, medium quality furniture (for the Sears-type customer), and higher quality furniture. Burlington fits into this latter category. In some ways, it is similar to Ethan Allen furniture, but it is a smaller firm than Ethan Allen.

Essentially, Burlington specializes in colonial–New England furniture, both primitive and later styles. Many of its pieces are reproductions of museum pieces. Burlington's advertising stresses quality New England craftsmen using quality Vermont wood to recreate a glorious and worthwhile past.

Burlington ships most of its furniture to large Eastern markets such as Boston, New York, upstate New York cities, Philadelphia, and so forth. It does have a few high quality dealers in certain important furniture centers such as Chicago, Los Angeles, Houston, Dallas, Denver, and so forth. But this second category represents only 25 percent of its business.

The firm advertises that it produces items to order and "will duplicate great grandmother's favorite chair or bed for you." Many customers and potential customers tour the plant while on vacation or when they are ordering their furniture.

To compete at all in this day of mass merchandising and middle-brow tastes, Burlington must have outstanding quality merchandise. This, in turn, requires expert workmen, some with the quality of artisans. This has become a problem in the days when more and more young people go to college.

Recently, Burlington has had to institute a fairly extensive technical training program. Essentially, it is designed to upgrade the semiskilled workers to the skilled jobs as the latter retire. It is also designed to take men and women with little or no experience and train them sufficiently well so that they can do some of the simpler tasks. The latter will have been selected on the basis of recommendations from high school shop teachers. These people also take a battery of tests including vocational interest tests and physical ability tests as well.

Burlington's organization chart is given in Exhibit 1.

One of the major jobs Clifford Fawcett, director of training, has been working on is the design of this training program. Arthur White, president, and James Newport, vice president–operations, have urged C. R. Lewis, vice president–staff, to get the ball rolling. Newport has promised his fullest cooperation.

Stanley Hoover, vice president–finance, has suggested that one way to

EXHIBIT 1
ORGANIZATION CHART OF BURLINGTON FURNITURE COMPANY

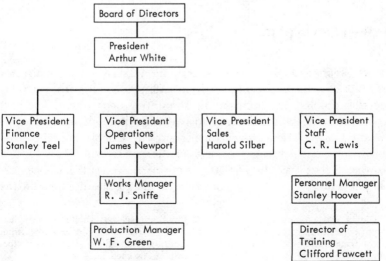

motivate good performance in these classes is for the trainers to assign grades to classroom performance: excellent, average, and poor. If the trainees are long-term employees being given an upgrading from semi-skilled jobs to skilled jobs, he suggests that those receiving the grade of "excellent" be given a raise at the end of the program and the first promotions available. Those receiving poor should be told they will not be promoted to the skilled jobs. If the trainees are new employees, those receiving poor grades should be terminated, those receiving excellent grades should be given first choices on jobs and a raise.

Newport wonders if the union would like that system, and Fawcett wonders if he could grade it that closely, considering the consequences.

Fawcett was ready to schedule the classes. He went to W. F. Green, production manager, and mentioned that the "higher ups" are really pushing the training program. He asks for a list of the semiskilled workers Green's chosen to take the course. He also has asked for the release of several workers and supervisors to help instruct in the courses. They are Jan Matteson, Charles Shell, and David Stone. Green replied, sarcastically: "You don't want much, do you, Fawcett? You just want the cream of my workers to do your instructing and a bunch of my guys to be your students. What do you think this is, a school? I've got to get these orders out by Friday. If I do what you want, they won't make it. Then the work's manager will be after me as to why. See me later when I'm not so busy!"

Requirement. You are Fawcett. How do you proceed to staff your courses? How do you decide on the question of grading the trainees? How do you seek the support of the line supervisors?

7. Stephen Doyle (A)*

In 1969, Stephen Doyle, director of training, was asked by the director of personnel at a medical center in Manhattan to assist with a serious and pressing problem in the hospital's accounting department. The post office was returning bills addressed to patients who had received treatment in the hospital's emergency room stamped "Unable to Deliver because of Insufficient Address." An examination of returned bills for one week revealed that 145 bills, or 30 percent of those sent, had been returned. The cause was either incomplete or inaccurate histories on the

---

* This case was written by Lynda Diane Baydin, research assistant, under the direction of Associate Professor Alan P. Sheldon as a basis for class discussion rather than to illustrate either effective or ineffective handling of an administrative situation.

emergency room reports which lead to incorrect mailing addresses. Sometimes the name which appeared on the report would be correct, but the street address incorrect; sometimes numbers were not transcribed carefully. The resulting loss to the hospital was estimated at a minimum of $1,089.50 per week or $56,654 per year, assuming a minimum charge of $7.50 a visit.

The directors of training and personnel were considering several options. Among these were (1) to conduct a traditional training program that would (*a*) emphasize the importance of the report to the medical center and (*b*) teach the clerks how to fill out the report completely and accurately; (2) to replace the clerks, who were union members earning approximately $106 per week and had been at the medical center on the average of two years; or (3) to conduct a systems analysis that would (*a*) indicate why the clerks' performance was below standard, and (*b*) develop an economical solution that would guarantee improved on-the-job performance and consequently reduce the number of uncollectibles from emergency room cards.

Stephen Doyle (B)*

Mr. Doyle's concern was to figure out how he could impact on the performance of the emergency room clerks. First, however, he wanted to make sure the problem was not one that could be corrected with further training. In order to do this, he had to determine how well the clerks could complete the patient report forms.

Under a test situation, each clerk was asked to complete an emergency room report for six hypothetical patients. To his surprise, the finished forms were 98 percent complete and correct. Further training was obviously not needed, and Mr. Doyle decided to look at the job environment and the background of the clerks themselves. He found that the clerks were generally high school graduates. He then asked himself the following critical questions: Are the clerks aware of what they were supposed to accomplish; that is, (*a*) Were performance goals made clear and measurable? (*b*) Were they receiving daily feedback on progress in relation to these goals? and (*c*) Were they receiving adequate rewards for achieving these goals?

Further inquiry led Mr. Doyle to conclude that the emergency room

---

* This case was written by Lynda Diane Baydin, research assistant, under the direction of Associate Professor Alan P. Sheldon as a basis for class discussion rather than to illustrate either effective or ineffective handling of an administrative situation.

Copyright © 1973 by the President and Fellows of Harvard College.

clerks had little idea or interest in the accuracy of their completed tasks. When one of the clerks was asked if the reports she had completed the previous day were accurate, she replied: "I don't known . . . I think I did okay, and no one has said anything to me. Have you heard of any problems?" Mr. Doyle concluded that the clerks assumed their performance was acceptable because they had received no indication to the contrary. Furthermore there was no incentive to improve performance because there was no reward system operating. As one clerk put it, "Sometimes I don't have a chance to complete the forms, but it doesn't seem to make too much difference. Once in a great while one of us will get bawled out, but no one tells us when we do a good job either." Mr. Doyle therefore concluded that from a clerk's point of view there were no significant differences in consequences if she did a job well or poorly. The rewards were nonexistent, and the punishments consisted of an occasional bawling out.

Stephen Doyle (C)*

Mr. Doyle's strategy was to establish a program that would provide immediate feedback to the clerks and the appropriate rewards for correct completion of the emergency room reports. He was fortunate in that the assistant director of the hospital, Mrs. Sylvia Hale, supported Mr. Doyle completely throughout the program. The emergency room employees, clerks, and nurses reported directly to Mrs. Hale through their supervisors.

First Mr. Doyle designed a job aide to assist the clerks in evaluating the accuracy and completeness of their reports. Exhibit 1 is a sample of the job aide. The second step was to provide feedback and self-measure-

EXHIBIT 1

JOB AIDE—PATIENT INFORMATION REPORT

Did I fill in the following information:

☐ Patient's first, last, and middle name?
☐ Apartment number, street?
☐ Borough, zip code, state?

---

* This case was written by Lynda Diane Baydin, research assistant, under the direction of Associate Professor Alan P. Sheldon as a basis for class discussion rather than to illustrate either effective or ineffective handling of an administrative situation.

ment. Upon completion of a report, the clerk was to evaluate it for completeness and accuracy. Errors were to be corrected immediately upon discovery. At the end of the shift, each clerk would compute the percent of reports filled out without error and submit the results to the supervisor on a Patient Information Feedback Report, Exhibit 2. Third, a process of rewarding the clerks for completing the task accurately was initiated. Mr. Doyle taught the supervisors how to use positive reinforcement. The supervisors were to reinforce the clerks with praise, for example, "Nice work, Hilda. Today you achieved 97 percent." Mrs. Hale similarly encouraged the nurses to reward the clerks with praise and gave positive reinforcement herself whenever possible. Weekly letters from the hospital's accounting department were forthcoming which said such things as "Congratulations, girls! You have made your weekly target."

EXHIBIT 2

PATIENT INFORMATION FEEDBACK REPORT

Hilda Jones   June 9, 1970

    100   Number reports filled out.

     97   Number complete and correct.

    97%   Today's performance

Standard = 95% filled out complete and correct

Did I meet standard today?   Yes   No

The entire cost for developing the program was $800. This amount covered the training department's cost for analyzing the cause of the problem, designing the job aide and feedback form, and time spent in instructing the supervisors how to use positive reinforcement.

Stephen Doyle (D)*

The director of personnel was very pleased with the results of Mr. Doyle's application of behavioral systems analysis to the problem which had arisen in the emergency room. In one week's time, the percent of

---

* This case was written by Lynda Diane Baydin, research assistant, under the direction of Associate Professor Alan P. Sheldon as a basis for class discussion rather than to illustrate either effective or ineffective handling of an administrative situation.

accurate and complete reports submitted by the emergency room clerks to their supervisors rose from 67 percent to 95 percent. The clerks for their part were experiencing increased job satisfaction. As one clerk put it, "I used to go home evenings wondering what I had done. . . . Now I look at my feedback report and can see what I have accomplished."

Because of the success of Mr. Doyle's program in the emergency room, a similar process was begun in medical records and admitting. In the case of medical records, Mr. Doyle set up an interaction schedule by having the supervisor praise the good performance of the group that pulled the records from 12 to 8 A.M. A nightly evaluation of performance was recorded for the crew on a chit sheet. The evaluation was based on how many records were requested and how many were pulled. The change in work performance was almost immediate. In the case of admitting, Mr. Doyle implemented a similar feedback and self-measurement system. Here, however, he was not as successful in providing positive reinforcement. The admitting department reported to the accounting office. Nobody in the accounting office would reward the admitting personnel on a consistent basis, and after a week, the program was dropped.

Three months after Mr. Doyle began the program in the emergency room, and two weeks after he began it in medical records and admitting, he resigned his position at the medical center.

Discussion questions

1. Evaluate the programs implemented by Mr. Doyle.
2. What problems are involved in using behavior modification for training employees?

E. MANAGEMENT DEVELOPMENT

1. Alberta Mobile Homes, Ltd.

Alberta Mobile Homes, Ltd., is a small manufacturer of mobile homes and modular homes located in Calgary, Alberta, Canada. The firm has about 250 employees.

Alfred Butkus, president of AMH, recently attended a seminar on personnel administration in Calgary conducted by Professor Warren Simpson of the University of Calgary's business school. After the session was over, Butkus approached Simpson and asked him if he'd be willing to come to his place and provide consulting help for several personnel problems.

"Sure, I'd be delighted," replied Simpson. A few days later, he went to AMH to begin the project.

Butkus introduced the problem this way: "Look, Warren, we seem to be having problems with our promotion and evaluation system here. Let me describe two incidents that have come up just in the last two months. We're in a growth industry. We've doubled our work force in the last year and a half. This means we need to move some people up, but we are having the darndest time with it.

"Recently, George Drester, the head of our plant, came to see me. He said he'd been wrestling with this problem for months. He'd promoted Jay Gilbreth to supervisor about six months ago. Jay was good at his job before, but he's not a good supervisor. His employees don't like or respect him. Jay himself seems aware of the situation. George is wondering what he can do about Jay.

"Then there's the case of Ed Bankhead, the head of marketing. He needs to recommend someone for promotion to sales manager. I've been asking him to do so for weeks, and no recommendations yet. See what you can do about it, will you?"

With this send-off, Simpson went to meet Bankhead. After some preliminaries he came to the point. "Look, Ed, I'm here to see about establishing some policies about promotion. Frankly, Al gave you as a case in point. He's wanting to know what you've done about the sales manager's job."

Bankhead shifted around in his chair. He then described in some detail the men he was thinking about:

1. James Prior: ten years' experience in construction sales, lots of personality, no supervisory experience, high school graduate.
2. Harley Cortney: four years' sales experience for AMH, the best salesman of the bunch, college degree in business, no supervisory experience, very quiet, almost introverted.
3. Matt Dotler: older, 12 years' experience selling, 5 of it for AMH, outgoing personality. He did supervise two men with his previous company.

"Frankly, Warren," Bankhead said, "I'm leaning towards Harley. I figure the best salesman is bound to make the best sales manager. But, I really don't have a lot of facts and figures to back up my choice. How should I go about this, anyway?"

Simpson said he would make a recommendation on this shortly. Next he visted Drester. "What am I going to do about Jay?" asked Drester. "He's not cutting it."

Simpson pressed Drester and asked him how he "knew" that Gilbreth's employees didn't like or respect him. "How wasn't he cutting it?" he asked. He quickly determined that these were just Drester's general impressions, not based on a lot of evidence. He also learned that Drester had not tried to discuss the issue with Gilbreth or try to counsel or help him.

Requirement. You are Professor Simpson: Write the report to Butkus, copies of which will go to Drester and Bankhead. The report should include recommendations on:

1. How to decide on a sales manager and if possible whom Bankhead should recommend.
2. What to do about Drester and Gilbreth.
3. Recommendations for improving promotion, evaluation, and counseling at AMH.

2. Sudbury Shoes

Ronald Bell has just been employed as a management trainee at Sudbury Shoes. Sudbury, a medium-sized manufacturer of quality shoes and boots, is located in Sudbury, Ontario, Canada.

Bell came from a small town between Sudbury and London, Ontario. He attended the University of Western Ontario and took the honors degree in business and commerce. Bell's father is in agribusiness; as a result, Bell worked around the business much of his life. For example, he spent all of his summers working in his father's business. His father naturally expected him to enter his firm. But Bell felt that he first should make it on his own. If he didn't, he wasn't sure that he would be respected at home. All he knew was agribusiness; he felt he'd like to try something else for a while.

Bell worked his way through college. He took his summer income and added funds from jobs he had held in London on weekends and on several nights a week. He also had taken out bank loans. He now owed the Toronto Dominion Bank $4,000 (Canadian). He plans to pay this loan off as soon as he can, preferably in the first year. He plans to live modestly. He has taken a flat with two other bachelors, where his cost per month will be $85. He has purchased a small Ford car and his monthly payments will be $80. His beginning salary at Sudbury will be $600. The company personnel manager, Richard Mason, who recruited Bell to Sudbury, promises Bell a raise if he does well in the first six months on the job.

Mason said that Sudbury had been a family-owned and run firm. But the last family member in management, H.T.L. Sawyer, had just died of cancer at age 49. Sawyer had been president. His son was a United Church of Canada clergyman and had never shown an interest in Sudbury. Sawyer's daughter was married; her husband was a career officer in the Royal Canadian Air Force. Mrs. Sawyer, the Rev. Mr. Sawyer, and Group Captain Higgins were on the Sudbury board of directors. But none of them had the capacity or interest in managing the firm.

Sawyer had begun to develop a professional management team. He was young enough that he wasn't overly concerned. Then he became ill. He appointed as president his long-time associate, James Lawrence, who had been vice president.

Lawrence saw the need for developing a professional management team, too. Table 1 summarizes the characteristics of the current management.

TABLE 1
SUDBURY'S MANAGEMENT TEAM

Management level and number	Age distribution					Educational background		
	<25	26–35	36–45	46–55	>56	High school graduate	Some college	College degree
Top (6)	0	0	0	2	4	4	1	1
Middle (10)..	0	0	3	4	3	2	6	2
First line (44) ..	1	7	11	13	12	44	0	0

Bell was to be the first of several college graduates brought in to professionalize Sudbury's management.

Because of its size, Sudbury did not really have a formal management training program. For the first several weeks, Mason arranged for Bell to spend several days in each department and area. Mason asked the supervisors to familiarize Bell with the operations of the department.

Then, Bell was assigned to the sales department. It was thought that he should spend a year as a salesman, calling on Sudbury's trade. Bell was assigned to John Knotts, a regional sales manager for Sudbury. Knotts has been with Sudbury for 15 years. He is a high school graduate who has worked his way up from the job of office boy at Sudbury.

Knotts introduced Bell to the Sudbury line and handed him price sheets and sales records of all the customers into the Toronto area. After a two-day introduction, Knotts drove up in front of Pay-Less Shoes, a store in one of the lower income areas of Toronto.

Knotts said: "Ron, I'm sure this is all simple stuff to you. I'd be in the way. Why don't you make the call on this store. It will be on your list of customers. The owner's name is Azimian."

What Bell didn't know was that Azimian was known in the trade as "the crazy Armenian," because of his unique style of dealing with salesmen. Ron entered the store.

Bell: May I please speak with Mr. Azimian?

Clerk: He's busy.

Bell: I'll wait.

Clerk: What do you want to see him for anyway?

Bell: I'm Ron Bell from Sudbury Shoes. I'd like to talk to him about our new line.

Clerk: You're wasting your time. Azimian doesn't buy Sudbury shoes. They screwed him in the past when he was smaller. Besides, they charge too much.

Bell: Look, I don't want to argue with you. I'll just wait for Mr. Azimian.

Azimian: You *are* talking to him, you little punk!

The man turned. Azimian was tall, burly, about 45 years old. He was wearing work clothes.

Bell: Oh, I'm sorry, I didn't know that.

Azimian: That's obvious. Now go away.

Bell: If I could just have a few minutes of your time, we really do have some outstanding new items for the new season and . . . .

Azimian: Too bad you got physical defects. You must be deaf. I told you to get the hell out of here. I mean it. Conversation ended.

At this, Azimian went into the store room. Bell picked up his materials and left. He got in the car.

Knotts: How did you get along with my good buddy, Joe?
Bell: Not so good. No sale.

Later, Knotts was discussing the matter with another regional manager, Ray Kittrell.

Kittrell: Why did you throw Ron at the crazy Armenian. You know he didn't have a chance. Nobody has ever sold him anything from Sudbury; I doubt they ever will. Ron seems like a nice kid.
Knotts: Listen, they sent me the new crown prince, didn't they? With all that college and all, he ought to be able to handle anything. He hasn't cut it as far as I am concerned.

Kittrell repeated the conversation to Mason.

Discussion questions

1. You are Mason. What, if anything, do you do about the orientation of Bell?
2. Examine the psychology of the orientation from Ron and John's point of view.
3. If you were Ron, how long would you stay at Sudbury?

3. Parks Electronics, Inc.

Parks Electronics is a large electronics firm, one of the industry's leaders. The firm maintains a research and development laboratory adjacent to a large factory it operates near Wichita Falls, Texas.

Alfred Page is an engineer in this lab. He met the casewriter at a party and began to talk about his job. He is a young, dedicated, hard-driving type. Yet, he couldn't believe what was going on at his lab.

Page had never had a full-time job before this one at Park Electronics. It appeared that he thought that the world of work was populated with highly competent, highly motivated persons pulling together to help achieve the lab's goals, thus the company goals as well.

After Page graduated from Georgia Tech, he was sent to Savannah, Georgia. The company's best lab was located near Savannah. He received his company training there. After going through the orientation program, he was assigned to the first location needing a person with his training, which was Wichita Falls.

Page's impression of the Savannah lab had been very good. It was an exciting place, where a lot of activity had been going on. New things were being tried, and it was challenging to be with people having such experiences and making such contributions.

The lab at Wichita Falls dealt with more applied problems than the one at Savannah. But Page felt he was suited to applied research, not theoretical research.

Page reported to his lab on a Wednesday. He was introduced around the section (see Exhibit 1 and Table 1) and was given a small project to work on by his new section leader, Edward Sandberg.

EXHIBIT 1
R&D SECTION, PARKS ELECTRONICS

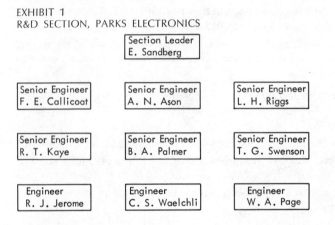

TABLE 1
R&D SECTION, PERSONNEL CHARACTERISTICS

Name	Degree	School	Date
Callicoat	B.S. (Eng.)	Cal. Tech.	1948, R.P.E.
Ason	B.S. (Eng.)	U. of Cincinnati	1939, R.P.E.
Riggs	B.S. (Eng.)	U. of Missouri-Rolla	1949, R.P.E.
Kaye	B.S. (Eng.) M.S. (Eng.)	Harvard	1954
Palmer	B.S. (Eng.)	U. of Wisconsin	1951, R.P.E.
Swenson	B.S. (Eng.) M.S. (Eng.)	Virginia Tech	1960
Jerome	B.S. (Eng.)	Texas A&M	1968
Waelchli	B.S. (Eng.)	Rice U.	1971

The morning went by rather quickly, and soon it was lunch time. Page was invited to join a group of young engineers for lunch. This was a much quieter group than at Savannah, and they had a tendency to talk mostly about football and sex. At Savannah, there had been much more shop talk and talk about some of the latest findings from the newest editions of the engineering journals. Instead, he was already bored with how much better the Red Raiders of Texas Tech and Texas Longhorns were than Georgia Tech. He also heard enough about how the southwestern conference was the toughest in the country, if not the world!

As Page continued telling his story to the casewriter, he related how when he returned from lunch Callicoat, Ason, Riggs, and Palmer were not there. They drifted in a half hour later than the end of the lunch hour. They had obviously been drinking. Slowly, as the afternoon passed, Page realized that these four had gone to sleep at their desks. He discovered this was not a one-time occurrence. It happened several times every week.

Page was astonished. At a party after three months on the job, he cautiously asked Bob Kaye about it and finally asked, "How do they get away with it?" Kaye replied, "Look, Ed Sandberg's got a problem. These guys made a real contribution to this company. Some of their inventions and modifications helped build the guts of our product line. But let's face it, engineering is a rapidly changing field, and they are out of the mainstream now. So after a morning of small projects which they can still handle, they've done all they can. They can't go home and let the whole world know what's going on. So they coast."

Discussion questions

1. Page is still upset by the situation and wonders if you, the casewriter, a specialist in personnel development, have any ideas on how to handle these five.
2. Why do supervisors let situations like these continue?
3. How would the four respond to attempts to retrain and motivate them?

4. Charlie Adams*

As Charlie Adams pushed determinedly through the door from the reception room, Bill Franklin, president of Spirox, Inc., took one look at Charlie's face and felt his stomach sink. He almost knew what Charlie was going to say. "Bill," Charlie began, "you won't believe this but Frank Pillsbury seems to think he reports to you, not to me. Isn't that the craziest thing you ever heard? I can't seem to shake him of this idea so I thought I better turn to you to straighten him out." With this statement, Charlie stopped and looked confidently at the president.

Charlie Adams was 62 years old, one of the more senior of Spirox's executives, having joined the company as a graduate engineer directly from college in the late 1930s. He had been promoted through several engineering grades in the then small company, thence to several production management positions, including plant manager. By that time,

---

* This case was prepared as the basis for class discussion rather than to illustrate either effective or ineffective handling of an administrative situation.

Copyright © 1968 by the President and Fellows of Harvard College, for use within the Harvard Business School and Library of Congress only.

the company had begun to grow rapidly and to diversify. As a result, Charlie was placed in charge of manufacturing and sales for one half the company's product line, Bill Franklin, a few years Charlie's junior and also an engineer, in charge of the other half. A few years and several acquisitions and mergers later, Bill became executive vice president and Charlie vice president in charge of manufacturing. Marketing responsibility was assumed by a young manager from an acquired company while research and engineering direction was given to another young executive.

When the president died suddenly two years later, Bill Franklin was voted president. As he surveyed his company's situation at that time, it was clear that the dominant focus had shifted from engineering and manufacturing on the one hand to marketing and research on the other. While the two young vice presidents in charge of marketing and R&E were well suited to this shift in emphasis, Bill felt that Charlie Adams was somewhat of an anachronism. Charlie was an extremely conscientious manager, loyal to a fault and highly competent as a practical engineer. He had tended to become immersed in technical detail as his manufacturing post broadened in scope and to require considerable supervision in dealing with the wider aspects of the manufacturing job. He was highly respected by his subordinates, though Bill felt they were frustrated from time to time by Charlie's absorption in engineering problems.

When Bill Franklin talked with Charlie Adams about some of his observations of Charlie's work, Adams inevitably interpreted Bill's remarks as commendation of Charlie's engineering work. Bill could find no way to correct this interpretation, and not wanting to hurt Charlie's feelings, he tended to let the matter drop. He did decide, however, to give Charlie a more restricted job than he had had and to counsel with Charlie frequently in the future. He further decided to send Charlie to a management course and to see that Charlie was well supported by competent juniors. He advised Charlie that he was to become vice president for corporate services, a new post of importance in the expanded Spirox company. As such, Charlie would have charge of corporate capital expenditures and engineering. The former marketing vice president was promoted to executive vice president, the former head of R&E was put in charge of manufacturing, and junior men were given charge of research and marketing.

Despite frequent discussions between Franklin and Adams, as well as schooling for the latter, Charlie's conception of his job continued to narrow in scope. In response, Bill took to regularly appraising Charlie's performance, although the discussions with Charlie which resulted had no apparent effect. Even when a general bonus system was inaugurated, based upon annual appraisals, Charlie's behavior continued as before. Thereafter, Charlie's raises shrank in comparison to others at his level. Still, there was no change. Bill Franklin assumed that Charlie's already comfortable financial situation simply made monetary incentives ineffective. Charlie's good humor in the face of these events seemed indomitable.

During this period of ineffectual attempts to get Charlie Adams more interested in change in his area of responsibility and in a broadened concept of that responsibility, Franklin discussed the problem with the vice president of research who was about to assume the new role of director of corporate planning. They determined to promote one of the latter's more promising assistants to a new position as manager of research and engineering, to whom would now report the research department, the chief engineer, and the corporate patent department. This move seemed to the two men to pull the entire R&E effort together in a way not heretofore possible. Since Charlie Adams still had three years to go to retirement, it was decided to have the new R&D director, Frank Pillsbury, report to Charlie. However, in order to have this new position function effectively, Bill Franklin told Frank Pillsbury: "You, of course, understand that you will work with Charlie Adams until he retires three years from now. However, I would like you to keep in close contact with me, and you know I expect you to be in full charge. I am sure you'll have no problems, but let me know if you do." The president also discussed the new organizational arrangement with Adams, stressing the importance of a coordinated research and engineering effort. Adams seemed to share the president's point of view and expressed his pleasure with the new arrangement.

Soon after Pillsbury assumed his new duties, he attended an organizing meeting with Charlie Adams and their several immediate subordinates. Charlie said: "I have no desire to become inactive, and I still have something to contribute in the engineering field. So, you, Frank, will continue in charge of R&D where your experience lies, and I will continue to take responsibility for corporate engineering. With this division of labor, we should be able to get the best from our departments and be of optimum service to the divisions." Frank, however, responded: "Wait a minute, Charlie, I understood that the whole idea behind this organizational change was to integrate research and engineering. Bill Franklin is holding *me* responsible for doing that." Charlie replied: "Frank, obviously you've misunderstood your assignment. Obviously, we'll have to postpone these discussions until I've had a chance to get Bill to clarify this situation for you. I'll go see him right away."

As Bill Franklin listened to Charlie Adams' recital of his conversation with Frank Pillsbury, Bill's mind flashed back to his many discussions with Charlie, how he had been tempted to seek Charlie's early retirement, yet feared to do so because of its effect on others in the company who liked and respected Charlie and who might see in Charlie's treatment some prospect of their own. For the same reason and for simple considerations

of cost, he had refrained from trying to "kick Charlie upstairs." And,
after all, Charlie was still a damned good engineer and proud of it, too.
Now, how the hell was he going to respond to that confident look on
Charlie's face, a look that plainly expected the president to verify Charlie's interpretations of Frank Pillsbury's new job?

Discussion questions

1. How would you handle Charlie Adams?
2. Could the company have prevented this situation from occurring? How?
3. What effect would the forced early retirement of Charlie have on other
   senior employees in the company?

F. COMPENSATION AND BENEFITS

1. Nudd Aluminum Works—I

The Nudd Aluminum Works is a large aluminum smelter located at Butte, Montana. Nudd is one of the largest smelters for the very large aluminum company which owns Nudd.

An aluminum smelter essentially converts bauxite ore through various processes from ore to aluminum ingots. The process involves high technology operations called potlines. Potlines are very expensive to build. Thus, the company finds it more expensive to build additional potlines than to run the Nudd works on overtime.

Recently, because the parent company closed some less efficient plants and because aluminum sales have been increasing, Karl Pollman, operations manager at Nudd, has had increasing difficulty filling order requirements.

He got his backlog figures together and went to see Daniel Junckerstorff, the work's manager, about his problems.

Pollman: Essentially, Dan, we have three choices: (1) continue to have these long backlogs and take a chance losing some of the business to competitors, (2) go to overtime and pay the time-and-a-half or double time as our union contract calls for, or (3) build another potline. I think the first choice is impractical. We've lost some big orders recently. Our competitors just built a new smelter, and they have slack capacity. They can give better service. We might lose all the business, 20 percent of our tonnage, if this keeps up. The third choice won't do either. When I chatted with Arnold Cudd at the home office, he told me that because of recent tax write-off rulings and the profit squeeze, it is quite unlikely that any capital expenditures will be approved for a year or two. That leaves the second choice. It will raise our costs some, but I don't think we have any other choice. What do you say?

Dan: Let me think it over and get back to you, Karl.

After looking at the figures, Junckerstorff decided to go ahead with what Pollman suggested. Junckerstorff called Pollman and said: "Karl,

I've given your problem a lot of thought. Go ahead on the overtime project. See Bob Shaller, plant personnel manager, and get the ball rolling. Keep me posted on the cost situation."

Requirement. You are Pollman. What do you do now? What problems do you anticipate having?

Nudd Aluminum Works—II

A few days later, Pollman asked Shaller to have lunch with him. Pollman explained the need to go to overtime.

Pollman: Initially, I suspect we'll need about a third of the employees for an extra Saturday every other week. Later, it'll be every Saturday. How do you think we ought to handle this, Bob?

Shaller: First off, I'll see Norm Edge, the plant's union representative, as to how he wants to allocate the overtime. He'll probably go for a seniority bidding system, but we'll see. I'll let you know how that works out.

The next day, Shaller saw Edge in his office. Shaller gave him the facts.

Edge: Well, Bob, that should be good news for the employees. With inflation and all, my guess is they'll be glad to have the money, especially the younger ones. I think we should allocate the overtime on the basis of the most senior employees who bid for it. Do you agree?

Shaller: You know the company's policy on that, Norm. We'd rather have the best people than the most senior. But we need you help on this, so I'll go along with you on it this time.

The two parted amicably.

The distribution of the Nudd Work's work force by age was as follows:

	Age of workers						
Levels of workers	*<25*	*26–30*	*31–35*	*36–40*	*41–45*	*46–50*	*>50*
Skilled 2	0	0	0	3	17	30	50
Skilled 1	0	0	11	16	35	26	12
Semiskilled 2	5	8	14	21	27	17	8
Semiskilled 1	9	12	16	18	26	19	0
Low skill 2	24	36	27	15	6	2	0
Low skill 1	35	32	24	6	3	0	0

A few days later, Edge dropped by Shaller's office. After a brief discussion about the weekend's pro football game, Edge said:

I don't know what plans you've made about that overtime yet, but I hope not too many. I've asked around the plant. You were right about some of the young employees—they'd hop at the chance. But, you know, we're running three shifts now. We can't get hours added on during the week. What you may not know is that the older skilled employees think of this job as a supplement to their farming or ranching income. Most of them run marginal enterprises. They use their off hours, especially their weekends, to catch up on their farming and ranching chores. When I asked the crucial employees how they felt—the skilled people that you can't do without—the typical response was: "No way! I got the best paying jobs here. That plus my farm (or ranch) and I'm making it. I don't need the money and don't have the time."

Discussion questions

1. You are Shaller. Junckerstorff and Pollman are depending on you to get the overtime program started. How do you proceed?
2. Is this problem solvable without retraining some younger employees? Would the union agree to that?
3. Could the senior employees be forced to work on Saturdays?

2. Bronson Paperboard Company

The Bronson Paperboard Company is a branch of a national pulp and paper concern whose home operation is in the Middle West. It is located in a small southern community which had experienced little industrial growth prior to World War II, but which has expanded quite rapidly since then. In fact, Bronson was the first national concern to find its way into Blairsville, just as the Blairsville plant was the first branch established by Bronson, although several others have been organized in the last five years.

The principal product turned out by Bronson at Blairsville is small cardboard and paperboard boxes. Some 80 to 120 workers are employed, depending on the volume of business available; these consist of males and females in about equal proportions. Most of these are hourly rated employees. At first no incentive wage system was used. Jobs were simply classified by management, which utilized for this purpose primarily the company's experience in the Middle West; hourly rates were assigned to each class of jobs in proportion to the relative amount of skill required.

In mid-1950 the question of shifting to an incentive payment plan was raised by both local and top management people; by fall a fairly firm decision had been made to go ahead. Key workers were kept informed of developments on this front, and, in general, worker response was favor-

---

* This case was developed and prepared by Professor Howard R. Smith, College of Business Administration, University of Georgia. Reprinted by permission.

able. Indeed, only one resistance point developed as plans proceeded, and that came from a totally unexpected quarter. When it appeared that labor costs in Blairsville would be increased by this move by a greater amount than had been at first thought, top management began to drag its feet. However, strongly backed by his own people at all levels, the local manager, John Johnson, insisted that the transition be completed, and his absentee superiors ultimately gave way.

The incentive system established was orthodox in structure. On each job a standard of output was set up, for which the worker would receive a base hourly wage. Above that level of output a bonus was to be paid, so calculated as to average approximately 25 percent for the entire hourly rated group. And as a team of home-office standards people worked out the details of the new pay system, there was no hint of the difficulties so shortly to follow. Local executives accepted the responsibility of acting as shock absorber between top management on the one hand and the work force on the other, and a spirit of give-and-take characterized the entire transition period.

At one point in the Blairsville operation, printed box material is fed into several machines which perform a number of precision operations: final trimming and making special incisions, creases, and peforations as required. As the material comes off these machines in a single flat sheet, it is caught up in bunches by female operators, who give it a partial inspection and load it onto a pallet.

Both the company's experience to date and the experience of the operators then doing this work in Blairsville suggested that in arriving at a standard for this job a "grab" of 25 sheets was a reasonable basis for calculation. Accordingly this figure was agreed to by all parties, and the incentive rate thus established was used without significant incident for about a year.

About the middle of 1952 a minor design adjustment was introduced into the manufacture of the Blairsville plant's largest volume item. The effect of this change in the production operation was to reduce the inspection responsibility of the employees taking the finished flat pieces off the machines. The thought immediately presented itself to management that a new standard must now be set up for this job, and thus it was that during this summer home-office standards people again spent considerable time in Blairsville.

But what seemed so obvious to management was much less immediately clear to the workers most directly involved. And perhaps only a part of the reason for this was the fact that a readjustment would significantly affect either work output or take-home pay. Over and above this difficulty, there was at issue here a fundamental difference of understanding about basic company labor policy.

Although no particular point had been made of this with workers as the Blairsville hiring and training program had gotten under way some years before, it was fully understood by local management that the basic labor policies followed in the home operation would also be followed by the Blairsville plant. More specifically, it was taken for granted that whenever a job was changed—whether in methods or equipment used, or in work actually being performed—management possessed an inherent right to alter the payment structure accordingly.

However workers might have reacted to an announcement of such a policy several years earlier, they certainly did not accept it enthusiastically now. Indeed, when the standards people concluded after a new study of this operation that a grab of 50 should now be considered the basis for computing a standard, the operators quickly concluded that management was playing the age-old "speed-up" game.

Tempers did not explode at this point. Rather, the operators argued that they had never performed their jobs this way, had never seen this job done in this fashion, did not believe it could be done effectively as the home-office representatives was suggesting—and that the proposed change would make it impossible for them to earn a bonus comparable with that which their friends would be receiving. And local management, concerned primarily about the consequences of an adverse worker reaction on the entire operation, reluctantly conceded that the inspection function might not be satisfactorily performed if the employees felt too pushed to earn at least the average bonus. Confronted with resistance on both of these fronts, top management's spokespersons backed away from their proposal —despite solid evidence that workers in other plants were satisfactorily performing their work in the way suggested—and the existing standard was retained.

The consequences of this decision were apparent almost immediately. Output by these operators increased dramatically, and a casual investigation was all that was required to demonstrate that the principal factor in this jump in productivity was an increase in the number of sheets the operators were handling in a single series of movements. Twenty-five was no longer an acceptable number with any of the employees, and 50 was by no means uncommon. Moreover, this development was not accompanied by any discernible deterioration in quality. And the other side of all this was that the wage earned by these operators regularly amounted to more than that of many other employees with higher skill ratings. Recognizing that it had a major problem on its hands and faced with the need to adopt some sort of expedient immediately, the local manager decided as his first move to slow down the pace of the machines. This brought the out-of-line bonus back into a more acceptable relationship with other bonuses, and the employees themselves were more or less mollified for their loss of earnings when this step was justified to them on the basis of the company's need to make certain that its product was properly inspected.

But for the longer pull this would hardly suffice. Certain fundamental principles were at stake here, and the fact that a slower machine meant reduced net earnings was not the greatest of these. Even more important to management was the question of who was to have the deciding voice in the determination of wage policy.

Still a third time the standards department, the workers directly concerned, and local management sat down to thresh this matter out. And now real tension was in the air as the two branches of management stood shoulder to shoulder. However, after angry words had been spoken on both sides, a moderate and distinctly unenthusiastic agreement was reached—not as to how the issue could be definitely settled, but on a mode of procedure for settling it. Worker assent was secured for a two- or three-day tryout on a revised incentive program, after which another discussion would be held to arrive at a more permanent arrangement. Stated broadly, the system now to be experimented with would require this group of workers to produce at a rate 15 percent greater in order to earn the same take-home pay.

Having by now limped along with this unadjusted rate for more than a year, management was understandably eager to work through this problem promptly. Unfortunately for that desire, however, the fates still seemed to be decreeing differently. Orders were low at the moment, and increasing the speed of the machine at this time might have had the result that some of the workers involved would lose hours. And so action was delayed until this particular seasonal lull was over.

And even when orders did pick up in the fall, a wholly convenient time to make this trial run did not appear. For one thing the rush of business at the peak of the year's operation was not the most opportune time to risk antagonizing a significant proportion of the work force. Then, too, local management preferred to inaugurate this change when home-office standards people were in town—in order to place on the out-of-town folks the blame for whatever ill feeling might develop.

In this process of waiting for just the right time to act, another year slipped away.

Discussion questions

1. You are Bill Thompson. The home office has hired you as a consultant to help solve the problems at Bronson. How would you proceed?

2. Did the conflict between the local management and the home office have any effect on the employees' actions? If so, how?

3. How can management prevent similar situations from recurring?

3. A Secret Pay Policy: A Ticklish Issue*

Lake County Community College was set to open its doors in the fall of 1975. The town was waiting expectantly for its first exposure to higher education, the building was nearing completion, the grounds were in order, and the advertising for students was well under way. Yet, there was no faculty, and the task fell to the president and the dean of instruction to recruit a faculty of 35 to provide the college preparatory, technical, and basic vocational training needed. Although neither of these two administrators had ever been trained to do this job, they set out in the characteristic way through advertising both nationally at various colleges and universities and locally at neighboring high schools and colleges. The response to this approach was adequate, and the faculty began to materialize. Each prospective faculty member's application blank was examined, and he/she was interviewed by the two administrators and other faculty members as they joined the faculty. Unfortunately, neither of the two administrators had any knowledge of varying demand in different fields and, in fact, had very little knowledge of other fields than their own, respectively, physical education and theology.

As each prospect met the rather intuitive criteria of the two administrators, he/she was asked, "What salary do you expect for nine months?" and in almost all cases whatever salary was requested was granted. In a very few cases, some bargaining took place. The year got off to a smooth start, and the two administrators felt proud of their accomplishment, even though occasionally some lack of understanding of the rigors of other disciplines the college taught caused problems. For example, the administrators could not understand why students in the accounting and statistics courses had problems with poor grades as they had never been exposed to these types of courses.

All in all, though, things went very well until one faculty member visited the state capitol and copied the page from the "blue book" of state employees salaries that gave all the Lake County College faculty and staff salaries, and distributed a copy of this page to all employees.

The administrators were furious with the faculty member but were not nearly as upset as the faculty in general who found major salary discrepancies upon examining the document. They discovered, for example, that Ph.D.s with several years of experience in many cases were making less than people with only master's degrees and no experience. They also found that lesser experienced faculty members in several cases were making more than their colleagues in the discipline, yet with more experience and college coursework.

---

* By Jerry L. Wall, Western Illinois University, reprinted with permission.

Finally, a committee was selected from among the faculty to discuss the issue with the two administrators. When the two were confronted with the evidence, they could only say, "We gave you what you asked for! We had no knowledge to base our salary decisions on but what you told us, and you seemed happy with what you got." To this the committee replied, "We came from various educational backgrounds, various geographical areas with differing salary structures, various types of experience with the job market, and expected you to give all of us a fair shake." The two administrators promised they would try to do something about the problem but were at this point locked into the salary figures because the legislature met only biannually in the state.

Discussion questions

1.   What was wrong with this approach to wage and salary administration?
2.   What is a secret/open pay policy?
3.   Can an organization fire an employee for divulging his/her pay?

4. Leidecker Drugs, Inc.

Samuel Heisch, president of Liedecker, a medium-sized manufacturer of proprietary drugs, believes Johnstown, Pennsylvania, is a good place to work. Leidecker produces products both for its own brand "Healthy," and also under the brand name of various drug store, grocery store, and department store groups.

Life has treated him well, Heisch thinks. He's worked hard, but he's prospered and reached his goal of the presidency. At 63, Sam is wondering what he can do as a legacy to all the fine employees who helped him "make it."

Maybe Izzy Siegel, vice president—personnel, is right. The way to improve the employee's lot as a legacy is to improve the benefits package. Siegel argues that raises just disappear, but that important new benefits are longer lasting, often tax free as well.

At present, Leidecker's benefit package includes the following items:

1.   Social Security.
2.   Worker's compensation.
3.   Paying two thirds of health insurance premium.
4.   Paying one half of major medical insurance.
5.   Group auto insurance.
6.   Paying one half of term life insurance up to $15,000 per employee.
7.   Cafeteria where good lunches (for example, salad, meat, two vegetables, dessert, and drink) cost 70¢.

8. Generous vacation plans.
9. Usual holidays and rest periods.
10. Paying one half of pension plan costs.

Heisch thinks these are all good. Siegel is proposing that he add these benefits:

1. Free day-care centers for working mothers or, where applicable, for working fathers.
2. Dental insurance.
3. Longer vacations.

Heisch is not sure that these additional benefits will do much for employee morale. The trouble with so many benefits, as he sees it, is that once the employees get the benefits, they accept them as their right. The employees are not particularly satisfied and don't work any harder for having gotten the benefits.

Heisch would rather put in a profit-sharing plan. He'd like to plan along these lines: One third of profit in dividends; one third retained for improved machinery, and so forth; one third profit sharing.

Probably the best way to compute the profit sharing is directly; that is, if the employee's wages or salary equals 1 percent of the payroll, he'd get 1 percent of the profit-sharing pool.

In fact, Heisch said to himself, "That's what I'll do! That will be my legacy." He rang for Siegel and explained his plan to him and his rationale that the plan would lead to harder working employees.

Seigel replied: "Sam, this is a very generous plan. But do you think we ought to ask the employees about this—whether they'd rather have that or dental care, and so forth? Not all profit-sharing plans have proved to work the way you say you expect this one to work. Do you want to see some studies of that before you go ahead with it?"

Heisch sat there stunned at Siegel's words.

Requirement. Is Siegel right in asking these questions? Could he have handled it better with Heisch? What will Heisch do now? How can Heisch find out how the employees feel about the plan without promising them the additional benefits in the beginning?

5. Taylor Bicycle Manufacturing

The Taylor Manufacturing Company is a medium-sized manufacturer of quality bicycles. It has specialized in ten-speed and racing bikes made

from the finest materials. Taylor bikes are light and relatively mainte-
nance-free because they are so well made.

Taylor has plants around the United States. It has one in Santa Ana,
California, one in Trenton, New Jersey, one in Spartanburg, South Carolina, and one in Decatur, Illinois.

The company has a good accident and safety record. The Decatur plant
has won the company's award for years because of having the smallest
number of accidents of any of the plants.

Recently, Eugene Schultheis, an employee of a little over a year, had an
accident at the Decatur plant. He reported it immediately to his supervisor,
Tony Kubicek. Kubicek made out the accident report after sending the
injured man to the doctor the plant had on retainer, Dr. Allen Schmuckler.
The plant is not large enough to have its own medical staff. It has had so
few problems that even if the plant were larger it is doubtful that it would
have a full-time medical staff.

Dr. Schmuckler treated Schultheis and furnished the information for
the work's compensation claim. The doctor told the personnel manager,
Mike Juhn, that although Schultheis had hurt his wrist and hand badly,
he would not lose them nor would he lose the use of them. It was Dr.
Schmuckler's estimate that Schultheis could return to work in about six
weeks. He was to report to the doctor weekly.

About the fifth week, Dr. Schmuckler reported to Juhn that Schultheis
was demanding plastic surgery for certain areas of his hand. He also said
that Schultheis felt he needed physical therapy to restore the use of his
hand. Dr. Schmuckler told him to follow certain exercises, but Schultheis
said he couldn't.

About the seventh week, the doctor did send Schultheis to the physical
therapist for treatment. The company questioned the need for plastic
surgery, but not wishing to look cheap and heartless, it gave approval.
This surgery was scheduled for the ninth week.

Schultheis also reported to Dr. Schmuckler about the eighth week
that he was having terrible nightmares about the accident. He wondered
"if he could ever return to that job," he said. Schultheis wondered if he
needed some psychiatric care.

When Dr. Schmuckler heard that, he reported it immediately to Juhn.
Juhn went immediately to Kubicek.

Juhn: You know that Schultheis has been giving us a hard time on this worker's compensation case, Tony. Now Schultheis wants to see a psychiatrist.
He is fairly new. I don't know him too well. What is he like?

Kubicek: I was afraid of this. I never liked that kid and he is a kid. He is 23
years old. We were talking one day. You know he's never held jobs long.
After high school, he hitched across the country for over a year. Then the
army got him—for 14 months. He got a bad conduct discharge. Then he
lived in communes and "around," as he told me. This is the first real job
he ever had.

Juhn: How did we ever hire him?

Kubicek: Well, I was never asked. Your personnel interviewer hired him. He was a walk-in. They said that with the tight labor market, it was the best they could do. He never really did a good job here.

Juhn: Well, what do you think he's up to now?

Kubicek: It's obvious he wants to ride a gravy train. I overheard him asking Jack Badawi detailed questions about benefits one day, including worker's compensation. That's very rare. Young workers never ask about benefits, just pay. Even the once-a-year briefing you people in personnel give them usually finds the young ones in the back talking football and telling dirty jokes.

Juhn: Thanks for your help, Tony.

Kubicek: If you want me to, I'll go over to his house and straighten him out and get him back to work. Psychiatrist! That's a good one.

Juhn: Thanks again, Tony. But we'll try to handle this one my way, first.

Then Juhn and Kubicek both laughed.

Requirement. You are Mike Juhn. How do you proceed in the case of Eugene Schultheis?

6. The Gladstone Company*

The company

Gladstone, a family-owned company, has been in the textile business for the last 50 years. It has grown from a small firm struggling for existence in 1926 to a national company in 1976 with gross sales in excess of $100 million. Gladstone has always been a paternal organization, concerned with the personal welfare of its employees while demanding a high level of productivity. For years Gladstone has enjoyed an excellent reputation for its efforts toward social betterment in the community. Many members of management are actively involved in community programs and projects with the full support of Gladstone's top management.

The company manufactures a complete line of textile products and has its own national sales force selling to both wholesalers and retailers. Gladstone's products are sold for commercial use and to ultimate consumers. Both branded and nonbranded items are sold. In general, Gladstone's product line is considered to be of moderate to high quality. Nine

---

* This case was prepared by Professors Ronald M. Zigli and W. Daniel Rountree of Appalachian State University as a basis for class discussion rather than to illustrate either effective or ineffective handling of an administrative situation. The names of the firms and employees have been changed so that they remain anonymous.

Copyright © Ronald M. Zigli and W. Daniel Rountree.

major plants produce most of Gladstone's line. Most plants are located in Burnsville, a small town of approximately 60,000 people in the southeastern part of the United States. A few plants are scattered in other parts of the eastern United States.

Each of Gladstone's manufacturing plants carries on most of its operations autonomously. Only questions involving marketing and sales, major financial investments, or other issues of companywide impact are decided at the company office. All other decisions remain the prerogative of the plant manager, whose effectiveness is usually measured against profit for his plant. Some plants manufacture intermediate items that are subsequently converted into finished products by other plants. Even in these instances, where profit cannot be measured directly, decisions are still largely the prerogative of the plant manager.

Gladstone employs 3,000 people including management. Most of the labor force (nonsupervisory) at Gladstone would be classified as skilled or semiskilled. There are some jobs, however, that can and do utilize unskilled workers. Typically, these jobs are either not challenging or unpleasant, or both.

The industry

The textile industry is rather unusual in several respects. Perhaps most apparent is the fact that it is one of the few industries that approaches pure competition in the economic sense. Even the largest firm captures no more than 10 percent of total industry sales (in dollars). Another characteristic of textiles is the concentration of firms in the Southeast. From a marketing standpoint, competition in the marketplace is fierce. "Cutthroat" practices are not uncommon. Finally, the textile industry is quite sensitive to buyer preferences and endeavors to produce what the customer wants. As a result, textile products are constantly changing in style and composition.

In the last several years, the industry has undergone a number of changes. More and more companies have expanded their operations. Many have merged with other companies (in and out of textiles), diversified and "gone public." Many of the largest manufacturers are actively investigating vertical integration. In addition, billions of dollars have been spent on plant modernization in an effort to become less labor intensive and more capital intensive. Nevertheless, most experts agree that some art or craftsmanship will always be an integral part of the industry.

Changes in raw materials and raw material sources have also occurred in the last several years. Synthetics are being substituted for more basic materials. Although, many buyers still prefer the use of "natural" materials, more and more consumers are convinced of the superiority of synthetics from the standpoint of durability and strength with no discernable difference in appearance.

In spite of all these positive changes, the textile industry still has several major problems to resolve. One of the more important and difficult issues facing many textile manufacturers is that of high turnover. This problem is particularly acute in areas where unemployment is low and a shortage of needed labor exists. In fact, availability of labor in some areas is so low that many companies have turned to less conventional sources for labor. Other companies have changed fringe benefit programs hoping to induce a greater sense of loyalty and tenure on the part of employees; still other companies have tried a wide variety of financial and benefit oriented nonfinancial incentive programs. For almost all of these firms, success has been minimal. A comparative statewide study of benefit programs was conducted by the state in 1974. The results of this study for selected industries are shown in Table 1.

THE SITUATION

Casual-wear plant 5

Gladstone is one of several large textile manufacturers in Burnsville. As a group, these firms represent the dominant industry and major employer in the area. Because of this, competition for the existing labor force has been fierce, and at any one time, a sizable proportion of textile employees are intransit from one textile manufacturer to another.

One of the largest manufacturing plants in the area for Gladstone is Casual-Wear Plant 5. Employment at this plant fluctuates over the year from roughly 300 to as high as 700 employees. One of the most frustrating problems has been the high turnover rate experienced at Casual-Wear Plant 5. Although the rates are not atypical for other similar plants in the area, the plant manager has been pressing hard for answers to the problem. Clearly, the costs of turnover are high. The personnel processing costs of recruitment, selection, and training, not to mention interruptions in production, have a serious impact on profitability. A number of things have been tried to reduce turnover, but none have been successful thus far.

One such experiment has been the employment of prison labor. Essentially, the program consists of releasing prisoners during the day to work at Casual-Wear Plant 5. Each evening these employees return to prison. These workers are paid comparable wages and are excused from other prison work. The only additional expenses incurred by prison workers are travel expenses, which are paid to the state by the prisoner from wages earned.

For the past eight years under the direction of Dave Packet, plant 5 has employed between 5 and 30 prison workers. In addition, several other efforts have been made to reduce the turnover rate including a merit

TABLE 1
FRINGE BENEFITS FOR SELECTED INDUSTRIES ON A STATEWIDE BASIS

	All Industries	Textile	Primary metal industries	Furniture and fixtures	Paper and allied products	Chemical and allied products	Rubber and miscellaneous plastics products	Stone, clay, glass and concrete products
Percent coverage of establishments in survey	12	17	20	9	31	10	20	6
Paid vacation of one week or more (less than 1 year service)	21	25	0	28	17	42	24	4
Paid vacation of two weeks or more (1–5 years service)	26	18	31	30	36	83	40	25
Paid holidays five days or more	72	51	100	53	93	100	96	83
Paid rest periods of 20 minutes or more	79	80	85	79	78	50	88	54
Annual or semiannual bonus plan	45	58	31	52	22	29	40	46
Annual savings or stock purchase plan	15	13	15	14	7	46	16	4
Cost-of-living pay increases	13	10	23	9	7	13	24	8
Paid sick leave (less than one year service)	9	2	15	2	15	25	28	8
Paid sick leave (1–5 years service)	13	3	23	2	15	33	38	21
Life insurance (employer paying more than 50 percent)	77	74	84	75	85	88	92	88
Hospital insurance (employer paying more than 50 percent)	76	75	92	69	85	95	92	96
Income protection plan (employer paying more than 50 percent)	31	23	38	38	46	71	40	33
Retirement pension plan (employer paying more than 50 percent)	55	53	69	55	74	95	56	67

Note: Statistical data compiled by state agency. Identification withheld for reasons of confidentiality.

review system whereby merit pay raises are given throughout the year. Also, Casual-Wear Plant 5 has had for years an "open-door" grievance system which allowed any employee to walk right into the plant manager's office with any complaint. In spite of all these efforts, turnover remains high as evidenced by Table 2. Until recently, the prison release program has been moderately successful. However, Dave Packet was just informed that the state plans to move the facility housing prisoners that participate in the release program at Casual-Wear Plant 5 to another geographic location which would be too remote for a continuance of the program. As a result, the entire issue of turnover has been raised again.

TABLE 2
GLADSTONE ANNUAL
AVERAGE TURNOVER

Year	Turnover rate percent
1965	100.00
1966	110.00
1967	115.00
1968	110.00
1969	126.00
1970	140.00
1971	140.00
1972	110.00
1973	125.00
1974	144.20
1975	75.49
1976	N.A.

N.A. = not available.

Source: Company records.

The plant meeting

The plant manager, Frank Brumbley, has called a meeting in his office. Attending are Dave Packet, Jean Britton, and all shop foremen. The pros and cons of the prison release program becomes the first order of business. It is pointed out by one foreman that prison workers are not accepted by other employees socially. As a result, problems have occurred on the job from time to time. George, another foreman counters this argument saying that these problems are minor and are more than offset by the fact that prison workers learn fast, are the most reliable, and are among the top 10 percent in productivity. Most of the other foremen agree with this observation. Jean asks Dave how long the average prison worker stays at Gladstone. Dave replies, "Approximately fifteen months." The basic purpose of the use of prison labor also comes up. "Are we interested in rehabilitation, profit, cost savings, or an assured labor source?" asks one foreman. After some discussion Dave, Jean, and Frank Brumbley agree that business interests must come first; however, the two issues are not necessarily mutually exclusive. Dave asks the question, "Do any employees show any resentment toward prison workers, perhaps feeling that a job has been taken away from someone else by the prison workers?" Again, most foremen indicated that they found no evidence of that on the job. Frank Brumbley suggests that the discussion of prison labor may be a moot argument since this source was not going to be available in the future. He then asked Dave and Jean whether there were any alternative sources of prison labor. Dave indicated that a younger group of prisoners, most of which were serving terms for drug abuse, would be close enough to the plant for employment. At this point, several foremen raised objections, citing a number of problems experienced by other companies that attempted to use such labor. On several occasions, other firms found these younger prisoners "pushing" narcotics and generally creating disharmony on the job for other workers.

The challenge

Frank Brumbley asks the question "Is it necessary to seek employees from less conventional sources? Could we offer additional direct and indirect financial and nonfinancial inducements to draw and develop a stable labor force?"

"Possibly," says Jean, "however, we will have our work cut out for us." She shows the group the annual average rates of employment for the United States and the county for the last 14 years. (See Table 3.) Jean goes on to point out that job for job pay scales are comparable to any in

TABLE 3
ANNUAL AVERAGE UNEMPLOYMENT

Year	Capitol County (percent unemployed)	United States (percent unemployed)
1963	4.5	5.7
1964	4.2	5.2
1965	2.8	4.5
1966	2.2	3.8
1967	3.1	3.8
1968	2.1	3.6
1969	2.0	3.5
1970	5.0	4.9
1971	5.2	5.9
1972	3.4	5.6
1973	2.9	4.9
1974	4.9	5.6
1975	N.A.	8.5
1976	N.A.	N.A.

N.A. = not available.

Source: State Employment Agency and Manpower reports to the President in 1971 and 1975.

the county or the state. She also cites a personal observation that the highest turnover seems to be in departments that have the most unpleasant jobs and highest unskilled labor ratios. Frank Brumbley finally charges Dave, Jean, and two of the senior foremen to develop a plan to reduce turnover and stabilize the work force.

Discussion questions

1. You are on the committee appointed by Frank to reduce turnover and stabilize the work force. What suggestions do you have?
2. Evaluate the advantages and disadvantages of Gladstone continuing to use prison labor.
3. Compare and contrast the benefits for the textile industry with the other major industries in the state.

7. Southwest Sporting Goods

Beach Losky, president of Southwest Sporting Goods, is sitting in his office thinking about a conversation he has just had with one of his most loyal employees. He is to spend a lot of time in the next few weeks on this issue.

As president of this medium-sized firm, he is responsible for all policy issues there. He has to keep in mind the welfare of his 2,200 employees.

Southwest's headquarters is located in Albuquerque, New Mexico. The firm manufactures items such as footballs, baseballs, basketballs, volleyballs, and allied equipment for recreational, school, and personal use. It has plants located near Los Angeles, New Orleans, Minneapolis-St. Paul, and Camden, New Jersey.

Robert Kamerschen, age 48, from the accounting department, has just talked with Mr. Losky. He pointed out that SSG was no longer the small firm of 150 employees Losky had inherited from his father 25 years ago. Robert had given SSG 25 years of his service, too. He said: "Other firms our size and smaller provide programs for loyal employees like me that give a person a feeling of security for his old age. In these days of inflation, you know social security and the savings I've tried to amass won't be enough. And SSG has no pension plan, no stock option plan, or anything. It's true, Mr. Losky, that you've given big bonuses the past year or two to retiring employees. But taxes eat much of this up. Don't you think it's time to set up a SSG pension plan? It has tax advantages for you, too."

Questions ran through Mr. Losky's mind: Can we afford a plan? Which kind? Can our five-person corporate personnel department set one up? Legally must I set one up in each state where I operate? He wrote a memo including these and other important questions to Carmen Smith, the corporate personnel director, asking his comments on them.

Requirement.   You are Carmen Smith. Make recommendations regarding a pension plan to Mr. Losky.

G. SAFETY

1. Hartley Conglomerate (A)*

The Hartley Corporation is composed of ten autonomous divisions and corporate headquarters as Exhibit 1 indicates. The case focuses on the Bien Works. Its organization is given in Exhibit 2. (See page 99.)

Bien Works is housed in a building erected in 1904. The building is five stories high. The top two are not used since the floors are too dangerous. The second and third floors have holes and rotted places in them.

The third floor holds the rack shop, lab, and marketing departments. The second floor contains the rack shop, office, some warehousing, and some buffing compound production lines. The first floor contains the warehousing for heavier materials and the rest of the manufacturing lines. The main operation is manufacturing. The rack shop is a support unit to make racks for drying chemicals. The works is nonunion.

Jesse Fuller has been with Hartley for 20 years, all of it in conjunction with the Bien Works. He holds a B.S. in chemistry from City University of New York. He worked his way through college. He's done almost everything at Bien. He started as a foreman in the manufacturing unit. He's run the rack shop, supervised the warehouse for two years, sold the compounds. The office and lab are white-collar or technical jobs so he's not worked there. His employees like him, although they are a bit afraid of him, too. He has a terrible temper which he loses about once a month. When that happens, everyone tries to get out of the way.

Jesse is now 53 years old. He's happy with the Bien Works. He likes the town and wouldn't move. Bien is like his own firm since he's isolated geographically from Hartley.

Since Bien makes more money for Hartley than his budget calls for, they let Jess alone. He has lower turnover than expected. Absenteeism is also low. His safety and health record is about average. All in all, Hartley and Jess are happy with the Bien Works.

---

* This is a disguised case—for obvious reasons.

EXHIBIT 1
HARTLEY CORPORATION ORGANIZATION CHART

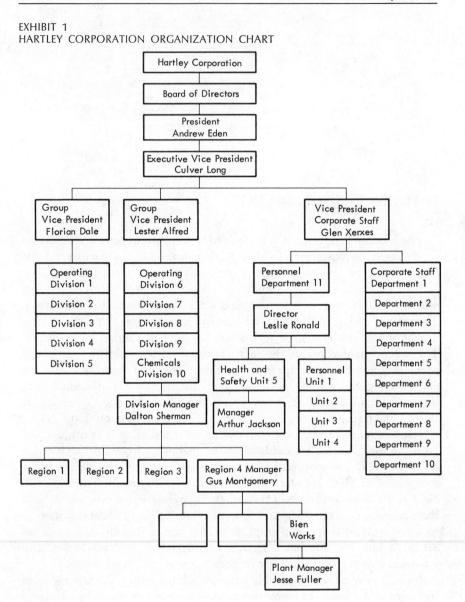

Then OSHA was passed. For some reason, the OSHA inspector came around Bien often. The local inspector was James Munsey. In April, James came to Bien when Jess was at a meeting at Hartley. He determined that the buffing manufacturing was producing unsafe gases. As is his right, he shut the plant down that day. Jess flew back and modified the gas filters. James passed the filters, and Bien started production again.

EXHIBIT 2
ORGANIZATION CHART: BIEN WORKS

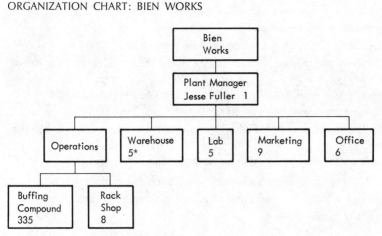

* Indicates number of employees in the unit.

In May, James came back and shut the plant again when Jess was at Rotary meeting. Again, the filters were cleaned and modified. This time Jess was really angry. After the plant was reopened and James gone, Jess held a meeting of all employees. At the meeting, he said:

Look, this OSHA guy is killing us. This is an old works. We can't afford to be shut down. At my recent meeting at corporate headquarters, I tried to make the case that we needed a new building here. The sharp pencil boys pointed out that we are profitable now, but not if we have to build a new plant. The industry is overcrowded, and Hartley will close this plant rather than spend money on it. If we get shut down or have to buy a lot of antipollution crap, they could shut us down. That OSHA guy is the enemy—just like a traffic cop. We've got to pull together, or we could all sink together.

The employees had never seen Jess so angry before, and they feared for their jobs now more than ever. There was a lot of unemployment in the area.

Hartley Conglomerate (B)

It is July now and James Munsey appeared at the Bien Works office. The office girls saw James coming and headed for the powder room. Melanie Smith, one of the lab technicians, greeted him. Melanie has just been hired in June and didn't know James.

Munsey: I'm the OSHA inspector. I need to talk to Mr. Fuller. He should accompany me on my inspection.

Smith: Just a moment, sir. I'll get him.

Smith (to Fuller): The OSHA inspector is here to see you.

Fuller: Oh my God! (pause) You go out there and tell him I'm too busy to see him today.

Smith (back in office): I'm sorry sir. He's too busy to see you today.

Munsey: Ask your boss if he's too busy tomorrow.

Smith (on the intercom): Mr. Fuller, are you too busy tomorrow to see the inspector?

Fuller (on the intercom): What do you want this time, Munsey?

Munsey: Because of previous violations, you're due for another inspection.

Fuller: Look, I'm busy. But come and inspect first thing in the morning.

Munsey: I'll be here at 8:30.

The rest of the day was a red alert.

No work was done. The whole plant was cleaned up. The lab was put in order. Bottles which leaked were secured. Shelves were straightened. The rack shop was cleaned up. Machine guards were put on—they weren't used otherwise. Machines without guards were moved and covered up as if they were no longer used. Machines too heavy for the third floor were moved.

The filters were cleaned. The water bath was cleaned. The slippery flood made of metal that was supposed to be neutralized and *scrubbed* daily (though it usually got it monthly) was neutralized and scrubbed. Everyone helped. Even the secretaries and lab technicians helped clean.

The next day, the inspector came back. The prettiest secretary was assigned to get him coffee and "chat him up." James and Jesse toured the plant and the inspector passed Bien Works. But the employees wondered if the inspector didn't have to realize what happened.

Hartley Corporation (C)

On August 15, James Munsey returned to Bien. This time Melanie knew who he was. She got him a cup of coffee and then went to Mr. Fuller's office.

Fuller: Tell him I'm out—that you can't find me. Stall!

Smith: Mr. Fuller seems to be out. As soon as he returns, I'll tell him you're here.

James drank his coffee. While James was drinking coffee, Jess called all departments and told them to clean up in a hurry. They started to.

Forty-five minutes later.

Munsey: Miss, I can't wait any longer. Let me talk to whoever is here.

Melanie got one of the foremen. Together Munsey and the foreman did the inspection. The foreman took the inspector to the warehouse first to give the other areas more time to cleanup. It didn't help. James issued four warnings and gave Bien 24 hours to comply.

Jess was so angry that this time he set up a plan. One of his foreman, Harry Coat, was moving to another division because of his wife's health problems.

Fuller: Harry, I want you to do me a favor. You're moving to Arizona anyway. That SOB inspector is bound to be back before you go. When he comes back, it's worth $500 to me to pick a fight with him and cold cock him. Don't worry, I'll cover for you.

Coat: Sounds like fun.

Hartley Conglomerate (D)

On October 13, James appeared for another inspection. Jess called Harry.

Fuller: Harry, it's D-Day. Get ready for the assault.

Coat: I'm ready.

As James walked through Coat's work area, Harry came up to him and started a fight and knocked James cold. James went back to OSHA to report the incident.

Fuller (calling the OSHA office): This is Jesse Fuller at Bien Works. Let me talk to the boss.

Grubb: This is Mr. Grubb, I'm in charge of this office.

Fuller: Listen this fellow Munsey has been giving us fits. Now he's picked a fight with one of my managers. I fired my manager. I assume you'll do the same.

James Munsey was transferred to another OSHA unit shortly thereafter.

Hartley Conglomerate (E)

In January, the new OSHA inspector, Pamela Morton, appeared at the Bien Works. After her inspection, she ordered it closed and issued five warnings.

The Health and Safety Division: Hartley

Arthur Jackson is manager of the health and safety division of Hartley's personnel department. Arthur is a graduate of Case Western Reserve University with a B.S. in industrial engineering. He has taken additional short courses in safety management offered by various professional associations. He had five years experience in the safety department of Allied Chemical before coming to Hartley a year ago. He was safety manager for several operating divisions (this division) prior to coming to the home office staff last year. He has tried to visit each division and plant since then, although he has never been to the Bien Works. Hartley has over 150 plants, and he has personally visited about 50 since he went to the home office.

The role of corporate level health and safety office is to set policy for the corporation. The office keeps the divisions and plants informed on the latest information, trains divisional and (where appropriate) plant level people, and is responsible to the president for safety for the whole company. It also is responsible to see that all operations meet all health and safety standards of the company and OSHA. Jackson has three professionals on his staff.

Arthur has received word about Bien's recent experiences with OSHA and has decided to go down to Bien and see what's going on. He arrives the week after Pamela Morton. Jess is sick that day. He inspects the works and finds numerous OSHA violations. The works also violates a number of Hartley's own safety and health regulations.

Requirement 1. You are Arthur Jackson. You've questioned employees about Bien's recent experiences on safety and health. You are to meet with Jess at 8:30 A.M. tomorrow. Outline how you will proceed to improve conditions at the Bien Works.

Requirement 2. You are Mr. Grubb at OSHA. Outline how you will deal with Bien Works in the next year.

2. OSHA and the A. B. Chance Division*

A. B. Chance Company, organized in 1907, is a manufacturer of electrical power and communication products, mostly for utilities. One of its

---

* This case was written by Sam Daudy and Bill Burnett under the supervision of Professor William F. Glueck. Reprinted with permission of the A. B. Chance Division.

major products is the "never creep anchor" for telephone poles. At the time of the case, A. B. Chance employed 3,000 employees in 15 plants in the United States, Canada, Mexico, and Brazil. Sales (1974) were over $100 million.

The case focuses on the utility systems division with its three plants in Centralia, Missouri. These plants have 680,000 square feet.

SAFETY PROGRAMS AT A. B. CHANCE

The safety program at ABC begins with top management support. The president has issued a safety policy to show his support for safety:

Because accidents are painful, wasteful, and expensive, it is the policy of the A.B. Chance Company to maintain a continuous program on safety. Management is responsible for education, promotion, and improvement of equipment with the goal of preventing accidents. No job shall be considered completed unless each employee has followed every precaution and safety rule. For these reasons it is imperative that all supervisors and employees work toward maximum accident prevention throughout the company.

The Centralia plant has a safety director, W. E. Allen. Allen has been with ABC for nine years. His prior occupation was as a navy medic. He spent three years of his college work in safety related courses such as industrial safety, industrial hygiene, and heavy conservation. Allen is a certified emergency medical technician, a certified audiometric technician, and a certified optician. This training has qualified him to set up three first-aid rooms, one in each plant in Centralia, which enables him to treat many injuries on the spot without calling a doctor.

The company does, however, have a doctor on call for serious injuries. His office is just across the street from the plant. In addition to emergency duties, the doctor does routine physical examinations (one a year for each employee), laboratory tests based on hazard exposure, chest x rays, and checks for cancer on those who work in the plastics department.

A. B. CHANCE'S SAFETY ACTIVITIES

The first thing ABC tries to do is inform employees about safe working conditions and their importance. The first method is a safety booklet, "The Answer Book." It is 62 pages long. The center spread, pages 30 and 31, makes a list of 18 "Safety Reminders . . . for your Protection," specifying safety rules and regulations of the company.

ABC also produces "safe practices" sheets for each job in each department. When a new employee or a transfer from another department reports on the job for the first time, the foreman of this particular operation goes over each item listed on the "safe practices" sheet, explaining in detail the safe way to perform. The employee signs two copies, indicating that he or she knows how to function safely on this job. He or she keeps one copy, and the foreman files the other. The employee can never say, "I wasn't informed." An example of these sheets is given in Exhibit 1 for the punch press job.

Communication also takes place in the weekly safety meeting with the

EXHIBIT 1

SAFE PRACTICES

These are the rules that will help you do your job safely. Please study them --- remember them --- follow them!

JOB: Punch Press   **DEPARTMENT:** 3100

I. Safe operation
    1. Keep hands out of die area.
    2. Use all guards and safety devices provided:
        a. Be sure they are adjusted properly.
        b. Be sure they are in good condition.
    3. Shut off and lock out machine before adjusting or maintaining.
    4. Use proper hand tools:
        a. Be sure they are in good condition.
        b. Be sure you know how to use them.
    5. Before setting up or removing dies:
        a. Clear away all obstructions and tripping hazards.
        b. Disconnect or shut off power and lock the switch.
        c. Clean off die with a brush.
        d. Use ladder for adjusting ram.
        e. Inspect die before starting run.
        f. Keep dies straight in racks, when stored.

II. Material handling by hand
    1. Check material for hazards.
    2. Get a firm grip on the object.
    3. Keep fingers away from pinch points.
    4. When lifting large or heavy objects:
        a. Lift with your legs — not your back.
        b. Never lift with the body in a twist.
        c. Be sure footing is firm.
        d. Get help with heavy or awkward loads.

III. General
    1. Report damaged or faulty equipment immediately.
    2. Be completely familiar with operating procedures.
    3. Watch out for others in your area.
    4. Keep obstructions clear of work area.
    5. Report all injuries, no matter how slight.

managers. In this meeting, proposed capital improvements programs for safety are submitted. On the first Monday of each month, each department supervisor holds a 20-minute safety meeting with the employees. A list of topics for discussion is selected a year in advance, so the 20 minutes will be fruitful and not wasted.

Recently, in a plantwide survey by Mr. Allen, he found that most accidents occurred among employees with one year of seniority or less and among those with 20 years or more. He is wondering how to create a company communication program aimed at reducing accidents among these groups.

Safety is stressed in frequent union-management meetings. These are very open meetings where the representatives of the employees can present safety hazards they see in the plant or on company property to management and ask when these can be expected to be corrected.

A. B. Chance tries to make safety fun and rewarding to its employees with various contests and awards. In 1974, for example, regular monthly safety meetings were held for all workers. Each department was allocated from $15 to $50 per quarter for a jackpot. If a worker completed a quarter without an injury, his name went into the jackpot, and a drawing was held to pick a winner. It cost the company $750 a quarter, or $3,000 for the year's program. The previous year green stamps were awarded for safe performances. This cost about $4,000. In addition, each department that completes a year without an accident is the guest of the management at a banquet.

In addition providing adequate medical facilities and keeping complete records, ABC supplies personal protective equipment to its employees. Each employee is required to wear safety glasses, which the company supplies at no cost. Originally any glasses worn were considered safety glasses. But OSHA regulations require that safety glasses must be 3 millimeters thick, heat treated so that a small ball may be dropped on the lens without the lens breaking, and the manufacturer's monogram must be on a corner of the lens. Eye protection costs the company about $1,000 a month, and employees may have an eye examination each year. The company also supplies the ear plugs and ear muffs necessary for those working in areas with high decibels of noise. Rubber aprons and hard hats likewise are provided for those working in the galvanizing area. At present no protective footwear is offered.

Company managers make safety inspections. Once a year the company exchanges managers among the plants. They then inspect each other's faults and errors. The foremen do the same thing quarterly. Quarterly inspections are made by two person teams from the safety director, factory managers, foremen, and insurance company representatives.

So that machines and equipment are safe, each Saturday the maintenance crew makes inspections and repairs. The safety director makes periodic inspections at any time and once each year makes a plantwide safety inspection, department by department, and makes a complete written report for top management, making suggestions for repairs, replacements, and improvements. The February 1975 report was eight single-spaced pages of detailed items to be corrected. Excerpts of this report are given as Exhibit 2.

EXHIBIT 2

Page 3
Annual plantwide safety inspection: A. B. Chance division

Department 3043 and 3047:
  A.   Press 47–316—Employee had hand in point of operation.
  B.   Tool crib needs general straightening and cleanup.
  C.   Drill press 4331 has frayed air line.

Department 3079:
  A.   Acetylene tank not secure on cart in flame spray area.
  B.   Operator of aluminum saw needs ear protection on some operations. Noise level ranges 100–102 dbs.

Department 3042:
  A.   Belt grinder 4251—Noise level 94 dbs. continuous. Operator needs ear protection.
  B.   Connections loose on dust collection system.

Department 3045: (PermMold)
  A.   Hoist hooks need safety catches.
  B.   Fire extinguisher on east wall was blocked.
  C.   Water fountain on north wall needs cleaning and front cover.

Department 3045: (Main Foundry)
  A.   Wires frayed on fans in coreroom.
  B.   Empty oxygen cylinder in machine shop not secured.
  C.   Pallets stored on end in this area.
  D.   Overall housekeeping in this department good—at time of this inspection.

Department 3045: (Iron Foundry)
  A.   Ear protection may be required, especially when operating abrasive cut-off saw.
  B.   Material storage is a problem in this area.
  C.   Housekeeping could be improved.
  D.   Need to check regulations for additional exits for second floor. Fire escape ladder may be required.

Whenever an accident occurs that involves sending a worker to the doctor, a complete accident investigation is carried out. Both sides of the story are heard. The accident is reported on state form 1020 which is exactly like the OSHA form, and thus is used for the OSHA report also. The injury likewise is recorded in the firm's log of occupational injuries and illnesses (OSHA form 100) and at the end of the year with all company injuries listed on the OSHA summary of occupational injuries and illnesses form and posted for the employees to see.

Exhibit 3 is the summary form posted for 1974. The totals for previous years are summarized in Exhibit 4. (See page 109.)

CASEWRITERS' INSPECTIONS

To assess the safety of the plants, the casewriters personally inspected two representative departments: the drop forge and punch press departments.

The drop forge department

The drop forge department is noisy. OSHA prohibits noise above 90 decibels (dbs.) per eight-hour work day. When the casewriters questioned ABC officials about the noise problem, this is what they found out.

The company had made plantwide surveys to check the decibel level for an eight-hour day in each department. It invested $700 in a sound level meter and calibrator. A. B. Chance's insurance company provided an industrial hygienist to make the plant survey and to teach Mr. Allen how to use the meter. OSHA also requires audiograms in high noise conditions. So the company would have to either bring in a consultant or do the testing itself. Feeling that it would be best and more economical to do its own testing, the company sent Mr. Allen to the St. Louis Hearing and Speech Clinic, where he became a certified audiometric technician. The company also purchased the necessary equipment (an audiometer and a sound room) to perform the test properly.

Those employees working in departments with a sound reading of over 85 dbs. were tested first, followed by the other company employees. This testing of other employees was to establish a base from which to judge changes in hearing resulting from a job transfer. These first audiographs showed that 30 percent of the employees had significant hearing loss.

Each employee now gets a hearing test each year with his physical, and records are being kept. If an employee is found to have an industrial induced hearing loss, a letter is sent to the employee notifying him of this fact. Mr. Allen and an audiologist go over the case with the employee and try to educate him on what can be done. The company has an audiologist consultant come from Mexico, Missouri, once a month to interpret the audiograms, help in the hearing conservation program, and to calibrate the equipment. This fee is $1,200 a year. The company instituted this program not only for the welfare of its employees, but also for its protection against lawsuits in case of suits for hearing loss.

The companywide decibel level check revealed that the drop forge department had the highest noise level—a reading of 115–120 dbs.

EXHIBIT 3

OSHA No. 102

Form Approved
OMB No. 44R 1453

Summary
Occupational Injuries and Illnesses
(From January 1, 1974 thru December 31, 1974)

Establishment name and address: A. B. Chance Company, 210 N. Allen St., Centralia, Mo.

			Lost workday cases			Nonfatal cases without lost workdays*	
Injury and illness category							
(1) Code	*(2) Category*	*(3) Fatalities*	*(4) Number of cases*	*(5) Number of cases involving permanent transfer to another job or termi- nation of employment*	*(6) Number of lost work- days*	*(7) Number of cases*	*(8) Number of cases involving transfer to another job or termi- nation of employment*
10	Occupational injuries	0	7		99	152	
21	Occupational skin diseases or disorders					9	7
22	Dust diseases of the lungs (pneumo- conioses)						
23	Respiratory con- ditions due to toxic agents						
24	Poisoning (sys- temic effects of toxic materials)						
25	Disorders due to physical agents (other than toxic materials)						
26	Disorders due to repeated trauma						
29	All other occupa- tional illnesses						
	Total—occupa- tional illnesses (21–29)						
	Total—occupa- tional injuries and illnesses	0	7		99	161	7

* Nonfatal cases without lost workdays—cases resulting in: medical treatment beyond first aid, diagnosis of occupational illness, loss of consciousness, restriction of work or motion, or transfer to another job (without lost workdays).

The above summary is true to the best of my knowledge and taken from the log of occupational injuries and illness form 100. Prepared by _Gene Allen_ 1/6/75

EXHIBIT 4
OCCUPATIONAL INJURIES AND ILLNESSES REPORT

Category	1971	1972	1973
Occupational injuries			
4	7	10	7
6	151	361	162
7	49	126	151
Occupational illnesses			
5	0	1	0
6	0	12	0
7	2	0	10
8	1	2	6

Obviously, this became the chief problem for correction. The drop forge shop employs 40 to 50 people in three shifts, usually 25 on the day shift, 15 on the evening shift, and 7 on the night shift. The employees are machine operators, material handlers, and housekeeping personnel, and all are subject to the extreme noise in the area.

OSHA states that in order to curtail the noise a company can:

1. Engineer out the noise.
2. Administer out the problem.
3. Supply ear protection.

The A. B. Chance Company attacked the problem on all three levels. First, it tried to engineer out the problem and decided that because of the factory arrangement, that is, the positioning of the machines in the forge, this would be nearly impossible or very costly. Even if a few machines were quieted in one section of the shop, the noise from the forge hammers would still be heard throughout the building. Even if a machine is semiquiet, when it is placed next to several like it, as at ABC, the noise is compounded. Several of the machines run by piston vibrators were converted to rotary vibrators, and this did decrease the noise level significantly from 115–120 dbs. to 92–94 dbs., but this is still too high.

The only way to administer out the noise is to shift personnel around evey two hours, so that employees would not be subject to this high noise level for long periods of time. ABC feels that administrative problems and higher production costs of this shifting makes this impractical.

The third remedy to the noise pollution problem in the drop forge department is to supply ear protection. This is the approach in use at ABC. In the drop forge department the employees are required to wear ear muffs because of the noise level of between 92–94 dbs. per eight-hour day. The noise is almost deafening. It is difficult to talk even when shouting in one another's ear. Ear plugs lower the decibels about 15 dbs., while ear muffs will lower noise level about 30–40 dbs. Wearing plugs alone does not bring the workers within the acceptable range of 90 dbs.

or less per eight-hour day, whereas the ear muffs do. Therefore, ear muffs are required. A worker may wear both ear plugs and ear muffs. The company supplies both the plugs and the muffs to the workers.

The department supervisor or foreman is responsible to see that employees are taking proper safety precautions by wearing the ear muffs. An employee can be fired for not wearing his muffs, but this is usually not the case, as a verbal reprimand generally suffices. EAR PROTECTION REQUIRED BEYOND THIS POINT signs are prominently displayed as reminders.

The second major health and safety hazard in the forge shop is heat stress. The temperature is 120 degrees in the summer time. The company is attempting to engineer out some of this problem by replacing gas furnaces with electric furnaces. Besides reducing heat, these save energy and reduce noise. A. B. Chance tries to administer out this heat problem by allowing employees to work 20 minutes, break 10 minutes, thus reducing time exposure to the heat. Air-conditioned suits are available. If the company were to buy these suits so the men could work an eight-hour day, it would cost $1,800 per man for each suit and $30 to $40 a day to operate them. Since there are 80 men involved, the cost is great.

The punch press department

The punch press department consists of presses, the main function of which is to press pieces of metal into different shapes for use in the overall production of anchors. At present, it consists of one shift of 15 workers and a foreman. Usually, there are two shifts. The employees are press operators, material supply handlers, and housekeeping personnel. The employees are "general laborers" of high school education or less and have developed their skills through experience within the company. These operators are paid a base salary plus an incentive rate for each pound of finished product they produce per day.

The chief hazard from a physical injury standpoint in the punch press department is the press machines. Besides their noise, they can injure, cripple, and even kill if the operators are careless. For safety to the operators, most machines require guards so that hands, fingers, or arms are not injured.

OSHA regulations state that operators of punch presses cannot place their hands in the "point of operation" of the machine. The casewriters believe that is not in compliance with the "letter of the law" as stated but is in compliance with the intent of the law; that is, that when the machines are in operation, the operator's hands are free and clear from the point of operation.

To make sure that the operator's hands are free and clear from the point of operation, the company has used a variety of safety devices and gadgets in the department, and each one has been more effective than the one before it. First of all, a "pull-out" device was used. In this case two cables are attached to the machine at one end and two leather gloves at the other end. The operator uses his hands in the "point of operation" area by first placing his hands in the gloves. As the employee trips the foot lever, the cables would pull the worker's hands away from the "operation" area as the press came down. This was not a fool-proof system, as the gloves have become caught in the machine and tension in the cables sometimes varied and hands were not pulled away. Both cases meant severed fingers.

Another safety device used was the single trip foot pedal. With this system, the operator has to step on the pedal each time he wants the machine to operate. This prevents him from keeping his foot on the pedal as he tries to speed up work by feeding parts through the machine between successive punches. The problem with this single trip foot pedal safety device was that the worker could learn to sychronize his work to such a routine that he no longer thought about what he was doing and, therefore, might inadvertently step on the pedal while his hands are still under the press.

Adjustable U-bolts are another safety device used. These U-bolts are placed all around the point of operation so that nothing can get under the presses except what the operator puts there. This offered no more protection to the operator than the single trip foot pedal, and it takes 15 to 20 minutes to set the U-bolts properly. The operators are reluctant to do this because it takes away from their production. This system also requires more supervision.

One of the newer safety devices developed is the double synchronized hand buttons." With this system, to activate the machine, the operator must reach out with both hands, one on each side, and touch buttons at the same time, thereby removing his hands from the danger area. John Elsbury, foreman in the punch press department said most of the workers originally complained when this change from foot lever to hand button was made. However, later they were happy when they saw the decrease in injuries and were proud of the company for taking an interest in them.

The newest device for safety protection on machines is the "electronic light beam" which automatically stops the press if any part of the worker's body breaks the beam. ABC has installed these beams on two of their newer presses at a cost of about $3,000 each. The company also follows a policy of replacing machines as older ones wear out. In some instances, the new machines are bought with safety guards. In others, the company is designing and making its own guards to meet its own needs and for the savings advantage.

At the present time, the company is using a mixture of all the safety devices we have discussed except the "pull-out device." The presses in the department are versatile enough to use any of some 300-plus different dies, and different dies require different types of guards to protect the operator. The "single trip foot pedal" is used on some operations; U-bolts with others, and "double synchronized hand buttons" on still other processes. The type of machine guard used, therefore, depends on the type of operation the press is being used on any given day.

ABC has two problems connected with the machine-guarding requirements of the law. First of all is the expense of the guards and, second, is the practicality of the law requiring no hands at the point of operation. Plantwide, ABC has more than 2,000 dies for presses, all of which require "barrier guards" of the type discussed. The guards themselves are not expensive; the cost is in the time and work that goes into designing each guard individually. There also is considerable maintenance, for the guards are always being damaged in transport to and from storage areas as well as in set-up and take-down. So machine guarding is very expensive.

The practicality of the OSHA law will not be analyzed thoroughly here. But, briefly, the A. B. Chance Company would incur astronomical variable costs if operators were not allowed to use their hands in the "point of operation" of the presses. The company, therefore, has made working with the present system as safe as possible by using a variety of guards such as the "double synchronized hand buttons," the "single trip foot pedal," and the "electronic light beam."

By these actions, the company has lived up to the intent of the law rather than the letter of the law in guarding its machines and in protecting the health and safety of its employees in the punch press department.

THE OSHA INSPECTION

Recently, Larry Stewart, the OSHA inspector came to ABC for an inspection. Mr. Stewart gathered general information about the company, documented the type of safety equipment furnished to employees, and checked safety and health projects and improvements made by the company since the beginning of the OSHA law. After this, he made an inspection tour, taking photographs and notes as he progressed about the plant. R. A. Flink, works manager, Marvin Hombs, union president, and Harold Welborn, manager of the Allen Street plant accompanied him. The entire process of notetaking and inspection took two and a half days. Mr. Flink also made his own notes of possible violations in the Allen Street plant and later prepared a formal report for Mr. J. G. Everhart, his superior.

At the conclusion of the inspection, the OSHA inspector had an exit interview with Mr. Flink and informed him of potential violations to the law that he had found and the length of time given to make these corrections. He also gave Mr. Flink recommendations on other pieces of equipment and working conditions without issuing a citation for these possible violations.

About a month later on September 5, 1973, the company received its official report of the investigation. The report listed eight violations of "nonserious" nature. Four violations resulted in penalties totaling $195.

Excerpts from the OSHA report to ABC are given as Exhibit 6. (See pages 114 and 115.)

OTHER ASSESSMENTS OF SAFETY AT ABC

One way to evaluate the company's safety and health program is to look at the records for the tangible dollars and cents paid for medical and compensation expenses. While the company has always kept these records, two years ago these records were expanded to the point of breaking down the medical and compensation expenses by department. The figures on the drop forge and punch press departments were made available to us. Roughly, medical and compensation expense is made up of weekly benefits and lump sum settlements. These are given in Exhibit 5.

EXHIBIT 5
MEDICAL AND COMPENSATION EXPENSES DROP
FORGE AND PUNCH PRESS DEPARTMENTS

	Drop forge department	Punch press department
July 1974	$159.75	$ 0.00
August 1974	74.50	0.00
September 1974	95.00	0.00
October 1974	444.39*	0.00
November 1974	134.00	0.00
December 1974	81.50	93.00
January 1975	55.00	104.00
February 1975	42.25	0.00

* The high expense of $444.39 in October of 1974 consisted of $82 for a strained shoulder injury, $62 for a broken ankle, and $300 for an eye injury with two weeks' lost work.

Another way to look at ABC's results is to examine longitudinal safety data. There has been a safety program at A. B. Chance as long as the plant has been in operation. One department of 30–40 people, the assembly department, has had no disabling injury in 30 years, and this was before OSHA. The company has just received the "Award of Honor" from the National Safety Council for its 1974 operation. (Exhibit 7 on page 116.) This is the highest honor bestowed by the council. This award is based on frequency of injury, that is, the number of injuries per million manhours worked; and on severity of injury, that is, the number of days lost for each million manhours worked.

EXHIBIT 6
EXCERPTS FROM OSHA REPORT TO A. B. CHANCE

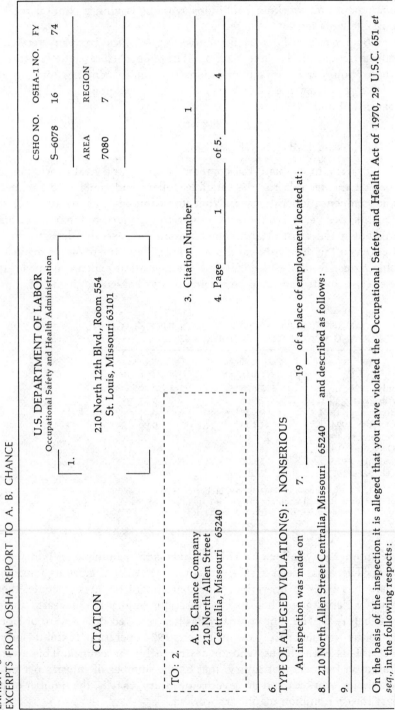

CITATION

U.S. DEPARTMENT OF LABOR
Occupational Safety and Health Administration

CSHO NO. OSHA-1 NO. FY
S-6078   16   74

AREA   REGION
7080   7

1.

210 North 12th Blvd., Room 554
St. Louis, Missouri 63101

3. Citation Number ____1____

4. Page ____1____ of 5. ____4____

TO: 2.

A. B. Chance Company
210 North Allen Street
Centralia, Missouri 65240

6.
TYPE OF ALLEGED VIOLATION(S): NONSERIOUS

An inspection was made on ____ 19 ____ of a place of employment located at:

8. 210 North Allen Street Centralia, Missouri 65240 and described as follows:

9.

On the basis of the inspection it is alleged that you have violated the Occupational Safety and Health Act of 1970, 29 U.S.C. 651 *et seq.*, in the following respects:

10. Item number	11. Standard, regulation or section of the Act allegedly violated	12. Description of alleged violation	13. Date by which alleged violation must be corrected
1	29 CFR Section 1910.178(m) (9), page 22257, column 2.	The only gasoline powered Clark high lift rider truck that was assigned to Departments 30–72 and 30–70 was not fitted with an overhead guard for protection against falling objects.	Oct. 9, 1973
2	29 CFR Section 1910.178(k) (1), page 22257, column 1.	Wheel chocks were not placed under the rear wheels of the truck at the plastics plant loading dock to prevent the truck from rolling while it was boarded with powered industrial trucks.	Immediately upon receipt of this citation
3	29 CFR Section 1910.212 (a) (3) (ii), page 22273, column 3.	The point of operation of the following machines whose operation exposes an employee to injury was not guarded: *a.* The 36–52 and the 36–77 riveting machines located in the center of the press shop. *b.* The 31–124 press located in departments 30 and 31 in the kim building. *c.* Twelve (12) of the fifteen (15) Bench master punch presses located in department 30–74 fuse link assembly.	Mar. 6, 1974

Penalties

Citation no.	Item no.	Proposed penalty
1	1	None
1	2	None
1	3	$85
1	4A–4B	$40
1	5	$30
1	6	$40
1	7A–7C	None
1	8	None
Total for all alleged violations		$195

EXHIBIT 7

NATIONAL SAFETY COUNCIL
EVALUATION OF INJURY RATES

•ATTN: SAFETY DIRECTOR   UNIT EVALUATED:

A B CHANCE CO   A B CHANCE CO
210 NORTH ALLEN ST
CENTRALIA MO   65240   CENTRALIA MISSOURI

The report of injury experience sent to the National Safety Council for the above unit has been evaluated in accordance with the procedure set forth in the Council's Award Plan for Recognizing Good Industrial Safety Records. The results of that evaluation are listed below:

	FREQUENCY	SEVERITY
1. This units injury rates for **1974**	3.10	44
2. This units injury rates for **3** prior years	3.87	109
3. HARDWARE AND HAND TOOLS Industry **1971-73** Rates	17.24	438
4. PAR Rates (½ the sum of lines 2 and 3)	10.56	274
5. Percent this unit rates for **1974** better than PAR. (W = worse than PAR)	71%	84%
6. Percent better than PAR required for this unit to achieve the { Award of Merit	48%	10%
{ Award of Honor	68%	30%

7. ** If asterisks are shown on the Award of Merit and Award of Honor lines in Item **6**, this means the requirements are not appropriate for this unit, which earned the Award indicated below for operating without a disabling injury during

man hours, from   to

AWARD EARNED

If an award is indicated below, it has been earned on the basis of a comparison with PAR as shown on lines **5** and **6**, or on the basis of the perfect record shown on line **7** if the PAR comparison is noted as not being appropriate. If the requirements for an award have not been met, this is indicated below in the box at the right. A copy of the award plan is available on request.

[X]	[ ]	[ ]	[ ]	[ ]
AWARD OF HONOR	AWARD OF MERIT	CERTIFICATE OF COMMENDATION	PRESIDENT'S LETTER	NO AWARD EARNED

If an award has been earned, it will be ordered on the basis of the award inscription form which was a part of the Summary of Industrial Injuries report from which this evaluation was made. Delivery will be in about four weeks after you receive this evaluation.

National Safety Council
425 North Michigan Avenue
Chicago, Illinois 60611

002460 0105 680   3/17/75

	Frequency	Severity
A. B. Chance injury rates for 1974	3.10	44
A. B. Chance injury rates 1971–73	3.87	109
Industry's injury rates 1971–73	17.24	438

This award shows that the A. B. Chance Company's frequency rates of injuries was 14.14 better than average; and its severity of injuries was 394 less.

In another attempt to check the effectiveness of the ABC's safety program, we have collected figures on disabling injuries, medical and compensation costs, and insurance rates, all factors indicating a good or bad safety program.

Starting with insurance, the A. B. Chance carrier estimated that accident cost for the company in 1974 would be $1.09 for every $100 of payroll. At year end, the actual cost was $0.43.

Exhibit 8 lists injuries for the A. B. Chance Company since 1966, when complete records were made:

EXHIBIT 8

Year	Average number of employees	Total hours worked per year	Med. treatment cases	Frequency rate	Severity rate	Number of disabling injuries	Days lost
1966....	900	1,843,099				1	12
1967....	925	1,932,634				8	290
1968....	N.A.	N.A.					
1969....	932	1,919,226				17	145
1970....	919	2,077,541	242	3.337	79.90	7	166
1971....	N.A.	N.A.					
1972....	1,051	2,184,191	139	5.4	170.77	11	373
1973....	1,043	2,192,868	171	3.19	87.96	7	162
1974....	1,209	2,258,739	168	3.10	43.83	7	99

N.A. not available

Note: Since 1970, better recordkeeping. OSHA requirement. Severity jumped in 1972 because of one injury (back injury) which cost the company $10,000. The worker was off the job six months with surgery and a disc removed. Cost was $3,000 medical and compensation plus $7,000 lump sum disability.

FINAL COMMENTS

The casewriters asked Mr. Flink if he felt OSHA was helpful in safety at ABC.

"No, I don't," he replied. "We received the safety award many times before. If you look at the data [Exhibit 8] you'll see that the number of injuries pre- and post-OSHA show little change. Our safety program always has been strong. OSHA is mainly an expense. It hasn't helped our safety and health record."

Requirement. Analyze A. B. Chance Division. Are A. B. Chance's employees safer as a result of OSHA regulations? What can A. B. Chance do to improve its safety program?

H. AFFIRMATIVE ACTION PROGRAMS

1. Indianapolis Community Hospital

Indianapolis Community Hospital is a medium-sized hospital with about 250 beds and about 650 full-time equivalent employees. In the hospital's admitting department, there has been a problem. Charles Striglia, the department head, is perplexed.

The hospital has been under pressure from the Equal Employment Opportunity Commission (EEOC) for inadequate representation of blacks in some categories. The blacks who work for the hospital tend to be in housekeeping, laundry, and janitorial categories. The administrator, James Dome, had signed an Affirmative Action Plan with the agency, agreeing to hire a major portion of new clerical employees from minority groups.

Thus when Striglia's department had a resignation, he looked for a minority person to hire. He hired Althea Jackson. She was a 23-year-old black from Indianapolis. She worked in various jobs for five years after leaving high school. Her clerical test scores weren't outstanding, but Striglia felt he should give her a try.

Almost from the beginning, Ms. Jackson was a problem employee. She came in late and left early. Her lunch hours were too long. Often she wouldn't return from coffee breaks for 45 minutes.

The people in the admitting department try to schedule their breaks and lunches when there are few persons being admitted. After all, sick people should not have to wait long to fill out the admission forms. Ms. Jackson refused to cooperate, and she took time off when she wanted to go.

Peggy Steed, one of the more experienced admitting clerks went to Striglia about two months after Ms. Jackson was hired. She said, "Look, Mr. Striglia, I and many of the others have had it with Althea. She doesn't do her share. She is inconveniencing sick people. We've tried to get her to cooperate, and she ignores us. Look, I'll admit I wasn't overly happy to work with a black, but I think there's a reverse discrimination here. If she were white like I am, you'd have had her fired long ago. I just don't think it's fair."

Striglia thanked Steed for her information and said he'd look into it. In a way, he'd pretended he hadn't known what was going on. He did, but he had hoped it would straighten itself out. Now he knew he had to act.

Later that day, he called Ms. Jackson in to have a chat. He told her about the positive results she'd had on some aspects of her job. Then he brought up her absenteeism and low-quality work. She broke down, cried, and told him she was upset because her boy friend was thinking about leaving her and Indianapolis. She said she would try harder.

However, during the next two months her work did not improve. Striglia counseled with her and asked if she needed more training. He wrote her letters of reprimand about her lateness and poor quality work. He even tried to enlist the help of the other blacks in admitting, but they weren't interested.

Finally, Striglia called Ms. Jackson into his office. He reviewed her record and gave her two week's warning. He spelled out what she had to do to keep her job. He confirmed this in writing with a carbon to the personnel department. She got worse. Striglia fired her.

Requirement. You are Striglia. Do you think you did all you could to help Ms. Jackson? Should you be concerned that the EEOC may not look kindly on your part of the affirmative action program? How can supervisors keep the morale of the majority of the employees high when they are placating another employee to meet EEOC goals?

2. Mount Haven University*

On March 17, 1975, Dr. Roland Malcolm, the chancellor of Mount Haven University, received a letter from Mr. Richard Farnwell, the district director for the Equal Employment Opportunity Commission (EEOC) office in Charlotte, North Carolina. The letter stated that Dr. Vickie Day, a female faculty member in the pathology department at Mount Haven University, had filed a charge alleging that the university's college of medicine tenure and promotion policies were sex discriminatory and biased against female faculty members. Consequently, the EEOC office in Charlotte would be investigating her complaint.

---

* This case was prepared by Professors Dev S. Pathak and Gene E. Burton of Appalachian State University to illustrate the issue of sex discrimination in higher education (based on EEOC decision 74–53, November 12, 1973).

BACKGROUND ON THE UNIVERSITY

Mount Haven University (MHU) is a private institution of higher education located in the state of North Carolina. Despite its status as a private university, MHU receives some state financial support. The total student enrollment for MHU stood at 34,562 for the academic year 1974–75. MHU employed a total of 8,543 faculty and staff personnel for the 1974 calendar year.

The academic programs of the university are organized under six colleges: college of arts and sciences, college of business, college of continuing education, college of education, college of fine arts, and the college of medicine.

The college of medicine consists of 14 departments including the pathology department. Dr. Vickie Day applied to the head of the pathology department, Dr. George Samuelson, in March 1969 in response to an advertisement (placed by MHU in the *Chronicle of Higher Education*) for an opening at the assistant professor level.

BACKGROUND ON DR. VICKIE DAY

Dr. Day received her Ph.D. in pathology from the University of Michigan in 1962. After graduation, she spent two years at Mellon Institute on a fellowship grant. After the grant expiration, she worked for two years as a senior analyst at Dow Chemical Laboratories in Bay City, Michigan. She then took a position as an associate professor at Grand Valley State College, located in Grand Rapids, Michigan. When Dr. Day applied for the assistant professorship position at MHU, she was still employed at Grand Valley State College and was a member of two medical honorary societies and five professional societies. She had published nine research papers and two monographs. Her application was thoroughly reviewed by the pathology department's personnel committee, and she was invited on campus for a visit together with six other Ph.D.s —all male—all candidates for the same job. At the time of her visit to the MHU campus, Dr. Day was quite concerned about the trends in tenure policies for academic institutions. When she inquired with Dr. George Samuelson, the head of the department, regarding the tenure policy at MHU, she was told that, according to MHU policy, no faculty member at or below the assistant professor level can be awarded tenure. However, promotion to the rank of associate professor would automatically result in a tenured position. Any faculty member who does not receive tenure by the end of the first five years of service at MHU is given a notice that his/her services have been terminated. After her visit, she was enthusiastically recommended by the departmental personnel committee, and she was offered the position of assistant professor in June 1969 in the pathology department at MHU. A copy of the letter containing the offer is shown in Exhibit 1. Dr. Day accepted the offer on July 5, 1969.

Upon her arrival on campus in August 1969, Dr. Day went through the new faculty orientation together with 72 other new faculty members who were joining the university. During her orientation, various policies

EXHIBIT 1

MOUNT HAVEN UNIVERSITY
CHARLOTTE, NORTH CAROLINA
28223

Office of Academic Affairs
Phone: 704/265–1153

June 11, 1969

Dr. Vickie Day
1572 Dearborn Street
Grand Rapids, Michigan

Dear Dr. Day:

Dr. George Samuelson, chairman of the department of pathology, has recommended that you be offered a position in the department of pathology, I support the recommendation and am pleased to extend an offer to you.

The policies developed and adopted by the faculty and approved by the chancellor and trustees specify that contracts for those who have not attained tenure may not be provided for more than three years. Accordingly, we offer you the position of assistant professor for the academic years 1969–70, 1970–71, and 1971–72 in the department of pathology at a salary of $17,500 for the 1969–70 academic year with raises for the year 1970–71 and 1971–72 dependent upon your future performance at Mount Haven University.

As discussed with you during your visit on our campus, you will be considered for promotion during your fifth year of service at MHU. However, in order to be considered for promotion, you must be elected into the American Society of Pathologists and publish scholarly research in your first five years of service at MHU.

The chairman of the department makes the teaching assignments. I am sure Dr. Samuelson has acquainted you with our policies and practices concerning employment, promotion, tenure, and the like.

We sincerely hope that you will accept this offer. We shall appreciate your letting us have your written answer as early as convenient and not later than July 11, 1969.

Yours truly,

Milton Curtis
Vice Chancellor for
Academic Affairs

and procedures of the university were explained. She was given an orientation package which included the materials regarding the university, scenic areas around Charlotte, and the faculty handbook.

DR. DAY'S CAREER AT MHU

From September 1969 to June 1972, Dr. Day's work was rated satisfactory by Dr. Samuelson. On March 15, 1971, she was elected to membership in the American Society of Pathologists. She published nine research papers in national and regional journals and presented eleven papers at various professional meetings between September 1969 and March 1972. However, her student evaluation, as conducted by first year medical students, reflected unfavorably on her teaching ability. Some students occasionally complained to other tenured faculty members about how unprepared she was when she came to class and how she never had time to answer students' questions. Students charged that she was too busy conducting her research and attending professional meetings and had very little time to devote to her classroom teaching or to her students' problems. Male students also criticized her "women's lib" attitude and complained that in the classroom she treated male students more harshly than female students. Despite the student complaints, her contract was renewed in 1972 for two more years, calling for a review during her fifth year in October 1974. During the next two years under her renewed contract, Dr. Day continued her scholastic and professional growth by publishing six more articles and presenting seven more papers at various professional meetings. Student evaluations of her teaching performance did not improve but stayed at the same level.

On June 1, 1974, Dr. George Samuelson, the head of the department, retired, and Dr. Daniel Miller was appointed as the new department head by the vice chancellor of academic affairs, Dr. Milton Curtis.

On October 2, 1974, Dr. Miller appointed a committee to review the applications of Dr. Day and Dr. James Zigi, a male faculty member, for promotion to tenured positions of associate professor.

PROMOTION PROCEDURE

The procedure relating to promotion of a faculty member to a tenured position as outlined in the faculty handbook was as follows:

1. Unless otherwise specified in the employment contract, a member of the faculty who believes himself to be eligible for promotion to a tenured position should apply to the department chairman.
2. The chairman will then appoint a committee of five tenured faculty members from the department to consider the application. If five

tenured faculty members are not available, the committee will consist of five senior members of the college of medicine.

3. If the committee recommends favorably, the head of the department
    reviews the case and sends his recommendations to the dean of the
    college.
4. The dean of the college of medicine sends his recommendation to the
    vice chancellor for academic affairs, and he, in turn, sends his recom-
    mendation to the chancellor.
5. If the chancellor approves, he submits his recommendation to the
    board of trustees.

Note: An unfavorable determination at any stage in the process can
result in denial of tenure.

The faculty handbook also specifies the evaluative criteria for the
various professional ranks. Criteria for the ranks of assistant and associate professor were described as follows:

Assistant professor: (a) an appropriate formal academic preparation
for a teaching position and/or special competencies in lieu of the formal
academic preparation; (b) evidence of ability in teaching, in research or
other germane creative ability, and in professional service to the university
and/or to the public.

Associate professor: (a) An appropriate formal academic preparation
for a teaching position and/or special competencies in lieu of the formal
academic preparation, and at least five years of appropriate experience;
(b) distinction and recognition in teaching, in research or other creative
ability, and in professional service to the university and/or to the public;
(c) ability to supervise teaching, graduate study, and research; (d) capacity for consistently mature performance in course and curriculum
planning, in the guidance and counseling of students and of junior staff
members, and in participation in routine institutional affairs.

THE ACTION OF THE PERSONNEL COMMITTEE

The all-male departmental personnel committee appointed by Dr.
Miller to consider the applications for promotion from Dr. Day and Dr.
Zigi obtained the candidates personnel files from Dr. Miller and found
the following:

1. The total number of papers published by both the faculty members
    in the last five years were approximately the same. However, the
    committee unanimously agreed that, although the number of papers
    published by Dr. Day met the quantitative criteria of research for
    promotion, the contribution of these papers to scientific thought and
    to the field of pathology was questionable and marginal, at best.

2. Although the two candidates for promotion presented papers to different professional societies, both of them had presented approximately the same number of papers during the past five years. Dr. Zigi had presented 20 papers, of which 13 had been in the last two years.
3. The grades, given by both the instructors to their students during the last academic year were as follows:

	A	B	C	D	F	Total
Dr. Day	72	84	155	9	4	324
Dr. Zigi	28	64	258	45	16	411

4. Student evaluations of both faculty members differed substantially. Dr. Zigi's evaluations were much more favorable than Dr. Day's evaluations. Dr. Day, in fact, had received the worst rating in the department for the criteria of student rapport, teaching ability, course content, course organization, and overall teaching effectiveness. However, Dr. Zigi and many other faculty members had received some negative, along with positive, comments in their evaluations.
5. The records showed that during the last three years Dr. Day had served on only 3 committees, whereas Dr. Zigi had served on 14 committees.

The committee also noted that Dr. Day, the only female member of the department, did not associate with her colleagues. She told the committee that it was difficult for her to understand how anybody who is a conscientious researcher could find the time to socialize with other members of the faculty.

After two months of deliberation, the committee recommended that Dr. Zigi, the male candidate, be promoted to the position of associate professor and that Dr. Day be denied the promotion. Dr. Day was verbally informed of the committee's decision by her department head, Dr. Miller. She also received a letter dated February 11, 1975, from the vice chancellor of academic affairs stating that because she did not satisfactorily meet the criteria outlined in the faculty handbook her services would be terminated at the end of the academic year 1974–75.

Dr. Day, after lengthy dicussions with various officials and other female colleagues at the university, decided to file a complaint with the EEOC in Charlotte on two grounds:

1. That the university has discriminated against her personally because of her sex; and
2. That the university is discriminating against women as a class by its promotion and tenure policies.

On both of these grounds, she charged that MHU had engaged in and continues to engage in unlawful employment practices in violation of Title VII of the Civil Rights Act of 1964. The charges were filed in the EEOC office at Charlotte, North Carolina, on March 17, 1975.

UNIVERSITY TENURE AND PROMOTION RECORDS

The records of tenure and promotion for the college of medicine and its various departments for both sexes are shown in Tables 1, 2, and 3.

TABLE 1
TENURED FACULTY MEMBERS IN THE COLLEGE
OF MEDICINE, CLASSIFIED BY SEX AS OF
JANUARY 1975

	Number	Tenured
Male	465	144
Female	52	7
Total	517	151

TABLE 2
TENURED FACULTY MEMBERS IN VARIOUS DEPARTMENTS WITHIN THE COLLEGE
OF MEDICINE BY SEX AS OF JANUARY 1975

Department	Total tenured male faculty members	Total tenured female faculty members
Anatomy	9	0
Biochemistry	11	2
Anesthesiology	4	1
Pharmacology	7	0
Microbiology	8	2
Pathology	24	0
Medicine	28	1
Surgery	11	0
Pediatrics	17	1
Radiology	8	0
Obstetrics and Gynecology	5	0
Physiology	4	0
Neurology	2	0
Psychiatry	6	0

TABLE 3
PROMOTION OF FACULTY MEMBERS FROM ASSISTANT TO ASSOCIATE
PROFESSOR RANK IN THE COLLEGE OF MEDICINE, CLASSIFIED BY SEX

Year	Number of assistant professors			Number of assistant professors promoted		
	M	F	Total	M	F	Total
1971–72	62	6	68	11	0	11
1972–73	89	10	99	9	1	10
1973–74	113	15	128	15	2	17
1974–75	142	17	159	24	1	25

Discussion questions

1. Do you think Dr. Day has a good case?
2. If you were the attorney for the EEOC and Dr. Day, how could you argue the case? For Mount Haven University?
3. On the basis of your answers to question two above, how would you rule on the case? Why?

3. Discrimination in Reverse*

On March 9, 1974, a vacancy was announced for the position of Equal Employment Opportunity Officer, GS–14 in the U.S. Department of Labor. A U.S. Civil Service Commission certificate of Eligibles was issued on April 13, 1974, listing nine (9) candidates who were found qualified for the position. All candidates from the Department of Labor were interviewed, but no official selection was made at that time. On May 12, 1974, an evaluation committee was convened. This committee added three new names to the Certificate of Eligibles. All three of the new candidates were interviewed, and Mr. Joseph Canedo, an American of Spanish ancestry who was an employee of the U.S. Civil Service Commission, was selected for the vacant position; however, he subsequently declined the appointment. On June 30, 1974, the official announcement of the job vacancy was cancelled.

A new vacancy announcement was advertised for the same position on November 13, 1974, and a new Certificate of Eligibles was furnished to the appointing authority containing the name of six (6) candidates on December 13, 1974. Mrs. Velma M. Strode, director, Office of Equal Employment Opportunity, selected a Mr. Leonel Miranda to fill the vacant job on February 26, 1973.

Mr. Robert J. Neyhart, program analyst, Office of Federal Contract Compliance, Employment Standards Administration, U.S. Department of Labor, Washington, D.C., who has been a government employee for 26 years, filed a complaint of discrimination through official channels on June 22, 1973, alleging that he was nonselected for the position of Equal Employment Opportunity Officer (deputy director, Office of Equal Employment Opportunity, U.S. Department of Labor, Washington, D.C.) GS–14, because of his national origin in that he *was not* Spanish surnamed. (See Enclosure 1 to the Appendix.) An investigation of the com-

---

* This case was prepared by Dr. Leo Rachmel of Virginia State College, Petersburg, Virginia, as a basis for class discussion. Cases are not designed to present either correct or incorrect handling of administrative situations.

plaint was conducted between the dates of July 9, 1973, and January 23, 1975.

By letter dated June 6, 1975, the U.S. Labor Department notified Mr. Neyhart of its proposed disposition of the complaint, ruling that the complaint was not substantiated by the evidence and that, therefore, a finding of no discrimination would be made. Mr. Neyhart was not satisfied with the proposed disposition and requested a hearing before the U.S. Civil Service Commission.

A hearing was originally scheduled for August 9, 1975; however, the case was remanded to the U.S. Department of Labor on two occasions by the U.S. Civil Service Commission examiner at the request of that department with Mr. Neyhart's concurrence. The hearing was subsequently held in Washington, D.C., on November 18, 1975, and the complainant was represented by Ms. Veronice A. Holt, attorney at law. The labor department was represented by Mr. David P. Callet, Office of the Solicitor, assisted by Ms. Shelia Cronan. Five witnesses, including Mr. Neyhart, appeared and testified during the hearing.

The complainant believed that he was discriminated against because of his national origin, because of a number of incidents which occurred during the selection process, and because of the climate with reference to the priority hiring of Spanish-speaking individuals during the time in question. Mr. Neyhart stated that he was found qualified for the position and was interviewed by Mrs. Strode after the March 1974 vacancy announcement was first advertised. He contended that Mrs. Strode gave him several indications that he had been selected, pointing out to him an office that would be assigned to him. (See Enclosures 2 and 3 to the Appendix.) Mr. Neyhart contended that after the interview with Mrs. Strode he was told that he was to meet and talk with Mr. Frank Zarb, Assistant Secretary of Labor for administration and management. (See Enclosure 4 to the Appendix.) He was also asked how much notice he would have to give to his current supervisors before leaving his present position for the new job.

After the interview with Mr. Zarb, another interview was held with Mr. Richard J. Wise, executive assistant to the Undersecretary of Labor and with Mr. E. Carl Uehlein, executive assistant to the Secretary of Labor. (See Enclosure 5 to the Appendix.) The complainant noted that he was the only applicant who was referred to higher authority for these interviews.

Based on these incidents, Mr. Neyhart believed that he was selected for the position but that because of instructions from the White House through the Cabinet Committee for the Spanish Speaking to place more Spanish-surnamed individuals in top administrative positions the agency decided to fill the post with a Spanish-surnamed employee, thus discriminating against the appellant because of his national origin. Both

Mrs. Strode and Mr. Zarb denied the allegations of Mr. Neyhart. (See Enclosures 2, 3, and 4, to the Appendix.)

The issue at stake is whether or not Mr. Robert J. Neyhart was discriminated against because of his national origin when he was not selected for the position of Equal Employment Opportunity Officer (deputy director, Office of Equal Employment Opportunity, U.S. Department of Labor).

Discussion questions

1. Was Mr. Neyhart discriminated against? Why?
2. Did Mrs. Strode handle the selection process properly? Justify.
3. Was Mr. Zarb sufficiently aware of his responsibilities in the EEO program? Justify.

APPENDIX
Extracts of Testimony*

1. Robert J. Neyhart (Enclosure 1 with attachment)
2. Velma M. Strode (of October 12, 1973) (Enclosure 2)
3. Velma M. Strode (of March 15, 1975) (Enclosure 3)
4. Frank G. Zarb (Enclosure 4)
5. E. Carl Uehlein, Jr. (Enclosure 5)

EXTRACT

City of Washington)

        ss:

District of Columbia)

I, Robert J. Neyhart, program analyst (EEO operations), GS–13, hereby solemnly swear:

* * * * *

I believe that I was discriminated against on the basis of national origin particularly by Mrs. Velma Strode, director, Equal Employment Opportunity, Office of the Assistant Secretary for Administration and Management, Department of Labor. Mrs. Strode discriminated against me when as selecting official she picked a Spanish-surnamed individual, Leonel Miranda, for the position of Equal Employment Opportunity Officer, GS–301B–14 and/or GS–0160–14,

---

* While testimony was taken from 33 witnesses by the U.S. Civil Service Commission Equal Employment Opportunity investigating officer, extracts of the most pertinent testimony is provided here for student consideration.

both of which are designations for the same job. The job in question is deputy director, Office of Equal Employment Opportunity, Department of Labor. Mrs. Strode selected Mr. Miranda although under the original announcement she had interviewed me and gave certain indications that I would get the job. The fact that extraordinary efforts were made to find a Spanish-surnamed individual constitutes unequal treatment of my application for the position in question. That is discrimination based on national origin since I am not a Spanish-surnamed or -speaking individual.

The situation which gave rise to my complaint grew out of several different factors. One specific factor was that the Department of Labor, as were all other departments, was ordered by the administration to put more Spanish-surnamed individuals in top or key positions in each agency. This information was communicated from the cabinet level committee for the Spanish speaking on the letterhead of the executive office of the President. These communications also told each agency to put more Spanish-surnamed people on the payroll. When any kind of directive or suggestion of a cabinet level agency is communicated on the White House letterhead it has the effect of becoming an order which must be carried out in its every detail. (See Attachment 1)

Enclosure 1

*   *   *   *   *

The vacancy in the position of deputy director, Equal Employment Opportunity, Departments of Labor, was first announced in March 1974 as being Equal Employment Opportunity Officer, GS–301B–14. The Civil Service Commission as yet had not put out the 0160 series for the specific role of EEO Officer. I applied in March 1974 and was notified on March 22, 1974, that I was qualified for the position. After I applied, Mrs. Strode interviewed me in April 1974. She was pleasant, interested in me as an applicant, and said that she would let me know the outcome. A couple of weeks later around late April 1974 she called, and I went back down to see her. On that occasion she reiterated that she liked my background and EEO experience. She said "This is the room you will have or be in." She further said that I would be able to select my own furniture and if I did not like the curtains I could get them changed. Our conversation continued, and she stated that she had talked to Mr. Frank Zarb, Assistant Secretary of Labor for administration and management, about me and that she wanted me to meet him and that she would arrange an appointment so I could go up and meet him. After that conversation I assumed that Mrs. Strode had selected me. During the same conversations she asked how much notice I would have to have to give my superiors upon leaving, and I told her about one week.

*   *   *   *   *

During the second interview with Mrs. Strode she had said that she would be in touch and that she would call me within the next week. In the meantime, I got a call from Mr. Zarb's office stating that I had an appointment with him on May 5, 1974, at 10 A.M. During the interview with Mr. Zarb he mentioned that Mrs. Strode had mentioned me and that she liked me. There followed a general discussion of the EEO program and how I would manage it. During this conversation he brought up my testifying on Capitol Hill before the Senate Post Office and Civil Service Committee concerning hearings on the Hatch Act. My testimony was given on April 16, 1974, after my interviews with Mrs. Strode. Mr. Zarb had a copy of the *Evening Star* open on his desk leaving the impression that he had read Joseph Young's column of May 3, 1974.

On that occasion I had taken annual leave and was there as a private citizen rather than from the Department of Labor; however, the newspaper named me as a career employee of the Department of Labor even though I had not been identified as such in the hearing. I did not tell anyone that I was from the Department of Labor.

The gist of my comments to Mr. Zarb concerning my testimony before the senate committee was that I felt quite strongly concerning the Hatch Act and that I felt that I had some contribution to make to the committee.

Cabinet Committee on Opportunity for the Spanish Speaking
(Formerly Inter Agency Committee on Mexican-American Affairs)
1800 G Street, Northwest, Washington, D.C. 20506 (202) 382–6651

Office of the Chairman

12 January 1974

Mr. Frank G. Zarb
Assistant Secretary for Administration
Department of Labor
14th Street & Constitution Avenue, NW
Washington, D.C. 20210

Dear Mr. Zarb:

I have recently learned of the creation of a new equal employment opportunities division in your office which will be headed by Mrs. Velma Strode. I am happy to hear that the Department of Labor is increasing its interest and activity in this vital area.

In view of the scope and mandate of the President's 16-point program for Spanish-speaking Americans, I would like strongly to recommend that the second position in this office be filled by a Spanish-speaking person. The Department of Labor employs only five Spanish-speaking persons in equal opportunity programs nationally; of these, only one is in the Washington office.

I would be happy to offer the resources of the cabinet committee to assist you in your recruitment efforts to identify a qualified and capable Spanish-speaking person to work closely with Mrs. Strode toward increased employment opportunities for Spanish-speaking and all other minority groups.

Sincerely,

Henry M. Ramirez
Chairman

cc: Secretary James D. Hodgson
      Mrs. Velma Strode

Attachment 1 to Enclosure 1

EXTRACT

Washington   )
)   ss:
District of Columbia)

I, Velma M. Strode, director of Equal Employment Opportunity, Department of Labor, GS–16, hereby solemnly swear:

*   *   *   *   *

In each case where I made a selection for the GS–14 vacancy in my office I was furnished a Certificate of Eligibles from which I made a selection. In the earlier case in the spring of 1974, I was furnished a list of eligibles containing about nine names, but I was not satisfied with those candidates who had been rated highly qualified and asked the personnel office what could be done. Mrs. Catherine Kernan suggested re-opening and re-extending the search for new eligibles. This added about three new highly qualified candidates to the original list. One of those added names was Joseph Canedo from the Civil Service Commission, and I selected him.

I selected Mr. Canedo because of his background in the complaint process and his knowledge of the overall EEO program gained through working in the Federal Equal Employment Opportunity Office at the Civil Service Commission. My selection was not affected by the fact that he was of Spanish national origin but was based on merit qualifications only.

Mr. Canedo accepted the position in late June of 1974 and later turned it down. Personnel had notified all other persons on the certificate that a selection had been made; therefore, I decided to cancel the certificate after Mr. Canedo declined the position. Since the other eligibles on the certificate knew of the selection I felt that it would be bad for human relations to make a second choice from the same certificate. That is the reason that I asked Mrs. Kernan to cancel that job announcement for deputy director of EEO.

During my interviews with the candidates on the certificate of eligibles, I asked specific questions of each concerning the complaint process, and I was looking for someone who had experience in the handling of EEO complaints and the overall EEO program-counseling, affirmative action, etc. I was also looking for someone with knowledge of communications with minority group organizations either locally or nationally.

Enclosure 2

In interviewing Mr. Neyhart, his discussion of his EEO experience was limited to the military and the Office of Federal Contract Compliance in the Department of Labor. His only minority contact that he made me aware of was the NAACP. He also talked a great deal about many other things. While he was a pleasant person and highly qualified, I felt that he did not have the above-mentioned things I was looking for. Therefore, I did not consider him as my first choice, and since I felt the same about the other eight candidates on the Certificate of Eligibles, I asked the personnel office, as mentioned above, what could be done with the results cited.

In regard to Mr. Neyhart, I was pressured by outside congressional personages from both major political parties by receiving glowing recommendations for him before making any selection for deputy director of EEO. This had an adverse effect on me.

One of the things I did when I interviewed each candidate was that I show them the layout of the office and introduced them to the staff. I was a little embarrassed with the drabness of the office and explained to each candidate the fact that my office would be on this side and that new furniture and curtains had already been selected by me. I said this so I could impress each prospective addition to my staff that we would have decent surroundings in which to work.

* * * * *

I do not recall asking Mr. Neyhart how much notice he would have to give his boss before being able to leave. This is an item I always leave up to the personnel office. I also do not recall saying to anyone, and certainly I did not put it in writing, any kind of comments that could have been interpreted as meaning that I was leaning toward picking Mr. Neyhart as my deputy.

As far as having Mr. Neyhart interviewed by Frank Zarb, then assistant secretary for administration and management, is concerned, he was not the only one so interviewed. Also interviewed by Mr. Zarb were Doctor Simons and Joseph Canedo. I do not know how long Mr. Canedo talked to Mr. Zarb, but I did introduce them and left Mr. Canedo in Mr. Zarb's office. Mr. Neyhart, Doctor Simons, and Mr. Canedo were introduced to Mr. Zarb because I considered them leading candidates for the position of deputy director in the case of the vacancy in the spring of 1974. In the case of Dr. Simons I am not certain it was this position or some other position that was involved when I introduced him to Mr. Zarb, although he was a candidate for the above position. The other candidates just did not come up to the standards I was looking for. I had Mr. Zarb meet Mr. Neyhart as a courtesy only because he was on the list of highly qualified candidates. This was in spite of the fact he was not my first choice. Who I select as a member of my staff is completely my own decision to make without regard to higher authority, except positions at GS–14 and above. This exception did, of course, apply to my EEO officer or GS–14 slot. However, this requirement, which is set out in a memo concerning clearing GS–14's and above through the secretary's office, is not to be construed as a constraint but is merely a formalizing of a courtesy system. This is an outgrowth of the President's average grade restrictions or policy. It was my interpretation during the time that Mr. Zarb was an assistant secretary that this courtesy notification should be made before selection. Under my current boss, assistant secretary Mr. Clark, it is my interpretation that the notification is to be made after selection. The selection in both cases of Mr. Canedo and of Mr. Miranda was entirely my own. Neither Mr. Zarb nor anyone else made either selection for me. There was no pressure on me to appoint a Spanish-suranmed person to either one of the two vacancies in my office at GS–14.

After receiving a certificate of eligibles (as a result of a merit staffing panel meeting in December 1974) with six names I interviewed all of the Department of Labor candidates in various parts of the country. It never crossed my mind to question the evaluations of the panel, and I therefore proceeded to conduct the above mentioned interviews. I selected M. Miranda because I felt he has the most experience, a firm commitment of EEO, communication with all minority groups, and his background in EEO was up-to-date in the areas of need in this office.

I objectively analyzed each applicant and made the selection of my choice in both instances without regard to race, creed, color, sex, national origin, age, or pressure from anyone.

EXTRACT

District of Columbia)

                                            ss:

City of Washington)

I, Velma M. Strode, director of Equal Employment Opportunity, Department of Labor, GS–16, hereby solemnly swear:

*   *   *   *   *

I have no particular comment to make concerning the letter from Henry M. Ramirez, chairman, Cabinet Committee on Opportunity for the Spanish Speaking, dated January 12, 1974, addressed to Frank G. Zarb, assistant secretary for administration, Department of Labor, a copy of which I received. I get many such letters and always read and file them. This letter does not stand out above any other such letter in my mind. I drafted the reply for Mr. Zarb as I do for all letters which apply to areas of EEO or civil rights. At the time of the letter to Mr. Zarb and my reply concerning the 16–point program portion of that letter, that program had not been transferred to my office, but since I was drafting the reply I added the response citing John DeLeon's name.

Enclosure 3

I recall no particular thoughts I had concerning Mr. Ramirez when I received the copy or when I drafted the reply. I am not aware of Mr. Zarb's thought concerning the Ramirez letter, and we had no discussion concerning it. I automatically drafted the reply. In drafting the reply, I did not have any reason to consider any course of action since none was required.

In view of the fact Mr. Neyhart was in the department, I did make an official appointment for him to see Mr. Zarb. If Mr. Canedo had been in the department and was readily accessible, I would have followed the same procedure as I did with Mr. Neyhart.

It was my understanding that I had to select one of the candidates referred; therefore, when I received the first candidate in April 1974, Mr. Neyhart was among those who were all highly qualified. Since he was on the certificate, Mr. Neyhart was a leading candidate before I made any consideration.

Mr. Zarb wanted to see candidates for jobs, and I referred only Mr. Neyhart to him from the first certificate because his credentials were the most outstanding of those candidates on that certificate before the addition of three names in May 1974. I referred Mr. Neyhart to Mr. Zarb as the then outstanding candidate even though I was dubious of his qualifications in view of negative references from Phil Davis, director, OFCC, Russ Binion, and Ms. Doris Wooten, also of OFCC. They were completely negative on him as far as his EEO qualifications were concerned. I received these references before I referred Mr. Neyhart to Mr. Zarb, and yet since I then erroneously thought I had to select one person from this certificate I made the arrangements for him to see Mr. Zarb on a courtesy call. I did not refer Mr. Miranda to my boss, who at the time (in February 1973) was Mr. Zarb. Mr. Clark, my new boss, was not here yet; therefore, I felt no need for a courtesy call by Mr. Miranda to the assistant secretary for administration's office.

EXTRACT

District of Columbia)

        ss:

City of Washington)

I, Frank G. Zarb, assistant Director, Office of Management and Budget, hereby solemnly swear:

* * * * *

I was Assistant Secretary of Labor for administration and management until December 15, 1974. The office of Equal Employment Opportunity was a new office around late 1974. Prior to setting up the office of EEO, there was no efficient EEO effort in the department. For instance, there was no orderly mechanism for handling EEO complaints.

To be precise in the recollection of events that took place a year and a half ago is not easy. At that time I did not attach major significance to each event concerning the office of EEO such as would help me currently to be more emphatic in my recollection of those events.

As a result of the cited lack of an organized EEO effort in the department, we determined to have an offce of EEO and began to build. However, we had no prior experience to go on. We started by hiring a director, Mrs. Strode, and a few staff members.

Enclosure 4

In organizing the office of EEO there were a number of discussions concerning the make-up of the staff, the budget, etc. For example, I was not immediately clear that we should have one deputy director or several. In the latter option, I considered the possibility of having "functional deputies" instead of one primary number two person.

In early 1974 when Mrs. Strode came up with some candidates for the job of deputy I thought it would be a good idea to go through the same process as when I hired her. In this connection I at first thought that any candidate for the deputy's slot should be seen by a number of people.

I talked with several candidates for various positions in Mrs. Strode's office so it is hard to separate one from another in trying to recall them as individuals. I do recall meeting Mr. Neyhart in the way of Mrs. Strode introducing me to one of the leading candidates for the position as deputy. However, I do not recall interviewing him as such, and I recall nothing in particular concerning what we talked about.

One reason I asked the executive assistants to the secretary and under-secretary of labor, E. Carl Uehlein and Richard Wise, respectively, to inter-view Mr. Neyhart was that they had assisted me and Mrs. Strode in drafting Secretary's Orders No. 14–74, No. 19–74, and No. 30–74, which replaced No. 14–7W, setting up the office of EEO. The intent was that they would help in interviewing all of the leading candidates as possible for leadership posi-tions in the office of EEO. As I recall one or both of them interviewed Mrs. Strode and other candidates for the top job in that office. This was not an unusual request directed to those representatives of higher officials of the department.

In this regard it is my best recollection there could have been some break-down in the system, as described above, of interviewing candidates because of time burdens on the schedules of Mr. Uehlein and Mr. Wise. Therefore, if Mr. Neyhart was the only candidate interviewed by the two executive assistants mentioned it may have been because they did not have the time to interview other candidates.

After the interviews I recall reaching some conclusions with Mrs. Strode concerning Mr. Neyhart's background and experience not fitting what we had envisaged for the person who would be her deputy or one other deputy. I do not recall whether these were my observations and I agreed. In any event we agreed he was not the best candidate of all the candidates, partly due to our feelings regarding what the ultimate structure of her office would look like and what would be the best qualifications for her deputy director(s).

Also involved in our decision regarding Mr. Neyhart was the dynamic or changing scene of the office of EEO. We were still in the process, described above, of finalizing our thinking regarding the leadership, organization, and function of that office. Therefore, our inability to settle initially on a candidate was partly due to our not having a firm understanding of what kind of EEO leadership structure was optimum.

It was Mrs. Strode's job to make the selection of her deputy, but I did approve vacancies in relation to resources available, etc. I regularly conferred with my office directors concerning candidates for top jobs under my juris-diction.

EXTRACT

City of Washington)

             ss:

District of Columbia)

I, E. Carl Uehlein, Jr., attorney, hereby solemnly swear:

* * * * *

I was executive assistant to the Secretary of Labor from September 1970 to February 1973. Because of my position I was asked to interview people from time to time both for my own opinion and for my knowledge of the secretary's opinion of what type person he would like to see in any position in which he might have an interest. While I was at the Department of Labor (D.O.L.) I interviewed maybe 10 to 20 people.

Concerning my interview of Robert Neyhart in connection with an EEO position at D.O.L., I have only vague recollections of that conversation. It was my impression that Mr. Neyhart was a candidate for the director of EEO position rather than deputy director. I was not even aware that the level of the position involved was GS–14. The interview had a rather informal structure or nature.

My interviewing candidates such as Mr. Neyhart was not necessarily a requisite to either approval or disapproval of the candidate so interviewed. It was more to get an informal opinion of the offices of the secretary and undersecretary without unnecessarily taking up their time. Richard Wise, then the undersecretary's executive assistant, sometime interviewed candidates in similar situations.

Enclosure 5

Frank Zarb's office, the office of the assistant secretary for administration and management, was the prime mover in establishing the structure of the EEO and under whose jurisdiction the EEO ultimately resided. This included determining such things as the number of job slots, whether there would be a deputy director or a number of assistants, etc. Of course, in this connection it was necessary for his office to cause the appropriate interviews to be conducted.

It was Mr. Zarb who asked me to interview Mr. Neyhart. I recall that for the interview I had a copy of Mr. Neyhart's resumé. It seems that he had a background in EEO work in the department of defense. I do not recall more specific details of the job he was applying for other than as cited above. We discussed general EEO policies and how he saw the overall EEO program. As I recall we discussed some specific details of the EEO program, but since I was only forming a general impression of him to give to Mr. Zarb, I do not recall the more minute details.

My general reaction to Mr. Neyhart was to give Mr. Zarb what he had asked for, a general impression. Mr. Neyhart neither impressed me as an outstanding candidate nor one who should not have been interviewed at all. I told Mr. Zarb in effect that I thought Mr. Neyhart generally had the appropriate background for the EEO office.

4. Carver State College

On May 13, 1975, Dr. Milton Cranston, the chancellor of Carver State College, received a letter from Mr. Richard Farnwell, the district director for the Equal Employment Opportunity Commission (EEOC) office in Birmingham, Alabama. The letter stated that Dr. Nicholas Erickson, a male faculty member in the department of English at Carver State College (CSC), had filed a charge with the EEOC, alleging that CSC had terminated his services because of his race (Caucasian) in violation of the civil rights act. Mr. Farnwell told Chancellor Cranston that, due to the discriminatory nature of the charge, the Birmingham EEOC Office would be investigating the allegation.

BACKGROUND ON THE COLLEGE

Carver State College (CSC) is a predominantly black state institution of higher education located near Birmingham, Alabama. CSC employed 214 faculty and staff personnel for the 1974 calendar year. The academic programs at CSC are organized under four colleges: college of arts and sciences, college of fine arts, college of education, and college of business.

The college of arts and sciences consists of seven departments, including the department of English. During 1974, the college of arts and sciences employed 81 faculty members, of which 12 (5 tenured and 7 nontenured) were in the department of English.

BACKGROUND ON DR. ERICKSON

Dr. Erickson was hired as an assistant professor in the English department on September 1, 1973. He had received a Ph.D. in English from the University of Florida in December of 1972. Prior to that, he had earned an M.A. and B.A. in English from St. James College in New York. During his Ph.D. program, most of his coursework and research were related to the study of British literature with emphasis on 17th and 18th century literature. His dissertation was entitled "A Study of Major Themes and Literary Techniques in England: 1700 to 1750."

---

* This case was prepared by Professors Dev S. Pathak of Ohio State University and Gene E. Burton of Eastern Kentucky University to illustrate race discrimination in higher education (based on EEOC decision 74–95, March 6, 1974, as published in *Topical Law Reports* [New York: Commerce Clearing House, Inc., 1973], par. 6432, pp. 4153–56).

FACULTY EVALUATION PROCEDURES AT CSC

The CSC faculty handbook describes in detail the policies and procedures relating to faculty evaluation, promotion, and tenure. The handbook specifies that every new faculty member be hired on a year-to-year basis for the first five years at the college, which amounts to the probationary period. Each faculty member is to be considered for tenure during the fifth year of employment. If he/she is not given tenure at the end of this probationary period, his/her services are terminated at the end of the fifth year of employment. According to the faculty handbook, nontenured faculty members are to be evaluated by the chairman of the appropriate department. The evaluation procedure is designed so that the individual faculty member may receive up to a total of 100 merit points based upon five criteria: (a) educational qualifications; (b) efficiency in performance; (c) character; (d) course and curriculum development; and (e) capacity to meet the needs of the community.

Unfortunately, there is no official grievance or appeal procedure and no morale committee through which evaluations or personnel actions may be reviewed.

DEVELOPMENTS AT THE COLLEGE

During the 1974–75 academic year, there was a state wide decline in college enrollments in Alabama. CSC was extremely hard hit, as its enrollment dropped 14 percent compared to the previous year. Projected CSC enrollments for the 1975–76 academic year indicated a further decline of 11 percent. The largest reduction in enrollments was in the college of arts and sciences, with the departments of English, History, philosophy, and biology (in that order) leading the list of declines.

After reviewing the situation, Dr. Harry Crawford, the vice chancellor of academic affairs, informed the dean of the college of arts and sciences on November 8, 1974, that he would have to terminate the contracts of four nontenured faculty at the end of the 1974–75 academic year. He also mentioned that, in accordance with the faculty handbook, those who are to be terminated must be notified prior to December 15, 1974. The dean, in turn, informed Dr. Daniel Raintree, chairman of the department of English, that due to the large decline in enrollment for his department, he would have to release two of his nontenured faculty.

Dr. Raintree (black) investigated the background of each of his seven nontenured faculty members (three Caucasian and four black) and then informed Dr. Erickson and Dr. Holt (both Caucasian) that their contracts would not be renewed at the expiration of the current academic year.

Upon the request of Dr. Erickson for an explanation of the chairman's decision, Dr. Raintree provided the following rationale:

1. For the past two years, Dr. Erickson had received a score of 75 (out of a possible 100 points) on his evaluation. His score was the second lowest of all the seven nontenured faculty members, with Dr. Holt's score being 72. Other scores from the highest to the lowest, as classified by race, were: 88 (black), 82 (Caucasian), 79 (black), 77 (black), and 76 (black).

2. During the 1973–74 and the 1974–75 years, the average student withdrawal rate for the classes taught by the English department faculty was 14 percent. This rate was comparable to that for the black nontenured faculty but was higher than that for the two white nontenured faculty who were being terminated. No specific breakdown of the rates of withdrawal between tenured and nontenured faculty was provided despite repeated requests from Dr. Erickson.

3. The faculty handbook requires that each faculty member provide the department chairman with a copy of all course outlines. During his four semesters at CSC, Dr. Erickson had provided 10 of the 16 outlines for which he was responsible.

4. One of the five criteria used to evaluate nontenured faculty members for continued employment at CSC is the capacity to meet the needs of the community. "The needs of the community" has been interpreted by the administration at CSC to mean that the total campus as well as each department should meet the needs of its students. Vice Chancellor Crawford told Chairman Raintree that, because the CSC body was predominantly black, the students' needs could be better met by black instructors.

5. Dr. Erickson's "friendly" behavior with students, especially black female students, had caused some concern among black male students. These concerns had been expressed by some students to Dr. Raintree in confidence.

Not satisfied with this rationale, Dr. Erickson argued that he had more seniority than two of the four nontenured black faculty members. He recognized that their evaluation scores were slightly higher than his, but he felt the difference in evaluation scores was not sufficient to justify termination out of seniority order. Dr. Raintree contended that seniority was not a recognized criterion to be used in the evaluation or termination of nontenured faculty.

Dr. Erickson supported his contention of race discrimination by declaring that almost all the faculty being released throughout the college were white. Dr. Raintree said that the actions of other department chairmen were none of his concern, noting that "we all have our problems."

CONCLUSION

Dr. Erickson, still dissatisfied with Dr. Raintree's explanation, talked with Dr. Holt (the other faculty member being terminated in the English department) as to what action, if any, ought to be taken. Dr. Holt, in his disgust, had already decided to accept a position at Youngstown College in his home state of Ohio. Dr. Holt suggested that Dr. Erickson would be wasting his time and energy in fighting the decision. However, after considerable consultation with friends, Dr. Erickson filed his complaint with the EEOC on May 5, 1975.

Discussion questions

1. Do you think Dr. Erickson has a justifiable complaint?
2. You are Dr. Cranston, how would you defend the university's actions?
3. You are the EEOC investigator, how would you investigate the case?

I. NEGOTIATIONS WITH EMPLOYEES

1. Guaranteed Appliances

Guaranteed Appliances is a large manufacturer of small appliances. It has plants all over the United States, usually in smaller towns. At present, few of these plants are unionized.

Plant no. 8 is located in a small town near Atlanta, Georgia. Many of the workers in the plant drive to work from Atlanta. The plant has been increasing rapidly in size.

The appliance manufacturing business is one of the most competitive in the United States. Many manufacturers compete for the business. Guaranteed Appliances is a firm which does some private-label business and competes largely on the basis of price. It does little advertising.

Because of the pressure of price, Guaranteed Appliances has tried to keep its wages and compensation low. The plant is new and modern, and the working conditions are good for this type of job. The hours are the usual 8:00 A.M. to 5:00 P.M. Monday through Friday, although occasional overtime is necessary for the new model year and Christmas and Mothers' Day sales pushes.

The benefits available are the legally required ones and a few others. Minimum medical insurance is available, partially subsidized by the company. There is no pension plan. Wages are close to the minimum wage law requirements. As a result of these factors, there has been a fair amount of turnover. To some extent, workers take a job with Guaranteed Appliances and leave if they get higher paying jobs elsewhere.

Recently, there has been a downturn in the economy. There are not many jobs available. The International Union of Electrical Workers (AFL–CIO) has taken preliminary steps toward organizing Guaranteed Appliances, including the Atlanta plant. Traditionally, unions have not been strong in the South, but they are growing.

Some of the workers have been signing the IUE petition for election. They include some of the longest tenured and best known workers in the plant. Guaranteed Appliances is frankly worried about Atlanta being a plant that might start a trend to unionization.

As usual, the IUE is promising that it can negotiate big improvements in pay and benefits. The home office of Guaranteed Appliance is sending in John Jackson from the personnel office to assist Leo Huffine, the plant personnel manager, in plotting the company's strategy to resist the union.

Requirement. You are John Jackson. What would you try to find out about the situation prior to designing a strategy for the company? What steps would you take in the development of a strategy for the company's handling of the union issue?

2. Jetronic Corporation*

Jetronic Corporation is a manufacturer of electrical and electronic products. Among its product lines are radios, stereos, components for television sets, components for industrial electronics equipment, and aircraft instruments. The company recently opened a new assembly plant in Topeka, Kansas, and from the beginning tried to instill in its employees an understanding of the significance of maintaining a high-quality product. Much of the work of the plant involves the inspection and testing of goods in process and final products in order to maintain the company's reputation for producing high-quality products. In fact, almost one third of the company's work force of 600 employees is directly involved in some type of testing or inspecting activities. The entire west wing of the plant is being used by the testing department. There are approximately 110 employees—all women—working in this area. These employees use oscilloscopes for checking out the finished products electronically. Such instruments have a scope that resembles the picture tube of a television set.

Shortly after the new plant had begun operations in a modern, attractive facility, some of the employees in the testing area began to complain that there was too much glare from the white fluorescent lights that were overhead in this section. The plant superintendent and the testing foreman agreed that there was too much light and glare for efficient testing. Consequently, they decided to replace the white tubes with blue tubes which diminished the glare considerably. Such blue lights were being used successfully by the testing departments in other Jetronic

---

* By Professor Cary D. Thorp, Jr., University of Nebraska.

plants. The most noticeable effect of the lights was that the entire area seemed to be bathed with an eerie blue mist.

The new lights were installed over a weekend so the employees truly experienced a "blue Monday" when they returned to work. The new lights had been in operation for less than an hour when two of the testers complained to their foreman of headaches. However, when a quick poll of 15 of the testers was made by the plant superintendent and the foreman, only 3 of them said that they wanted the white lights put back up for illumination. Thus, it was concluded that all that was needed was a period of adjustment, and the blue lights were kept on.

In the first half hour after the noon lunch break three employees from the testing department reported separately to the first aid department with various complaints, such as headache, nausea, and so forth. Each requested permission to go home, and such permission was given. At 1:30 P.M. the same day, seven of the testers, including the union steward for the department, abruptly shut off their oscilloscopes and left the plant. This was the first time that the plant management had experienced a violation of the "no strike clause" which appeared in the labor agreement. The employees of the plant had only recently organized and had elected to affiliate with the International Brotherhood of Electrical Workers (IBEW). The labor agreement negotiated by the local IBEW and Jetronic had been in effect for less than two months. The "no strike clause" read as follows:

There shall be no strikes, refusal to work, or slowdown by the union during the life of this agreement, and there shall be no lockout on the part of the company. No officer or representative of the union shall authorize, approve, ratify, or condone any strike, refusal to work, or slowdown, and no employee shall participate in any such activity. The company agrees not to lockout any employee or group of employees while this agreement is in effect.

The labor agreement also contained this "management rights clause":

It is recognized and agreed by the company and the union that the management of the company is and shall continue to be vested solely in the company, and the company, in its judgment may increase or decrease operations, remove or install machinery or appliances, determine work processes and procedures, to continue to subcontract in accordance with past practice, to maintain discipline, and to enact company policies, plant rules, and regulations which are not in conflict with this agreement, remove any plant to another location as circumstances may require, or close or liquidate any plant.

When informed of the walkout, the plant manager quickly called a conference with the plant personnel manager, the plant superintendent, and the testing department foreman. Three questions faced this group of managers: (1) What steps should be taken to prevent further walkouts from the testing department this afternoon? (2) What disciplinary action, if any, should be taken against the seven strikers? (3) What disciplinary action, if any, should be taken against the three employees who had checked out through the first aid department?

Though this was the first walkout that had occurred at the Jetronic Plant, management had established an unwritten policy—known to the union leadership—that violation of the "no strike clause" would result in automatic discharge of the employees involved.

Requirement. What should management do now to handle this walkout? Invoke the no strike clause?

3. Southern State University (A)*

Samuel Carlton, professor and chairman of the department of management at Southern State University, was engrossed in some of the paperwork which seemed to consume so much of his time when his secretary, Barbara Paulson, entered his office.

"Here's a copy of the new union contract," she said, handing Carlton a document. The secretaries and other clericals were the last of several groups at SSU to unionize within the past few years, and the contract had not been resolved until after a month-long strike.

Still preoccupied with other matters, Carlton briefly glanced through the contract, noting basic provisions common to such agreements. Barbara was an excellent secretary, and he wasn't particularly concerned about unionization affecting his operation. He returned the document to Miss Paulson with the comment, "I don't see any problem as long as you are here, but if you ever leave, that seniority clause will give us trouble in finding a qualified replacement." The clause in question gave preference to seniority of applicants from other areas of the university without regard to the job classification level, as long as they came from the secretarial-clerical ranks, unless it could be proved that one with less seniority had "clearly superior requisite skills." Such skills were not further defined in the contract.

Several weeks later Barbara Paulson came into Carlton's office, and it was obvious that she was troubled about something. Finally she blurted out, "I've been thinking about this for a long time, and I have decided to quit my job and go to school full-time." She had taken a secretarial job right out of high school and had done well in a succession of jobs at the university before taking the position in management, which represented

---

*This case was written by Professor Claude I. Shell of Eastern Michigan University to serve as a basis for class discussion, not to illustrate effective or ineffective handling of administrative problems. All rights reserved to the author.

another in her series of promotions. Carlton stared at her for a moment without comment as he mentally reviewed these things. Barbara was a very capable person with great artistic ability, and as much as he hated to lose her, he recognized that she should be encouraged to pursue a course of action to utilize such talent. He assured her that he thought she was taking the right action, even though all faculty in the department would greatly miss her. Then he recalled the union contract and its seniority provision. This was the first time he had had to deal with this type situation as it affected a secretary, and the prospects didn't reassure him.

Barbara had given Carlton a lengthy advance notice of her plans, so there was ample time to work on the process of getting her successor. The first thing Carlton did was to call the person who handled such matters, Carl Chavis, assistant director of personnel. Chavis was very reassuring and outlined the procedure that would meet contract conditions. The position was advertised internally, and seven applicants filed applications. After interviewing each applicant, Carlton prepared from his interview notes a spread sheet (Exhibit 1) noting for each applicant seniority, typing skills, and other qualities which Carlton considered to be important.

Certain things quickly became apparent and a little disturbing. The most senior applicants were obviously not qualified in Carlton's opinion, but he wondered how much backing he would get from personnel. These applicants had poor typing capabilities, and no academic department secretarial experience. After spending some time studying his information, it was obvious to Carlton that the best person he thought he could get under the contract was fourth on the seniority list. (Two of the more qualified were not in the bargaining unit, which excluded temporary employees and three offices on the campus. Carlton advised them to seek employment elsewhere where they would have opportunities to advance.)

Carlton made an appointment with Chavis and took his materials over. Chavis was very personable, young, and not too experienced. "This is the one I want," Carlton told Chavis, pointing to number four, Patricia Parsons. Chavis raised his eyebrows, so Carlton continued. "Number one has been at the university 17 years and still has not been able to reach a classification equal to that of a departmental secretary. She has had no experience in an academic department working directly with faculty, which I think is very important, and her typing is terribly inaccurate. She is reasonably fast, but she made 24 errors on the five-minute test. She will never get the job done." Carlton also pointed out to Chavis that he could not accept the personnel office practice of reporting typing scores on the basis of deducting one word per minute for each error made, instead of the more standard practice of measuring the amount of typing correctly done in a given period, or of deducting ten words for each

EXHIBIT 1
APPLICANT QUALIFICATIONS

Applicant	Seniority (years)	Current job classification	Typing Speed	Errors	Department secretarial experience	Acounting experience	Promoted on present job	Passed over for promotion	Supervisory experience	Education
1	17	3	79	24	No	No	Yes	U*	Yes	H.S.‡
2	10	4	80	18	No	No	Yes	U*	No	H.S.
3	7	4	59	6	No	Yes	Yes	U*	Yes	H.S.
4	6	5	72	3	Yes	No	Yes	No	Yes	H.S.
5	2	3	55	4	No	No	No	No	No	H.S.
6	1	4	81	7	No	Yes	No	No	No	2 years college†
7	Temporary	Temporary	83	5	No	No	No	No	No	H.S.

* Unknown. Many records, especially older ones, were incomplete.
† Two-year secretarial administration program.
‡ High School.

error. Chavis became defensive at the criticism of personnel policy and asked about the other candidates. Carlton continued, "Number two has eighteen errors on the test and likewise has not advanced to a secretarial level, although she has over ten years seniority. Number three has about a year seniority over number four, but her typing is slow and still not as accurate. Further, she has no departmental secretarial experience." At this point he paused, watching Chavis' reaction.

Finally Chavis said, "OK, I agree. These should be qualifications that we can defend under the contract. Go ahead and hire Miss Parsons, but you should realize that number one is also secretary of the union, and they will probably feel compelled to file a grievance. Write to each of the others telling them of your decision, but don't give any reasons." At this point Carlton felt relieved and agreed to follow the advice on the letters, although he normally followed a different practice.

Carlton returned to his office, feeling much better and thinking that maybe this union stiuation wouldn't be too bad after all. His own background and training made this difficult as it had all been on the management side, both in industry and in academic training. He informed Miss Parsons of his choice. She accepted the job and was transferred into the office. Miss Paulson had a week overlap with Miss Parson, and they worked very well together. Miss Paulson wished to stay on as student secretary. Carlton realized this was a potentially troublesome situation, but Miss Parsons requested it, and Miss Paulson wanted a job and was happy with the arrangement.

Carlton kept an eye on the calendar to see if a grievance were filed within the three weeks provided for in the union contract. He had heard nothing until almost the end of the third week when he received notice to appear at a step three hearing. (The grievance is filed, normally against the supervisory person allegedly committing a breach of the contract, requesting that the action be overturned, and the hearing of this grievance with this supervisor is a step one hearing. An appeal of the step one decision to the superior of the person being grieved against is a step two hearing. Step three is a further appeal, in this case involving the personnel office, and is the last step before binding arbitration.) This notice came as a surprise, as he had expected to have a grievance filed against him for a step one hearing for not hiring the most senior person, so he reread the contract. Only then did he realize that the contract called for the grievant to file against his or her present supervisor, regardless of whether this was the person being grieved against. In this instance hearings had already been conducted at steps one and two without his even being notified! He was dumbfounded to learn this. He was further disturbed when he learned that all three of the more senior persons had filed grievances and that in one case the supervisor, who was in the process of leaving the university, supported the grievant even though he was in a nonacademic department and knew nothing about the job in question.

Carlton immediately contacted Chavis, who told him not to worry as he, Chavis, would handle the hearing and that Carlton need only appear and bring records to support the decision. On the day of the hearing, Carlton was further disturbed. The union had four representatives from their grievance committee present, and Carlton noted a bit uncomfortably that the small talk exchanged between Chavis and Norton Dunn, committee chairman, seemed a bit "cozy." Both were relatively recent SSU graduates and chatted about their partying in their student days. The hearing went badly, as Chavis did not do a good job of presenting Carlton's case. Carlton wished he had done it himself, but he had assumed from the beginning that there would be a stalemate at each step short of arbitration, so he didn't think too much about it.

After about 45 minutes of discussion the union asked for a caucus, during which time Chavis attempted to allay Carlton's concerns by telling him the union was just going through the motions. At the end of the caucus, Dunn announced that the union wished to utilize a provision of the contract which called for an adjournment of the step three hearing until a representative of the international union (Mine Workers International) could be present. Carlton was beginning to feel depressed.

A few days later Carlton received through the mail a notice of resumption of the hearing. The meeting was scheduled for a time when he had a class. Chavis had not bothered to consult him before setting the time. Carlton tried to contact Chavis to get the matter resolved, but neither Chavis nor his secretary were in that day. The next day Carlton called again, and somewhat brusquely informed Chavis that he could not make the meeting at the time scheduled because he had a conflict. Chavis responded that David West, the personnel director, would be present and that it wouldn't be necessary for Carlton to appear. By this time Carlton had become very pessimistic about what he viewed as lack of support from personnel, and he felt the only way things could be turned around would be to take the matter to arbitration. Surely a qualified arbitrator would separate the facts in the case!

On the day of the hearing Carlton went to class as usual. He had just started when Miss Parsons appeared at the classroom door. She indicated that Chavis had called, stating that West had a conflict and could not make the hearing and that Carlton should come over as soon as he could. Carlton completed the class and then crossed the campus with a sense of foreboding. When he entered the meeting, he found three of the four campus union representatives and two from the international. The hearing proceeded in the same fashion as the first one, except that it was obvious that the international representative felt he had a good opportunity to make a good impression before the union membership and he was going to make the most of it.

At one point the representative raised the letter that Carlton had written to the rejected applicants and said, "Any time you write a letter like that and do not give specific reasons for passing over a senior person, you are going to get a grievance!" Chavis nodded and said, "Yes, I agree. That is a very poor letter." Carlton had great difficulty restraining himself, as that was the letter Chavis insisted that he write. The meeting adjourned without reaching a resolution of the issue, as neither side would yield.

Carlton waited until he and Chavis were some distance from the union representatives, and he literally exploded over the letter episode. Chavis numbly nodded, agreed the letter was his idea, and apologized for his handling of the matter. Carlton again stated that the matter obviously had to go to arbitration, but Chavis' reaction gave him great doubts that personnel would support him in the matter. A later meeting with West revealed that personnel was going to recommend that the matter be carried no further. West then wrote the union that although the university believed that Miss Parsons did indeed have "clearly superior requisite skills" sufficient to give her the job over less senior employees and that they rejected the union contention to the contrary they would, nonetheless, grant the grievance, return Miss Parsons to her former position, and give the management secretarial position to the number two applicant (number one had withdrawn from the proceedings by this time).

4. Discharge of Sleeping Beauty*

COMPANY: REYNOLDS METALS COMPANY,
                CORPUS CHRISTI, TEXAS.

UNION: ALUMINUM WORKERS INTERNATIONAL UNION,
            AFL-CIO.

On August 6, 1974, Allen Walston was discharged for sleeping while on duty. He filed a grievance two days later protesting his discharge and requesting full reinstatement with back pay. The grievance was not resolved, and the case went to arbitration in accordance with article VI of the union-management contract. The parties agreed that the grievance was properly before the arbitrator and jointly identified the issue as: Was the discharge of Allen Walston for proper and just cause? If not, what is the appropriate remedy?

---

* This case was prepared by associate professor I. B. Helburn of the University of Texas at Austin and assistant professor Darold Barnum of Texas Tech University as a basis for class discussion rather than to illustrate either effective or ineffective handling of an administrative situation. Real names of individuals in the case have not been used.

Copyright © 1975 by I. B. Helburn and Darold T. Barnum.

Background

Walston began working at the Reynolds plant in April 1969. Five years later at the time of his discharge, he was a trainee under area foreman, Ben Chavez. He had received no written warnings in the three months preceding his termination.

On August 4, two days before his discharge, Walston was working the midnight–8:00 A.M. shift. Chavez needed to see him and thus paged Walston twice using the public address system. Walston did not respond. Sometime later he did appear and said that noise had kept him from hearing the call. Chavez tore up the written reprimand he had intended to give Walston for sleeping on the job. He did, however, counsel Walston about failure to appear when paged. He also discussed Walston's generally poor work record with him, as he had already done on several previous occasions.

On August 6, 1974, Walston was again working the graveyard (midnight–8:00 A.M. shift. He had been taking aspirin and Dristan for several days as he had been bothered by sinus trouble. Chavez saw Walston at 5:45 A.M. when the employee came to the office for a piece of equipment. Then about 30 minutes later Chavez and General Foreman Clarke (in the hospital at the time of the hearing) found Walston in a prone position on top of a tool locker, his head on a makeshift "pillow."

The locker was located on the third and highest floor of a filter building across the street from Walston's work area. No other employees were in the locker area because no work was being done there on this particular night. There was a snack bar used for coffee breaks on the same floor about 50–75 yards from the tool locker. Coffee breaks were generally taken about 6 A.M., with employees allowed to be away from their worksites for approximately ten minutes.

After finding Walston on the locker, Chavez called plant security and had Walston escorted to the office. There Chavez asked for an explanation of the incident, but Walston gave him none. Chavez then told the employee that he was being discharged for sleeping on the job and that he could pick up his formal termination notice from personnel when that office opened in the morning. The security guard escorted Walston directly to his locker to collect his belongings and from there off the plant grounds. Walston was the first employee Chavez had fired in his 18 years as a foreman at Reynolds Metals.

On August 8 Walston filed a grievance through his union. It was later denied by the company, and the case was arbitrated on December 19, 1974.

Company Position

The company claimed the right to discharge under article XXIII of the agreement because Walston's sleeping was deliberate. It maintained that premeditation was shown by the resting place, the pillow, and the deep sleep in which Walston was found.

Chavez testified that upon finding Walston he first called Walston's name several times while standing next to him. Walston did not respond until after Chavez had shaken him four times. Then Walston sat up and said, "I'm sick." At that point the foreman called plant security.

Chavez further testified that Walston was resting his head on an army field jacket stuffed with rags. Chavez said he had never seen the jacket before, that with the warm August weather there was no need for a jacket, and that there had been no rags in the building or work area. Chavez also noted that Walston had what appeared to be a jacket with him when he finally left the plant grounds and that the "pillow" was gone the next day when Chavez checked the area.

The foreman knew that Walston had been taking medicine for his sinus trouble but noted that he did not ask to go to first aid. Had he done so, permission would have been granted.

Regarding the incident two nights earlier, Chavez said that when Walston did appear he looked as though he had been sleeping. The warning was torn up because the foreman hoped that talking to Walston and giving him the benefit of the doubt would encourage him to do better. The company attorney claimed that another employee, whom the company would not name nor call to testify, later reported that Walston had indeed been sleeping in a pickup truck.

Chavez also testified that Walston was "irresponsible, lackadaisical, and lazy" and that he needed much more supervision than other "problem" employees. The company attorney said that Walston was disliked by fellow employees because of his poor performance.

The company agreed that employees did doze on coffee breaks when they were in the snack bar or the operations shack and that such employees were simply awakened and sent back to work without being disciplined. It was argued, nevertheless, that such dozing was different from Walston's deliberate and premeditated sleeping and that Walston's behavior was serious enough to warrant discharge. The company cited an arbitration decision in another company, in which the arbitrator upheld the discharge of an employee found sleeping in a tractor he was supposed to be operating.

Union Position

The union responded that Walston had not preplanned his pillow, hidden himself, nor purposely fallen asleep.

Walston said he left his work area about 6 A.M. He took five to seven minutes to walk from his work site to the locker area, stopping to tell other employees he was going to rest rather than to have coffee, and to get him if he was needed. He wanted the rest rather than the coffee because of his sinus condition, which was bothering him considerably, particularly since earlier in the evening he had had to use a pistol grip compressed air hammer.

Walston admitted to resting on the tool locker but would only say that it was possible he was sleeping although he did not think so. He said he did not hear his name being called but did not feel Chavez shake him.

Walston denied having a jacket as a pillow, saying that his head was resting on a piece of cloth and some rags that he found on the locker. This piece of cloth had neither buttons nor sleeves. He further testified that he could not have recovered a jacket from the tool locker since he was escorted by plant security from the time Chavez found him until he left the grounds.

Also, the union argued that since Chavez had not seen Walston lie down, he could not say the bed had been deliberately made. And no company employee had ever been terminated for sleeping on the job.

Walston claimed that on the August 4 shift he had not heard Chavez call him because of the noise of some nearby pumps, which obscured the public address system. When he was told by Henry Cooper, a fellow employee, that Chavez wanted to see him, he went directly to the office. Cooper's testimony supported Walston's story.

Finally, the union pointed out that in the arbitration decision cited by the company the discharged employee had not been taking medicine and had been given one written warning and two short suspensions in the two weeks prior to dismissal. Thus the circumstances did not apply to the Walston case. Although the union did not dispute the company's right to discharge under Article XXIII, they argued that proper and just cause was lacking and that full back pay and allowances were due.

Selected Agreement Provisions

Article V, section 1. In the event an employee in the opinion of the company has acted in such a manner as to deserve discharge he may be immediately suspended, and the chairman of the grievance committee, or his designated representative, shall be informed of the reason for the company action. Such notice will be given on the same day as notice is transmitted to the employee involved.

Article V, section 2. Should the employee, within five (5) working days of the suspension, believe that he should not be discharged, he and/ or his union representative may present his complaint in writing to the company personnel representative (third step of the grievance procedure), who will give the matter prompt and thorough consideration.

Article V, section 3. Should it be found upon investigation as provided in article VI hereof that an employee has been unjustly treated, such employees [sic] shall be immediately reinstated in his former position without loss of seniority and shall be compensated for all time lost in amount based on his average straight time hourly rate of pay for the pay period next preceding such suspension, or other such adjustment as may be mutually agreed to by the company and the union, or determined to be proper by an arbitrator.

Article VI, section 1. Failing satisfactory adjustment by the director of labor relations, the grievance may be submitted to arbitration by either party.

The decision of the arbitrator shall be final and binding on all affected parties.

Article X. The following understandings shall apply to plant working rules number 9 to 17, inclusive:

When an employee receives a warning under one of the aforementioned working rules, he may have this warning removed from his record if he does not receive another warning under any of the aforementioned rules within three months after the date of this warning.

Article XXIII. It is recognized that, subject to the provisions of this agreement, the operation of the plant and the direction of the working forces including the rights to hire, lay off, suspend, and discharge any employee for proper and just cause are vested exclusively with the company.

Plant working rules (part of contract). For those persons who fail to conduct themselves properly, the following penalties have been established and will be enforced. Violations of rules 1–8 will result in discharge for the first offense. Violations of rules 9–17 will draw a written warning for the first offense and discharge for the second. Violations of rules 18 and 19 will draw written warnings for the first and second offenses and discharge for the third.

1. Fighting.
2. Refusal to obey orders.
3. Possession of a lethal weapon.
4. Possession or use of drugs or alcoholic beverages in the plant.
5. Theft.
6. Moral offenses.
7. Willful destruction of company property.
8. Deliberately tampering with or punching another employee's time card.
9. Violation of a safety regulation which could result in injury.
10. Failure to wear prescribed safety equipment.
11. Loafing.
12. Poor work.
13. Leaving work area without permission of foreman.
14. Leaving operating post without proper relief or without permission of employee's foreman.
15. Horseplay.
16. Failure to have badge in possession.
17. Soliciting funds without consent of company.
18. Unexcused tardiness.
19. Absence without leave.

Discussion questions

1. Evaluate the arguments of management. Of the union.

2. As the arbitrator, how would you rule? Why?
3. How can management prevent similar arbitration cases in the future?

5. Hidden Budget*

In early April 1972, the police department of Doylesville was the lowest paid law enforcement agency for class I cities (population over 200,000) in the state. At that time, the city council and city manager of Doylesville indicated to the Police Benevolent Association (PBA) that they planned to give a $125-a-month across-the-board pay raise to all local police officers, a move that would bring this department in line with police salaries in the state's other major cities.

City council elections were scheduled for May 15. Members of the old council told the police informally that they did not want to saddle the new council with the task of raising the funds for the pay raise. They advised, therefore, that the raise would not be included in the city budget which was finalized before the election. Once the election was over, however, these old council members, if reelected, would then provide each officer with the $125 raise.

The city manager informed members of the PBA at a lodge meeting that he had enough money "hidden" in the budget to assure the raise. The officers at this meeting agreed to cease their campaign for higher wages that they had been conducting through local newspaper and other media until after the election.

The nine city councilmen were reelected, and they held their first meeting on June 2. No action was taken at this meeting on the pay raise for the officers. At the next meeting on June 9, the council voted to give the police a hazardous duty pay increase in the following manner: patrolmen—$55 a month; sergeants—$65 a month; lieutenants—$70 a month; and captains—$75 a month. The police did not previously have hazardous duty pay. The Doylesville Police Department is comprised of 280 police officers, 225 of which are patrolmen, 31 sergeants, 15 lieutenants, 7 captains, one deputy chief and a chief of police.

All off-duty officers were in attendance at this meeting and several members of PBA's police wage committee voiced their strong disappointment at the raise, saying that this wasn't what they were promised both by the council and the city manager. Three councilmen told them that

---

* This case was prepared by Richard M. Ayres, FBI Academy, and Thomas L. Wheelen, McIntire School of Commerce, University of Virginia, as the basis for class discussion.

this was all they were going to get, and there would be no compromise. The council then unanimously passed the motion for the hazardous duty pay raise.

The next morning the police wage committee met and found that since the increase was labeled hazardous duty pay the city did not have to contribute to the officer's pension fund in matching amounts. Under the existing police pension plan, the policemen and the city each contributed 6 percent of the gross earnings of each officer. Furthermore, by labeling the raise as such, the increase was not added to the hourly wage scale of the officers, thus circumventing the requirement of the city to pay overtime at the rate of the raise. Also, the retirement pay an officer receives is 50 percent of their monthly wages based on their five highest straight-time earning years.[1] The pay raise would also be excluded from this calculation.

That night at 8 P.M., a special meeting of the PBA was called. All off-duty officers attended and voted to declare a "blue flu."

Beginning with the midnight shift on June 12, all officers called in sick, except the chief and 16 probationary officers. The latter were excluded from the job action because they lacked job security. The remaining 263 officers joined the job action.

The chief of police, in an attempt to combat the "blue flu" situation, immediately ordered all officers that called in sick to report directly to the city medical examiner in the morning. He further threatened to suspend all those officers who were found healthy. No one reported.

A special meeting of the council was called for 9 A.M. to handle the strike issue. Each council member had been notified by the chief of police of the strike action vote.

Discussion questions

1. Does the "blue flu" constitute a strike action? Should police officers have the legal right to strike?
2. What role does city politics play in public sector labor relations?
3. How should this labor relations crisis be prevented in the future?

6. Middle Management Ignored*

In 1967 officers of the Gardner City Police Department became affiliated with the American Federation of State, County and Municipal Em-

---

[1] The 50 percent was for 20 years of service. Each year in addition to 20 years, the officer received 1 percent more up to a maximum of 60 percent (30 years).

* This case was prepared by Richard M. Ayres, FBI Academy, and Thomas L. Wheelen, McIntire School of Commerce, University of Virginia, as the basis for class discussion.

ployees (AFSCME). At this time, the middle management ranks of the Gardner City Police Department, especially sergeants, lieutenants, and captains, decided not to be represented by the union.

At the beginning, the benefits AFSCME gained through the collective bargaining process were small and automatically given to middle management. AFSCME has now been in operation for six years and during the last two years has won some very good fringe benefits and wage increases for its members.

In 1973 AFSCME invited middle management to join the union. The middle management echelon of the police department was the only group in Garner City not affiliated with a union. The fire department has been totally organized since the inception of the firemen's union. The police middle management met and discussed the offer to join AFSCME. They decided not to join since it would be detrimental to the mission of the officers. They also felt that their affiliation with a union would cast a shadow of doubt as to where their loyalty rested. This decision on the part of middle management left them without any representation in regard to benefits and wages.

Up until this time, the city manager, through the city council, had immediately passed all union gains to middle management without a request from them.

One of the issues included in the 1973 contract was a 10¢ night-shift differential. This benefit, however, was not passed on to middle management.

In the 1975 negotiations, more new benefits were derived from union members. Middle management, once again, did not receive any of these new benefits. As a result of this action, middle management decided it was time to bring these inequities to the attention of the city manager. A formal letter (Exhibit 1) was drafted and sent to the city manager. All middle management members of the Gardner City Police Department signed the letter. The city manager then wrote a reply (Exhibit 2) to their letter responding to their expressed inequities.

EXHIBIT 1
LETTER TO CITY MANAGER OF GARDNER CITY

February 14, 1975

Dear Sir:

We, the members of the supervisory and management echelon of the Gardner City Police Department, would like to take this opportunity, with all due respect, to voice our collective opinions regarding several inequities which we believe may develop from our ranks which are not included in the bargaining unit.

EXHIBIT 1 (*continued*)

We consider our echelon, supervision and management, as an extension or arm of the city manager and the chief of police, and as such our loyalty must and does in fact remain with these administrators. We have vividly demonstrated this loyalty in the past by voting against our inclusion in the bargaining unit representing the operational echelon of the department.

Recently, in what appeared to be a job action by members of the department bargaining unit, the responsibility for providing police protection fell on the shoulders of supervisory personnel whose loyalty was demonstrated by reporting for duty and performing all required services for the citizens of Gardner City. We feel that in order to prevent a conflict of interests and perpetuate the strong loyalty to the administration we cannot and should not become affiliated with a bargaining unit. No man can serve two masters and be equally loyal to each.

However, self-preservation and self-esteem are two most intense behavioral drives possessed by men, and to these ends we have constructed this communication.

First and of long-standing concern to our numbers is the inequity which exists between bargaining unit members and our ranks with respect to the night-shift differential. The night-shift differential has been in existence for several years and was not initially offered to nonunion employees nor has it ever been discussed with our numbers. Currently, only eight supervisors would be concerned with this pay differential, but it is an inequity to the supervisory ranks of the department.

Next area of concern to nonunion personnel was the apparent fact that the bargaining unit has obtained an additional $35 uniform allowance. No additional allowances were forthcoming to supervisors which was embarrassing and thought-provoking. It was embarrassing since it was apparent on that payday when two checks were received by union employees and none for supervisors. "You guys don't rate," was a somewhat grating statement heard by most supervisors upon reporting for pay.

It was thought-provoking in that if intially we were not included in the night-shift differential, then not included in the allocation of funds for additional uniform allowance, it is apparent that the future is not getting brighter for supervisors who are loyal and nonunion members.

These inequities should not have accrued initially. To allow the initial oversight to carry over from year to year and to overlook the appropriation of funds to guarantee those additional benefits to supervisors is most detrimental to the morale of the supervisory echelon.

We respectfully request that the nonunion supervisors of the police department be placed on parity with other city employees and this be standard for each subsequent contractual agreement. This would eliminate the anuual apprehension and requirement that we must communicate inequities on a yearly basis.

We request these aforementioned conditions be considered in the light of fairness, equality, and an opportunity to provide a prideful environment for supervisors who are nonunion affiliated.

Respectfully,

Supervisors of the
Gardner City
Police Department

EXHIBIT 2
LETTER TO CHIEF OF POLICE OF GARDNER CITY

February 27, 1975

Dear Chief:

This is in reply to the letter dated February 14, 1975, signed by all of the sergeants, lieutenants, and captains, in which they set forth certain alleged inequities in the benefits offered to nonunion personnel.

I would point out that, with the exception of the chief and assistant chief, all other supervisors receive overtime pay at the rate of one and one half times regular pay. This benefit is not extended to any other supervisor in Gardner.

In addition, I must remind you that last year the classification for the chief and assistant chief was upgraded in order to compensate for the lack of time and one half provisions in these two positions.

In order for me to secure money to implement the requests contained in their letter, it will be necessary for me to request an additional appropriation from the city council. If you will provide me with the cost figures to cover the numerous requests made, I will present this to the city council.

Very truly yours,

City Manager

Discussion questions

1. What factors are present which would cause middle management to unionize?

2. What problems may be caused by permitting supervisory personnel to be members of a patrolmen's union?

3. What would middle management's expected response be to the city manager's letter?

7. Who Should Drive the Wagons?*

COMPANY: BETHLEHEM STEEL CORPORATION, SHIPBUILDING DEPARTMENT, BEAUMONT, TEXAS

UNION: INTERNATIONAL BROTHERHOOD OF TEAMSTERS, LOCAL 920

* This case was prepared by Associate Professor I. B. Helburn of the University of Texas at Austin and Assistant Professor Darold T. Barnum of Texas Tech University as a basis for class discussion rather than to illustrate either effective or ineffective handling of an administrative situation. Real names of individuals in the case have not been used.

On August 7, 1974, a salaried employee who was not a member of the bargaining unit drove a group of employees who were members of a union other than the Teamsters to an off-site work area in a company-owned station wagon. A grievance was filed the same day, contending that the driver should have been a Teamster. When no settlement was reached at the third step of the grievance procedure, arbitration was invoked. The parties agreed that the matter was properly before the arbitrator and that the issue in dispute was:

Did the company violate any agreement by allowing a salaried employee to drive a company station wagon on August 7, 1974?

Background

The primary function of Bethlehem Steel's Beaumont yard is building and repairing ships and offshore oil drilling platforms. Repair is done in the yard and at off-site (field) locations. Men, tools, and equipment are transported to off-site work in two ways. The first is with transportation department trucks driven by members of the Teamster bargaining unit. The Teamsters have exclusive representation rights for employees in this department.

The second source of transportation is general manager's department vehicles which include two station wagons. These wagons have generally been driven to the field by supervisors when both a supervisor and two or three bargaining unit employees were being transported.

Relations between the company and the union are governed by the August 18, 1972, agreement between Bethlehem Steel and the Beaumont Metal Trades Council, with which Teamster Local 920 is affiliated. Pertinent contract provisions are reproduced at the end of this case.

During the 1969 negotiations the union raised the question of supervisors driving bargaining unit personnel in company station wagons and introduced the following language for inclusion in the new agreement:

Transportation of tools, material and crafts will be made by personnel of the transportation department, inside and outside the plant, whether by car, bus, or truck.

No agreement was reached on this provision, and it was not included in the 1969 agreement.

On February 27, 1970, the union filed a grievance because two individuals who were not Teamsters used a company wagon to transport themselves and their hand tools to the field. The union business agent, Parson, dropped the grievance after the first step because he considered the incident an emergency.

The 1972 agreement was negotiated with no changes in the language regarding work assignments. However, the union alleges and the company denies that Mr. Lincoln, the chief company negotiator, told union members during conversations that if supervisory personnel were doing bargaining unit driving the practice would stop.

On September 26, 1972, the union filed a grievance after a salaried employee had transported a non-Teamster member of the bargaining unit to Lake Charles, Louisiana. Business agent Parson dropped the grievance after the first step, considering the incident an emergency.

On April 30, 1973, Don Hughes filed a grievance because a supervisor had transported a machinist and an electrician to an off-site job in his own car. This grievance was withdrawn by the Teamsters when Hughes picketed the yard in violation of the agreement. (The union did not sanction the picketing and withdrew the grievance because of it.)

On February 21, 1974, an hourly-paid leaderman, a union member other than a Teamster, drove a company wagon with other bargaining unit men and their tools and related equipment to an off-site job. As a result the Teamsters filed a grievance and ultimately invoked arbitration when no third-step settlement was reached. Prior to the actual hearing the parties reached an agreement on their own. The settlement of the grievance, which did not involve back pay, was stated in a June 25, 1974, letter signed by A. B. Julip of Bethlehem Steel and confirmed by Parson for the union. The letter stated:

This will confirm our agreement to enter into with you contemporaneously herewith concerning certain work performed by truck drivers.

In the future on jobs performed outside a radius of 50 miles of the yard when only hourly employees are involved it is management's intent to transport these employees in a transportation department vehicle, when such a vehicle adequate to the task is available with truck drivers. This does not preclude the use of commercial transportation, when applicable.

In the past, some jobs have been within and others outside the 50-mile radius. On August 7, 1974, the current grievance was filed as noted previously.

Union Position

The union argues that bargaining unit work cannot go unprotected and that the company wrongfully assigned bargaining unit work outside the unit. By this action the Teamsters have been deprived of the work and of the double-time pay specified for off-site repair work.

The union points to language contained in article XIII, section 10 and paragraph 3 of the appended letter as specific support for the grievance. They argue that the contract requires the assignment of work to the appropriate craft, in this case the Teamsters, and that the letter prohibits supervisors from doing bargaining unit work. The union further argues that all company-owned vehicles are included in the term "equipment" when bargaining unit personnel are transported in them. The grievances filed in 1972, 1973, and 1974 are offered as proof of the union's intent to protect its contract rights.

The union contends that in the June 1974 letter from Julip the company agreed not to assign driving of bargaining unit personnel to other than Teamsters. To construe the letter in such a way as to continue to allow supervisory personnel to drive would mean that the Teamsters settled the grievance without truly gaining their objective. The union business agent testified that this was clearly not the understanding he had when the grievance was settled. He understood the settlement to require that only Teamsters would drive the station wagons when bargaining unit personnel were being moved.

Finally, the union says that an oral commitment had been given by the company's chief negotiator during the 1972 bargaining. Parson testified that when he returned in August 1972 from convalescing from a heart attack he was briefed on the progress of negotiations by Braxton and Fonda. Included in the briefing was the information that Lincoln had said that driving by supervisors rather than bargaining unit personnel would stop if it was occurring.

Local 920 President Braxton and Steward Fonda both testified that Lincoln had indeed made the statement they reported to Parson and union counsel spoke of non-Teamster members of the bargaining committee who were also present when the remarks were made. The union does not dispute the right of supervisors to use the wagons by themselves, or to transport members of the bargaining unit for medical attention, or for other true emergencies. However, the union does claim that when passengers are bargaining unit members and there is no emergency the wagon driver should be a Teamster.

Company Position

The company argues that the practice of allowing supervisors to drive members of the bargaining unit in station wagons dispatched from the general manager's department is an established past practice which has not been changed by anything that the company has written, said, or done. Article II, section 1, refers to work "normally performed" as covered under the agreement. The company claims that the grievance does not involve work "normally performed" by the bargaining unit.

The company says that Teamsters have never driven the station wagons. Even Parson, under cross examination, said that he could not recall a Teamster ever driving a wagon, although he thought it may have occurred. The company also claims that the union's attempt to introduce new contract language in 1969 showed that they knew the existing language did not give their members the right to drive the wagons. When asked to define "equipment," Julip included trucks but excluded station wagons. Richardson, the supervisor who drove the wagon resulting in the present grievance, testified that he had made 15–20 trips in the 15 years he had been a member of the yard supervisory force and that his experience was typical of most supervisors.

The company notes that those grievances filed prior to 1974 do not establish past practice in the union's favor, since the three were all withdrawn prior to the second step of the grievance procedure. Neither is the June 25, 1974, letter from Julip viewed as serving to establish the right of Teamster members to drive the station wagons. The company points to specific wording granting the right of Teamsters to drive only when hourly-rated employees alone are involved and when the work is outside a 50-mile radius from the yard. The claim is also made that the absence of back pay indicates no wrongdoing on the part of the company.

Lastly, the company disputes the union contention that an oral agreement was made by Lincoln in 1972. The union did not mention the agreement during the earlier stages of the grievance settlement process. Julip testified that he too represented the company during the 1972 negotiations and to the best of his recollection was present each time Lincoln was. Julip stated that he did not remember Lincoln making an agreement such as that described by the union. Furthermore, according to Julip, he was responsible for local issues, Lincoln for national issues. Thus Julip and not Lincoln would have been the likely negotiator on issues which were local, such as this work assignment issue.

1972 Agreement Selected Provisions

Article II, section 1. This agreement covers the bargaining unit at the Beaumont yard consisting of hourly-paid employees, except watchmen and clerical, supervisory and building trades construction employees.

This includes work as normally performed by the various classifications in accordance with shipyard practices. . . .

Article XIII, section 10. In accordance with past practice of the company, supervisors shall allocate the work to the craft which normally performs such work as recognized by the unions involved.

Article XIX, section 7. The arbitration procedure shall not be used to change or modify any of the provisions of this agreement in any respect.

Letter, appended to the agreement, paragraph 3. Salaried supervisors will not work with tools or operate equipment in the performance of their duties or replace other employees, except to instruct in the use of tools or equipment or methods or performance of work, except in cases of emergency.

Also, Appendix 1 of the agreement includes job classification descriptions for chauffeur, bus driver and truck driver. The language of article XIII and paragraph 3 of the appended letter have remained unchanged since before the 1966 contract.

Discussion questions

1. Evaluate the impact of the contract clauses, the appended letter, and the June 1974 grievance on the arbitration case.
2. What must the company show to have its position upheld? The union?
3. Evaluate the company's case. The union's case.
4. As the arbitrator, how would you rule? Why?

8. The Grayson Construction Company*

A SECONDARY BOYCOTT PROBLEM

Jim: Well, that's the story. Is your position on the matter the same as indicated during our earlier discussion?

Dan: Yes, it is. I'm sure that you can count on our support for two weeks, but I can't promise you anything beyond that. Our management group meets in an hour, and I will have to tell them at that time what course of action you intend to follow.

Jim: Let me give it some more thought. I will call you back before your meeting.

This ended a telephone conversation between Jim Carter, vice president of a construction firm, and Dan Stokes, a member of the management group of one of his most important clients. Jim had to decide how to handle a difficult problem that had been developing for some time and that had finally come to head. The heart of the matter revolved around a conflict between his company, which did not employ union labor, and local construction unions who objected quite strongly to nonunion labor being used on jobs in the area. In the present situation Jim was in the uncomfortable position of having to meet the unions in a headlong clash or acquiesce to their demands. He could not predict with certainty the effect of his decision on relations with his client, who would be caught in the middle in such a dispute, nor could he ascertain the effect of his action on future efforts of the union to bring economic pressure against his company.

The Grayson Construction Company was the largest of several firms in metropolitan Philadelphia that handled contract work on a bid basis for the gas, electric, sewer, water, and telephone companies. Even though his father, who founded the company, was its president, Jim exercised active management direction of the firm. Much of their work involved

---

* This case was prepared by Professor R. H. Finn of the University of Georgia as a basis for class discussion. It is not designed to illustrate either effective or ineffective handling of administrative problems.

installation and maintenance of underground conduit, gas, steam, sewer, water, and cable systems. All of Grayson's competitors were organized, as were the utility companies. Jim attributed much of his company's success to the work flexibility and efficiencies they enjoyed as a result of not being organized. A concerted effort had been made about seven years earlier to unionize Grayson's employees, but this drive failed by a very narrow margin, and there had been no further attempt at union organization since then.

Even though no overt effort had since been made to organize the work force, Grayson continued to be subjected to economic pressure initiated by one or more of the local construction unions. A typical incident of this kind occurred a year or so earlier. Grayson was awarded a contract to complete certain phases of a larger construction project. Other contractors on the job employed union labor. Upon learning that a nonunion firm was on the job, the business agent for one of the unions threatened to pull all of his men off the project, thus bringing it to a halt, unless "that nonunion guy" was taken off. Upon discussing this situation with his client, Jim clearly got the message that the client wished to avoid union trouble and that it would be best if Grayson pulled off the job. Jim pointed out that the union was probably bluffing since, in his opinion, the threatened action was in violation of the secondary boycott provisions of the Labor Management Relations Act (see Exhibit 1). Nevertheless,

EXHIBIT 1

Section 8 (b) (4) of the Labor Management Relations Act says in part:
   . . . It shall be an unfair labor practice for a labor organization or its agents to engage in, or to induce or encourage an individual employed by any person engaged in commerce or in an industry affecting commerce to engage in a strike or a refusal in the course of his employment to perform any services when the object is to force or require any person to cease doing business with any other person. . . .

Section 303 (b) of the law says in part:
   . . . Whoever shall be injured in his business or property by reason of any violation of Section 8 (b) (4) may sue therefore in any district court of the United States and shall recover the damages sustained and the cost of the suit. . . .

---

the client preferred not to risk the consequences that could result if a labor dispute did in fact materialize. Thus, Jim pulled his men and equipment off the job. This kind of thing happened perhaps three times a year. About 15 percent of Grayson's contracts (in number and dollar volume) involved working at job sites where union contractors were also performing work. It was at these places that this problem sometimes, although not always, occurred. In addition, Jim noticed that he was sometimes not invited to bid on those jobs where Grayson's presence could provoke a labor dispute. Since Jim usually had a backlog of work, his business had not been substantially hurt by these tactics. However, he was quite concerned about the future if this pressure continued and especially if it should expand.

In April Jim had bid on, and won, a contract with the electric company (that represented about 20 percent or $500,000 of his annual volume) to relocate underground conduits at the intersection of two heavily travelled highways. This work had to be completed before an extensive highway construction program could proceed through the intersection. The relocation expense was borne by the electric company, since it was not reimbursible under state and federal laws. Jim knew that this job would be tailor-made for a labor dispute. Several road contractors, all larger than Grayson, would be working on various phases of the highway project in the vicinity of the intersection. He felt that one of the construction unions would try to get off the job.

A few days after work had been under way, the business agent for the Hoisting Engineers union came by the job site and asked who was handling the relocation contract. Upon learning that it was Grayson, he told Bill Hale, a state highway department inspector assigned to the job, and Jake Ross, an inspector for the general contractor, that he was going to stop all his men from working on the general contractor's project because the electric company was using a nonunion firm. Upon being informed of the above situation, Jim called his lawyer and discussed the problem with him. As a result of his earlier experience with unions, Jim recognized the value of competent legal advice when faced with the possibility of a labor dispute. This lead him to seek the advice of an attorney who specialized in labor relations matters. After describing the history of his situation and the tactics used by the unions, Jim listened to his attorney's response:

There are several aspects of this situation that you need to keep in mind. To begin with, the union pressure you describe is clearly in violation of the secondary boycott provisions of the L.M.R.A. If a union has a labor dispute with an employer and tries to bring pressure against him by directly coercing another party, through a work stoppage for example, then this is a secondary boycott. In your situation the unions have actually been violating the law by their threats of a work stoppage, since this amounts to coercion. In order for you to have the protection of the L.M.R.A., you would have to show that your business has a "substantial" effect on interstate commerce, as defined by the National Labor Relations Board. I would not anticipate any difficulty in that regard. Procedurally, you would file a complaint with the regional director of the N.L.R.B. who should hold a preliminary hearing. His office would subsequently petition a U.S. district court to issue a temporary injunction or restraining order against the union, pending final disposition of the matter by the

N.L.R.B. This order would instruct the union to discontinue their illegal tactics, and they would be subject to contempt proceedings upon failure to observe the order. The injured employer(s) may also sue the union for damages. In conclusion then, you would have a good case at law if the work stoppage does occur.

Unfortunately, however, the practical application is not as simple. An employer involved in a secondary boycott struggle is interested in immediate relief. Every day that passes without relief can result in losses that may not be recoverable through a damage suit. Even though the N.L.R.B. is directed by law to expedite secondary boycott cases, a good union lawyer may be able to cause delays in the procedure. The judge who hears the case is also an important consideration. One judge may be inclined to act quickly and to issue a strongly worded injunction, while another judge may not be quite as sympathetic with the employer. I know of cases where an employer finally won a suit but where the union had forced him out of business by that time.

In any event, you should be prepared to show that you would suffer substantial economic loss if appropriate relief were not forthcoming. I think the minimum time in which you could expect an injunction would be a week, and two weeks or more would probably be a more realistic estimate.

Jim then called Dan Stokes, manager of the electric company's construction department, who had let the contract. The essence of their conversation was as follows:

Jim: Have you been advised yet of the possibility of union trouble at the highway crossing project?

Dan: Yes. I was just getting ready to phone you about it.

Jim: Well, you know how I feel. I'm convinced that the union is just bluffing. My attorney, who specializes in labor matters, says that this would clearly be a secondary boycott and could be stopped with a court injunction.

Dan: I'm inclined to agree with you, and I for one don't want to let the union tell us who we can use as a contractor. Nevertheless, I think we must consider the possibility that they aren't bluffing.

Jim: I agree. What kind of spot would you be in if I stay on the job and if the union does strike the general contractor?

Dan: Well, it could be pretty messy, especially if a walk-out lasted more than just a few days. These developments are entirely possible:

1. Every day that a total work stoppage continues will cost the state and the other contractors a lot of money, about $250,000 a week. There will also be a public reaction due to the inconvenience caused motorists. Those two roads carry a tremendous amount of traffic. All of this could well result in increasing pressure being brought against the electric company by the state to do whatever is necessary to end the work stoppage. As you know, we could not ignore this pressure. To a great extent, our operations (rate structure, job specifications, construction programs, etc.) are regulated by the departments of public utilities and public works. We cannot afford to fight with time;

2. We could be asking for trouble with our own union. It is conceivable, although I think not too likely, that they would go out on a sympathy strike in support of the Hoisting Engineers. It's impossible to tell how this might develop. Then too, we might be tagged by the construction unions as being an "unfair" employer (due to hiring a nonunion contractor), which could lead to the use of harassing tactics such as picketing against us;

3. We could have some internal repercussions. I know that our top management group will be divided on the question with some, including the legal department, advocating that you be displaced from the job, and there will be others, including me and my boss, wanting to stick it out with you at least for a while.

Jim: I see. That's not a very encouraging picture. Well, what is your conclusion?

Dan: This is the way it looks to me right now. I can give you assurance that we will not displace you for two weeks. However, there will be some point beyond that when we would have to come in either with our own crew or a union contractor and get the job moving. How long would it take you to get an injunction against the union?

Jim: My attorney says we may be able to have one issued within a week. But the union would surely try to delay this so it's hard to tell precisely.

Dan: Why don't we sleep on it tonight. Let's meet at the job in the morning so that we will be on hand if the walk-out does materialize. If it does, you will have to tell me what you want to do—move your men out or stay and take the matter to court.

Jim: Okay. See you in the morning.

As he neared the construction site the next morning, Jim continued to be preoccupied with the preceding day's conversation with Dan as well as with some of the possible consequences for his own company.

He could take his men off the job, thereby avoiding conflict with the union and relieving the electric company of pressure. This alternative would not noticeably affect his own competitive situation, at present.

If he chose to fight and if he were able to bring legal action against the union to a successful and early conclusion, then this could be a real victory. Other companies, on whom he depended for business, might be less easily influenced by union pressure. This could mean more business for Grayson.

If he chose to fight and did not win or did not win quickly enough, he would have real problems. His relations with the electric company would be hurt and could well result in less future business from them. His other clients would very likely react in the same manner. And further, the unions might be encouraged to step up their pressure campaign against him.

It was with these thoughts that he arrived at the job and met Dan Stokes. Much to his relief and satisfaction, there was no work stoppage, and the day passed without incident. As several more days passed without any trouble, Jim began to feel that the crisis had passed and that he had accurately assessed the union's lack of willingness to carry out their threat. However, this respite was short-lived.

About a week later it was necessary for Jim to rent a special type of crane from the Rennick Equipment Company to do a particular job. Rennick, who was unionized, also supplied a man to operate the crane. Within hours after the crane had arrived at the site and was in operation, the Hoisting Engineers business agent came by and asked the operator whose job he was on. Upon being told that it was Grayson's, the agent told the operator to stop working since "we've had trouble with this outfit before." The operator called his supervisor at the equipment company who advised him to check with the local headquarters of the union. He did this, and the union officer there told him to follow the business agent's instructions. He talked again to his supervisor, who told him to "do whatever you have to do." The operator then shut down the crane and left the job.

Grayson's crew had to stop work since the job being done by the crane was a necessary preliminary to their continuing. Their inability to continue would have a chain effect on other contractors in the vicinity since they could not proceed beyond a certain point until the relocation work was finished. This effect would begin in about two week's time. Thus, in essence, Jim was now in the same position that he had contemplated a week earlier. He had to either pull off the job or stay and initiate legal action against the union. It was at this point that Jim phoned Dan Stokes (at the beginning of the case) and described the situation. Within the hour he would have to call Dan again and indicate what his course of action would be.

Discussion questions

1. If you were Jim, what course of action would you take? Why?
2. Using cost-benefit analysis, what effect will Jim's decision have on future business?
3. What is the union's objective in the work stoppages? What other methods might they use to accomplish the objective that would not be illegal?

9. Aspen County High School*

The following is part of a conversation between the superintendent of schools and Mr. Don Mason, Aspen County High School principal, that took place at the regular Wednesday meeting of the Aspen County School District board of trustees during the last week of March.

Superintendent: Don, it seems like every time you come to our meeting you've got your hand out for more money. Last month it was money for new band uniforms. Before that you were trying to tell us the athletic teams needed another $2,000 worth of equipment. Now you hit us with this across-the-board raise for your faculty. You know we're working on a very limited budget, and we have other demands that must be met, too.

Don Mason: Of course, it costs money to run a school district. I can understand your problems. But remember, the only way we're going to be able to offer good instruction to this community is by having well-qualified teachers on the staff. And good teachers cost money! Besides, remember you promised us last year when we asked for a raise that we'd get it this year, and . . .

Superintendent: Now, just a minute, Don. We never promised you that you'd get a raise this year. We simply said that it was impossible to give you a raise *last* year because Western Steel had closed down as a result of the strike, and the district's income was decreased substantially.

At that time we thought that Western Steel would soon be operating at full steam and that we would have the funds available for a raise *this year*. As everyone knows only too well, Western still is only operating at about one third capacity. This means that their payroll is only about one third. Quite a few people have moved from the area to get jobs. Business income is low and some of the shops have closed their doors permanently. We just don't have the money in the general fund, and we probably couldn't pass a special bond issue at this late date anyway.

Aspen County School District was a unified district comprised of four elementary schools, two junior high schools, and one high school. The district served the entire population of the county. The major source of income for this small western community was Western Steel. Strikes and slowdowns at Western Steel often had resulted in extreme fluctuations in the population and the financial well-being of the community. As a result of these problems and others the superintendent and the board experienced frequent discord with the teachers and administrators on financial matters.

This case was prepared by Assistant Professor Sherman Tingey of Arizona State University as a basis for class discussion. All rights reserved to the contributors.

At 8:30 A.M. the following Monday, the 37 faculty members and administrators of Aspen High School held their weekly faculty meeting. The meeting was called to order by the vice principal of the high school, Bob Lane.

Bob Lane (vice principal): We have a lot of business to cover in our meeting this morning, but first I think it is appropriate that we hear from Don. As most of you know by now, Don went to bat for the faculty against the board for a salary increase, and he wants to bring this item up first so that everyone will understand exactly how things are progressing.

Don Mason (principal): I met with the board last Thursday and asked about that raise they had promised us. They gave the same old excuse of no funds. It looks like we're going to have a tough battle on our hands if we expect to get an across-the-board raise this year. Since their major objection appears to be a lack of funds, the teachers' welfare committee has been working over the weekend on possible ways that the funds can be obtained. They have worked up a couple of alternatives that can be presented. The most attractive one involves not receiving your three summer month's checks in one lump sum in June as some of you have been doing. Phil, why don't you explain just how that is going to work?

Phil, the chairman of the teachers' welfare committee, then explained to the group that approximately one half of the teachers had been exercising the option to receive their three summer checks in a lump sum at the beginning of the summer. If receipt of these checks could be postponed until after June 30, the expense would appear in the next fiscal year. This could be a permanent postponement. If only 75 percent of those now exercising this option were willing to forgo this advantage, enough funds would be created to finance the desired salary increase. A hand vote of those who were willing to give up this option indicated that 16 of the 18 teachers involved would probably be able to rearrange their financial affairs to support the proposal.

Don Mason: Thanks very much for your support. I'll present this proposal to the board this Thursday and see if we can't work something out. Bob and I were talking just yesterday, and we both expressed the opinion that we have an excellent staff here at the high school, and we think that you deserve a raise in the salary schedule. Besides, Bob and I are on a schedule, too, and we'd benefit from a raise the same as you would. Both "X" County and "Y" County received schedule increases this year, and our county is falling behind.

The meeting was turned over to Bob who conducted the remaining business. That same afternoon a group of teachers were discussing the situation in the teachers' lounge after school.

Teacher A: I heard Bill [an English teacher] say that he was going to investigate the possibility of a position at Sacramento if it looked like we weren't going to get a raise this year. Do you think we'll get the raise?

Teacher B: Naw, we probably won't. But I wouldn't leave because of that alone. Money isn't everything. I think the kind of work environment we have here is worth something. Not very often will you find a school where both the principal and vice principal will stand behind their teachers and support them 100 percent. I think that's one of the reasons Don and Bob are so well-liked by the teachers.

Teacher C: I'll agree with that! I'll never forget that incident with Bob Lane when I first came here. You remember that he asked me to be the lettermen's club advisor? None of the coaches wanted the job because it takes a lot of time, and the kids are pretty rough to handle. Well, anyway, when he introduced me to the club members, he said that the administration would stand behind me in whatever I wanted to do as long as I thought it was for the best benefit of the club.

Later, when I told the club members that the initiation had to be toned down considerably because of the danger of seriously hurting someone, they stormed right into Bob Lane's office complaining. They figured that since they had to go through all that rough stuff to be initiated, it was only fair for them to "get revenge" against the new members. Boy, it really made me feel good when I found out Bob had told them "If that's the way your advisor wants it, then that's the way its going to be." It surely made my job a lot easier from then on.

Teacher A: Do you remember that problem I had in the boys' cooking class right at the first of the year?

Teacher B: No, what was that?

Teacher A: Well, it really wasn't a problem. I was nervous since this was my first teaching job. We were supposed to be making cookies. Two boys were laughing and goofing around, and somehow they broke a bottle of milk. I was so upset that I sent them to the office. Really, it was just an accident, but Don gave the boys a talking to anyway and told them not to goof off in class. I realized afterward that sending them to the office was too strong a discipline measure, but I was surely glad that Don stuck up for me anyway.

Teacher D: I really think a lot of Don and Bob. Remember last fall when I was teaching that adult evening class in bookkeeping? Dayle [another teacher] and I had gone out for a little deer hunting after school one afternoon. We shot a three-point near the top of Hogback Mountain, and it took us a lot longer than we expected to get that deer out. The class I was teaching was supposed to meet at 7:00 and we didn't get back to town until about 7:30. When Don phoned my home about 7:20 and found out that I was still out deer hunting, he said, "I'll tell the students to go ahead and work on their own. He's probably shot a big one and is having difficulty getting it out."

When I got to class 40 minutes late all my students were still there waiting for a deer hunting story. After class I met Don in the hall, and he asked just one question: "Did you get your deer?"

The following Thursday at the board of trustees' meeting, Principal Don Mason presented the proposal of the teachers' welfare committee in an effort to show the board members where they could get the funds for a salary increase. After considerable discussion of the proposal, the board said they would take it into consideration but still didn't feel a salary increase would be forthcoming.

At this point in the meeting, the board revealed to Don Mason that during the week they had decided to set his salary for the next year at $12,000. They emphasized that he would be receiving $900 increase in addition to the regular yearly increment of $400. They also emphasized that they expected a lot more cooperation from him in the future.

Mason expressed his thanks for the raise but also expressed his opinion that the teachers should also receive a salary schedule increase. He then rose to leave. As he was leaving, he heard one member of the board whisper, "Boy, talk about ungrateful!"

At the next board meeting, Mason had arranged for members of the teachers' welfare committee to meet before the board in an effort to convince the board members of the necessity of a salary schedule raise and that the means for the raise were accessible. After the presentation by the committee, the board said they would consider this information and requested time to verify the data the committee was using. They also expressed their opinion that there was little hope of obtaining raises this year.

Three days later all the teachers at the high school received notification of a special faculty meeting to be held immediately after school for the purpose of discussing recent events in the negotiations of salary increases.

As some of the teachers met in the hall on the way to the meeting, Teacher "G" was asked if he knew what was going on. He replied, "I don't know for sure, but Bob Lane said it was 'something big' and for everyone to be sure to attend."

Teacher H: Maybe we're going to get our raise after all!

Teacher G: Not a chance! You know as well as I do the board isn't going to let Don tell them what they should do. Something else must be in the air.

As Bob Lane, the vice principal, called the meeting to order, some of the teachers were commenting on the absence of Principal Don Mason.

Bob Lane: I think everyone is here now. We've called this special meeting because we think that you should know exactly what has been going on during the past few day. Apparently Don has pushed the board a little too hard for salary increases for the teachers. The night before last one of the board members called me at my home around 9:00 and asked me if I could come over to his house. When I arrived, three of the board members were there to greet me. They asked how I liked my job as an administrator in the high school, and I told them I really enjoyed my work here. Then they asked me if I would like to be principal of the high school next year with a nice increase in salary. [Several oh's and ah's were heard in the group.] All I could think of was: What about Don? I asked them if Don had quit, and they said, "No, but we aren't going to offer him a contract for next year." [Looks of astonishment and surprise appeared on many faces as a few teachers leaned over and whispered to each other.]

When I asked them why they weren't offering Don a contract, they said it was personal, and they didn't want to discuss it with anyone. Well, I didn't hesitate to tell them if they didn't offer Don a contract for next year, they needn't offer me one either because I wouldn't sign it. Now I think this is information that you should know. I think Don finds himself in this position because of his efforts to help you teachers. If there is any way that you can support Don in his fight, I certainly think you should, and I know that he would welcome your help.

At this point Bob Lane left the room, and Teacher "P," the president of the High School Teachers' Association, took over the meeting. The room was filled with loud talk and excitement.

Teacher P: May I have your attention, please! I know that this is quite an unexpected turn of events. It surprised me as much as it did you when Bob explained the situation to me about an hour ago. But you haven't heard the the whole story yet. Don met with the board in a special meeting that was called at Don's request last evening. He specifically requested reasons for his dismissal, but the board said they did not have to give any reasons for their actions.

Contracts will be offered on the first of May—that's about ten days away. What can we do to help Don?

Teacher D (jumping up excitedly): Well, I'll tell you one thing! If they fire Don they can find a replacement for me, too. I don't want to work for a board that can fire someone without any reason other than disagreeing with them.

Teacher E: I have no ties here. The main reason I stay is because I like to teach under Don and Bob. If they go, I'll go too, and I'd like to see the rest of you do the same.

The faculty meeting continued for another hour. It was determined by secret ballot that approximately 90 percent of the faculty would be able and willing to support Principal Mason in the following manner: If Don Mason was not offered a contract, the teachers would not sign their contracts. It was also decided that this information should be conveyed to the board immediately.

On May 1, the teachers received their contracts in sealed envelopes. Also in each mailbox was a mimeographed note saying Don Mason had not received a contract. All contracts were to be returned to the board of trustees by May 15.

During the next two weeks the following appeared in the local newspaper:

Dear Editor:

I read in the *Daily Times* this evening that Mr. Don Mason has requested four times a statement from the school board as to why his contract was not renewed as principal of the Aspen High School.

I do not know much about civil law, but I do know of a moral law that reads: "Do unto others as you wish them to do unto you." Any person who has been employed in a school system whether principal or teacher for a period of years is definitely entitled, as a matter of courtesy, to be given an explanation as to why his contract is not renewed.

I feel this very unjust to the man and the teachers as a whole. No teacher can feel secure under an administration of this caliber. I think the public should demand an explanation. Any innocent member of the school board who sits back and lets this go on is as guilty as the rest.

Sincerely,
A Parent

The following letter was signed by approximately one fourth of the 650 students at Aspen High School.

Dear Editor:

What is the school board trying to do by dismissing Mr. Mason without giving any reasons? We feel that Mr. Mason has done an excellent job of building up our high school.

We have been told that better than 90 percent of our teachers have refused to sign their contracts for the coming year. This would result in drastic conditions for our school system. If this happens, our school could possibly become a nonaccredited school. This could pose many problems for the seniors planning to attend college.

Parents! Are we the only ones concerned about these problems?

A citizens' committee had been formed to investigate the current school "crisis." This committee had requested the investigating services of Dr. Williams, an executive from the state education association. A special meeting was held at which Dr. Williams reported his initial findings to the citizens' committee. The newspaper printed the following as part of the report of that meeting:

It was stated during the meeting that there has been a complete breakdown of the communications between teachers, administrators, and school board members, thus creating a crisis in the education system. There has been unwillingness on the part of the school board, it was said, to discuss the situations as they arise with the persons involved. In addition . . . Dr. Williams stated that he had checked with attorneys on such a problem, and he was now certain that a school board has the right to refuse to give new contracts to teachers without having to give an explanation of the refusal. However, to prevent the type of breakdown that now exists here, that person should be called in and an explanation given as to the cause for action.

Five days prior to May 15, the date the contracts had to be returned to the board, the local paper printed the following in its editorial column:

This week appears to be the week of decision, for the contracts are supposed to be returned to the school board within five days. The board is apparently counting upon most of the good teachers signing up by the deadline.

Thinking on the basis of the present situation and eliminating what is already "water under the bridge," there seem to be three things that could happen: (1) The school board could reverse its decision regarding the principal, or (2) the teachers could decide they want their jobs even more than they want victory in this strange fight, or (3) the board and the teachers could remain adamant, and the board could attempt to recruit as many new teachers as needed.

Discussion questions

1. Analyze the possible reasons *why* the various parties (school board, principal, vice principal, and teachers) acted as they did under the circumstances.
2. In your opinion, what motivated the board to offer Principal Mason an increased salary initially and to reverse this decision later? If you were a teacher in the high school, how would you have reacted to these two board actions?
3. What incidents involving Principal Mason and/or Vice Principal Lane illustrate desirable or undesirable administrative leadership?
4. "Grave dangers exist for the individual in giving too much loyalty to a leader or a group." Discuss.
5. *a.* What, action, if any, do you recommend be taken by:
   1. The board
   2. Principal Mason
   3. Vice Principal Lane
   4. The teachers
   b. What action do you *think* each party took? Why?
6. What *policies* do you recommend be adopted to help eliminate future crisis situations such as this one?

J. MANAGING THE DIFFICULT EMPLOYEE

1. Epperson Foundry

Epperson Foundry is a small firm located in Huntington, West Virginia. It employs about 55 people, with most of them men in the foundry proper.

The company was founded by Harris Epperson in 1910 and is currently run by Douglas Epperson. The shop is run by three foremen and a plant superintendent.

Recently, the plant superintendent, Ken Fulhage, called a friend, Professor Gainey, at the nearby business school and discussed a problem with him at lunch.

Fulhage: You know, Jim, I've been around. I've seen all kinds of problems in my time. But I guess I'm getting old—I'm 59. I ran into a new one and ask your help. One of my foremen, Carl Idecker, called me over and told me about one of his men, Jerry Kiehl. Kiehl is a good worker, about 23. One day recently he was acting really strange. He seemed to be in another world, dropped things, and so forth. Idecker tried to smell his breath; he hadn't been drinking. But Carl found him in the rest room later, and he was almost out on drugs.

Kiehl's never done that before. We sent him home. I don't know anything about drugs except they scare me. I suppose Kiehl will become a zombie or something. What do I do? If he can shape up, I'd like to keep him on. You don't find many good young workers like him these days.

Gainey: What day did this happen?

Fulhage: Last Friday afternoon, and if it'll help you any in thinking about it, we got it out of him that he was "spaced out on coke," whatever that means.

Requirement. You are Professor Gainey: How do you proceed and what do you recommend? What policy should Epperson have about drug usage on the job?

2. Jack Shuford*

One of AMC's (Air Material Command) AMMA[1] operations was the setting for the events described. Actually, they occurred in a subdivision of the maintenance engineering division. This subdivision was made up of four branches, inline engines, reciprocating engines, training engines, and accessories.[2]

EXHIBIT 1
PARTIAL ORGANIZATION CHART—MAINTENANCE
ENGINEERING DIVISION

Jack Shuford was a maintenance technician in the inline engine branch. He was a disabled veteran, having been injured when his tank was hit by an enemy bomb in the E.T.O. Following the war he had completed three years of mechanical engineering in a large northern university; and, because of this technical training in his background, he was qualified for any maintenance position in the subdivision. However, Shuford was having difficulty in his position; and, from rumors circulating within the office, it was a result of personal differences between him and his section chief.

Now, Major Bates, chief of the reciprocating engine branch, informed Ralph Byrum, under his line of authority as section chief of Pratt & Whitney engines, that Shuford had applied for transfer to his section to

---

This case was developed and prepared by Professor Curtis E. Tate, Jr., College of Business Administration, University of Georgia. Reprinted by permission.

[1] Term used in referring to any single installation in the AMC.

[2] See Exhibit 1.

fill a vacancy that existed. Byrum requested Major Bates that he be permitted to interview Shuford before approving the transfer. It was agreed. But Byrum went on TDY[3] for three days, and when he returned, Shuford had been transferred into his section. He immediately sought out Major Bates with a question about the failure to grant his request for an interview. Bates arrogantly answered that as the branch chief he did much as he pleased.

The Pratt & Whitney engine section had been organized by Byrum into units in which each technician was, to some degree, a specialist. For example, one technician was responsible for the overhaul of the engines, one for in-service operation, another for accessories. The vacancy filled by Shuford was that of in-service operation.

Swallowing his resentment, Byrum left the branch office. He greeted Shuford and welcomed him into the section. He described the organization of the section and the responsibilities of the in-service operation unit. Also, since Shuford was new in this job, he was welcome to come to the chief's desk at any time to discuss his problems and to seek advisory assistance. But, when Byrum had completed his orientation remarks, he was almost knocked off his feet. Shuford made this comment:

I am a disabled war vet; I had my kidneys torn loose and I was hospitalized for six months. So, I have no intention of doing anything, because, the way I have it figured, "Uncle" owes me a living. Besides, my dad told me when I was a young boy that there are only two kinds of people in the world: those who don't work and the . . . fools who do.—'And, Son, I'm not raising a . . . fool.'

"Is this what I can expect?" asked Byrum.

The answer was affirmative.

As the results of the orientation were told to Major Bates, Byrum learned the problem was his and he would have to work it out.

Discussion questions

1. You are Mr. Byrum. How will you handle Jack?
2. Why is the company putting up with Jack's attitude? Is it for the benefit of the company?

3. How High the Doc?*

Ms. Barret was head nurse of the operating room at Mountain View Hospital. She was experiencing some difficulties in scheduling scrub tech-

---

[3] Temporary duty away from the installation.

* This case was prepared by Professor Richard B. Chase for the University of Arizona as a basis for class discussion. Presented at the Intercollegiate Case Development Workshop, University of Santa Clara, October 18–20, 1973. Reprinted with permission.

nicians and circulating R.N.s to certain surgery rooms. People who had been doing fine during one surgery had come to the nursing station during clearance of the operating room to ask to be relieved of their next surgery. They complained of feeling dizzy or just in need of a break. This often put the R.N. at the desk on the spot as she had difficulty in replacing personnel in the middle of the day. Requests were always granted, and the employees would break for 15 minutes to an hour and then ask to be reassigned.

After about two weeks of this, the problem was brought to Ms. Barret's attention, and she told the nurses to send all relief requests to her personally. Gary, a certified O.R. technician who had been with the hospital for two years, was the first to come to her with a request.

Barret: Gary, what seems to be the problem?

Gary: Well, Ms. Barret, I just don't feel very good, and I'd just like to lie down for a while.

Barret: If you don't feel good, you'd better take the rest of the day off.

Gary: I don't think I need to do that.

Barret: Gary, can you tell me what's going on around here?

Gary: Well, most people just don't like to work for Dr. Collins. He's pretty slow and seems to be out of it most of the time.

Barret: Have you talked to Ms. Johnston, the circulating R.N., about this?

Gary: I've talked to her and Dr. Martin. Ms. Johnston gave me a hard time as usual. She says I am getting too big for my britches, and if I don't like the situation, I can ask for a transfer. Dr. Martin says that he's with Dr. Collins most of the time, and he looks fine to him.

Barret: Thank you Gary, this will be kept confidential.

Ms. Barret went to ask Ms. Johnston to come in to see her. After four days without seeing her, Ms. Barret went to find her.

Barret: Ms. Johnston I'd like to ask you some questions. I asked to see you four days ago.

Johnston: I have been trying to find time to see you.

Barret: I have some questions to ask you about Dr. Collins. Do you feel he's competent in surgery?

Johnston: As far as I know.

Barret: Have you ever seen him overly tired or not feeling well?

Johnston: Well, he did come in last week hung over, but that was an emergency. He was on call and had just been to a cocktail party the night before. That's what those techs are complaining about, isn't it?

Barret: How many times has this happened?

Johnston: Well, I don't know. But if Dr. Collins has any problems, Dr. Martin is always there to take over. I always circulate for him, and I know my business. The techs are complaining because they don't like to be told what to do. They just can't take orders, and Dr. Collins gives it to them when they don't. They think just because they have been through a few cholecystectomies they can start questioning the doctors and R.N.'s orders.

Barret: Thank you, Ms. Johnston, that is all the questions I have.

Two days later Gary gave his notice and quit working three weeks later. Relief requests stopped coming in, but two other O.R. techs gave their notice. Absenteeism rose.

Ms. Barret scheduled Ms. Johnston to work under another doctor and assigned Ms. McEvers to circulate for Dr. Collins. Later that day Ms. Barret went to visit the O.R. room where Dr. Collins was working. There she found Dr. Collins, head anesthesiologist, Dr. Martin assisting, and Ms. Johnston circulating as usual. She inquired into where Ms. McEvers was as she was scheduled for this surgery. She was informed by Dr. Martin that this operation could involve complication, and they needed an experienced circulator.

Barret: Dr. Martin, you have every right to request certain circulators. I would appreciate some notice before you tamper with room scheduling.

Martin: I am giving you notice that I would like to have Ms. Johnston circulate for me and Dr. Collins.

Barret: Due to some difficulties in scheduling, Ms. McEvers will circulate for you for the rest of the week. After that if I have your request in writing, I will have no choice but to assign Ms. Johnston to you, scheduling problems or not.

Ms. McEvers worked out the week under the two doctors, and at the end of the week Ms. Barret asked to see her in her office to inquire into Dr. Collins' competence.

McEvers: I refuse to make waves here so I want this confidential. Dr. Collins often looks hung over in the morning when he does his patients preop. I wouldn't stand up in court and swear he had been drinking, but he sometimes smells of alcohol.

Barret: Have you ever inquired into his behavior?

McEvers: I asked Dr. Martin about it. He always has some story of Dr. Collins just being called in or not feeling up to par.

Later that week Ms. Barret confronted Dr. Martin with this information.

Martin: Those are pretty serious charges you're leveling at Dr. Collins.

Barret: No one is accusing anybody of anything at this point.

Martin: What you're saying could have serious repercussions around here. If anyone got wind of this, it could look very bad, not only for us but for the profession and the hospital.

Barret: I am concerned here with the patient's safety.

Martin: No one is in danger. Ms. Johnston and I are always with him.

Barret: That isn't the point.

Martin: Take it to the chief of staff, then, but let me give you some advice. You need some hard facts to make anything stick. You need the testimony of at least four nurses, and under the circumstances that might be hard to get. You might like to know Dr. Collins is retiring next year.

Discussion questions

1. You are Ms. Barret, how would you handle the situation?
2. Alcoholism is a problem in many organizations, but in a hospital the problem is magnified. How can the hospital make such situations easier to handle?
3. Why are Dr. Collins' co-workers covering for him? Are they justifiable reasons?

EXHIBIT 1
MOUNTAIN VIEW HOSPITAL (185 activated beds)

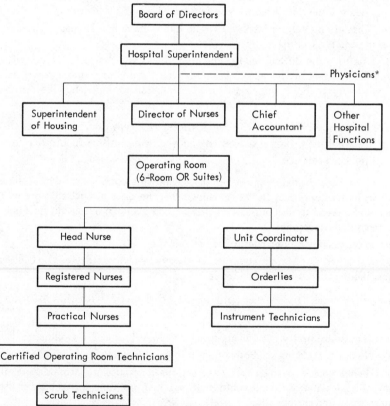

* Physicians are at this hospital to use the facilities and are often considered more in a staff than line position. They are answerable to themselves and the chief of staff.

EXHIBIT 2
PHYSICIANS

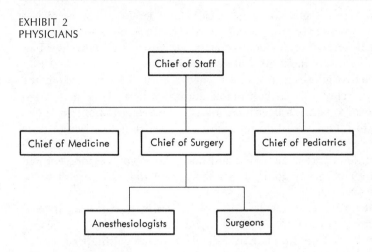

4. Paul Anyon

The personnel manager, Charles Mazze, has a problem. One of the symphony's best violinists, Paul Anyon, seems to be drinking to excess.

Paul is 42 years old, married with two teenage daughters, and lives comfortably in Hinsdale, Illinois, comfortably as a classical musician's salary will allow that is. Besides his position as third violinist at the symphony, he gives private lessons in his home and teaches music at a nearby college.

Paul had begun his career with the symphony in the seventh chair. By an extraordinary amount of practice, he had worked his way up slowly, a chair every other year. Until two years ago, he was second chair. About this time, a brilliant young (28) violinist had applied for a job with the orchestra. The conductor had hired him, R. Wu, as second chair. Paul was moved back to third chair at that time.

Charles had known Paul for years. They were good friends. Occasionally, they'd have "a few" after work. But he had no idea how badly Paul's problem had become until recently.

At a recent social event, Paul had become obviously drunk and was getting abusive with one of the ladies on the Women's Symphony Committee. Chuck decided the best way to help was to take Paul home. He had a terrible time getting him in his car. First Paul denied he was drunk and said he wanted to stay. Then he said he could get home himself and didn't want to leave his car there. Finally, he agreed to Chuck driving him home. But at every stop light, he'd roll down his window and yell abuses at drivers. In some cases, he'd get out of the car and try to punch the drivers nearby, all of whom were total strangers. There were some difficult moments for Paul that night.

About two weeks later, Chuck got a call about 9:30 P.M. Chuck picked up the phone downstairs and his wife Kay the extension. Paul, in a very slurred speech, said, "Hey Chuck, come on down to the McAreavy Bar. I've got two broads all lined up. It'll be a great time."

Chuck tried to joke him out of it. Then one of the girls got on the line. She said, "Hey, mister, you better get down here. This guy's been feeding us drinks, and it's been OK, but our dudes are about to show, and they'll kill him if they find him with us. They're both twice his size and half his age."

Chuck hung up. Kay came down and said, "Look you've done enough for that lush. You're not going down there with that drunk and those tramps. You stay home."

Chuck put on his coat and left. When he returned at 1 A.M., he had some explaining to do to Kay. He'd found Paul with two 21-year-old black girls in a back booth. He had a devil of a time getting Paul out of there. Paul insisted they bar hop 'til they find some more girls. By 12:45, he'd passed out in Chuck's car, and he and Paul's wife Rita got him in the house.

Recently, the concertmaster has asked Chuck about Paul and remarked that he might be headed for fourth chair soon.

Requirement. You are Chuck. Do you discuss Paul's problem with the concertmaster or the conductor? What, if anything, do you do for Paul?

5. Robert Miller—I

Robert Miller is employed as a sales engineer for a large computer manufacturer and distributor. Robert is the son of an engineer who emigrated from England after World War II.

His family is large (five brothers and sisters) so Robert had to work his way through high school and college. He went to a private high school and then to the University of South Carolina's pre-engineering. So he transferred to a small private college nearby and completed a degree in accounting and business administration. His grades were good, if not outstanding.

He had worked his way through college by working for a small manufacturer of conveyors. The firm offered Robert a good job at a high salary for the industry. They had been very pleased with his work.

Robert took a job with the computer firm instead, for he thought computers were a real growth industry that paid well and would make him a wealthy man.

Robert's politics were moderate Democrat. He belonged to a main line Protestant church and attended regularly. Most of his friends considered him to be almost staid. He had always worn his hair short, for example.

After the training program, he began his job of selling computers. The company enforced a dress code that required wearing of suits, hats, white shirts, and ties when calling on customers. Robert had heard that it had relaxed this regarding work in the office. So one day he wore his new suit with a yellow shirt and a nice tie to the office on a day where he had paperwork to do.

Shortly after his arrival, Janice Trueblood sent for him. Janice was his immediate superior.

Janice: Bob, you're not going to believe this, but Kemal has asked me to speak to you (Kemal Tschirgi is the manager of the operation at Columbia). I guess he's of the old school. But I am to remind you that this company's image is at stake when you don't wear white shirts, a hat, a suit, and half length dark socks.

Robert: Janice, it's Friday, you're pulling my leg.

Janice: No, in fact, he asked me to hand you a copy of the dress code—here it is—and note in your personnel file that you blatantly have violated the code. He suggests that you find a more mature way to exhibit your demand for individuality or at least a different time to do so.

Robert: In the army, we had an expression for this kind of thing whose first initials are C.S.

Janice: I agree with you, but believe me, he's serious. I pointed out that you were the best young salesman we had. That didn't cut it. He talked about the company spirit and all that. So be warned.

Robert: I feel warned all right.

Kemal Tschirgi is a man of 55, who graduated from the "school of hard knocks." He'd worked his way up from delivery boy when he was 21. He lets everyone know that. He's been characterized as a firm, but fair, supervisor who always lets an employee know where he stands.

Janice Trueblood is a career woman, aged 35, a college graduate in mathematics, well liked and considered quite competent.

Requirement. You are Ray Buffa, personnel manager at Columbia. Bob has just described the incident to you at lunch. Bob has asked you to comment on the whole incident from the company's point of view. Ray had just filed the memo on Bob in his personnel file.

Robert Miller—II

Robert didn't really take the incident too seriously. He was still doing by far the best selling job in the division, as Janice's reports made clear.

Employees at the company were expected to do their share of public service work. So when he was asked to go on a kids' show to explain computers for ten minutes to the audience, he accepted.

He'd read somewhere that blue shirts looked better on T.V. On his way to the studio, he stopped by to get a few mock-ups to use as training aids. He talked briefly with Janice and was on his way. He was at the office 20 minutes or so. On his way to the T.V. studio, his mind was occupied alternatively with what he was going to say and how much this publicity might mean to sales.

Back at the office, Priscilla Forsgren, Mr. Tschirgi's secretary delivered a memo to Janice Trueblood. It said:

Janice, I saw young Miller here in that blue shirt earlier. This was obviously a deliberate flaunting of my authority. No man can be a good company man and succeed here with his troublemaking attitude. Before you say anything about how good he is, I want to make it clear that this case is closed. You are to talk with Ray Buffa and arrange his immediate termination.

Janice was very upset. She dropped by to see her boss. But Mr. Tschirgi's response was to imply that she might have more than a supervisory relation going with Robert by the way she was acting.

Requirement. You are Ray Buffa. Janice has come to you and asked for advice. She also has hinted that you might intercede to save a good employee. How do you proceed?

6. Wilson Distributors Company (A)*

On October 24, 1967, Mr. Donald Wilson, vice president of personnel and labor relations of Wilson Distributors Company, was faced with the problem of deciding what action, if any, to take against a company truck driver, Thomas Bolino. Bolino had been hired by the company approximately six years earlier. He had worked for about one month as a delivery truck driver and then had been transferred to the warehouse where he had worked for approximately one year. At the end of that period he had bid for and received another delivery truck driver job which he still held. The job consisted of transporting the company's products from the warehouse to the customers.

Recently, the company had been informed by two of its customers

---

* This case was prepared by Michael Jay Jedel, research assistant, under the supervision of Professor Thomas M. Kennedy, as a basis for class discussion rather than to illustrate either effective or ineffective handling of an administrative situation. Copyright © 1968 by the President and Fellows of Harvard College.

and several of its competitors' salesmen that Bolino was offering to sell company merchandise to customers on his delivery route at prices far below the regular prices quoted by the company's salesmen. After reviewing the evidence presented to him by company officials, Wilson was convinced that Bolino was guilty of this offense. He wondered what he should do about it.

BACKGROUND

The Wilson Distributors Company was a family-owned wholesale distributor to lumber dealers of windows, doors, and related products. It was started in 1904 and in 1967 operated three warehouses, with overall sales of $15 million. Its main office and largest warehouse (sales of $8 million) were located in Chicago. Initially, Wilson was a retailer, then moved into wholesale distribution, and then into manufacturing, mainly through assembly. In recent years, company officials had decided to limit their operations to wholesale distribution because of the high labor costs they had incurred as a manufacturer. By 1967 incidental manufacturing operations such as the glazing of purchased glass and the finishing of various pieces of lumber were a very minor part of overall activity in each warehouse.

The company employed 300 people of whom 175 were in Chicago, including 55 shop personnel (of whom 30 were assemblers), 83 employees in warehousing and shipping (including 18 drivers), and 12 salesmen (classified as office personnel). All nonsupervisory warehouse and shop employees belong to the Carpenter's union, which had won bargaining rights in 1948. In the past five years, the level of employment had remained constant. There had been no layoffs or terminations because of lack of work and only four disciplinary discharges. The union had appealed only one of the discharges to arbitration, and in that case the company's action had been upheld by the arbitrator.

Since the company's primary activity was distribution of assembled products, the Chicago warehouse was usually full of merchandise. As orders were received, they were recorded on order forms which were forwarded to the appropriate departments for processing. When the materials for a particular order were ready for delivery, they were collected at the shipping dock. The shippers were responsible for what was then loaded onto each truck. Normally, the driver who was to make the deliveries then backed up his truck to the loading platform and the shippers loaded it.[1] Occasionally, the truck driver assisted the shipper.

---

[1] Drivers on the late afternoon shift might sometimes arrive at work and find someone else had already backed up their truck to the loading platform, and the shippers had begun loading it.

Sometimes there were no shippers immediately available, and the driver was trusted to load his own truck. Once the truck was loaded, the driver delivered the materials to the company's lumberyard customer. Under a company policy begun about eight years ago, employees who owned their own homes could purchase a limited amount of company materials at reduced cost for use in their homes.[2] With the exception of these personal purchases, all the materials were delivered from the warehouse in company trucks to the lumberyard companies.

THE PILFERAGE PROBLEM

In the latter part of 1965, management heard through numerous rumors and reports that merchandise was leaving the Chicago warehouse without accompanying order forms. When the annual physical inventory check was concluded in December, company executives discovered that they had suffered inventory losses of approximately $40,000.

Management was of the opinion that such a large loss could not have been due to errors in shipments. Likewise it was convinced that it was not the result of thieves breaking in from the outside because the warehouse was completely surrounded by a high fence and guards were on duty constantly. The company concluded that some of its drivers and warehousemen were colluding to steal and resell company goods.

The reports from customers and competitors regarding Bolino were not the first that the company had had concerning attempts of its drivers to sell its merchandise at low prices. In one earlier case a customer had reported that a driver had offered to sell merchandise to his yardman at ridiculously low prices. The customer had claimed that he had threatened his yardman with dismissal if he bought any of the "stolen merchandise." In another earlier case a customer had reported that a driver had approached him directly and had offered to sell him company products "for cash" at very low prices. In still another earlier incident it had been reported that one of the drivers had had business cards printed with his own name and that of a fictitious company through which he proposed to sell merchandise at below normal prices. Although management investigated all of these earlier cases, it did not believe that it had sufficient evidence to move against the suspected employees. The company tried rotating employees among the various routes in order to make it difficult for those who were suspected of selling to build up regular customers. This procedure, however, was discontinued because it worked against the company's desire to build long-term good relationships between the drivers and the customers.

---

[2] Bolino did not own his own house.

THE COMPANY HIRES A SECURITY CONSULTANT

Further checks in the spring of 1966 indicated that the inventory losses were continuing. That summer, an employee confirmed management's impressions that the pilferage was the result of collusion between some of the drivers and some of the warehouse workers. As a result, late that summer the company hired Security Advisers Associates (SAA), a firm which specialized in company security matters, to conduct a complete investigation and make recommendations. SAA's study which included a review of company policies and security practices was made known to all personnel. As a part of the study a number of employees were interviewed. As the study began, R. Steven Wilson, Jr., president of Wilson Distributors, sent the following letter to the company's supervisory personnel:

In recent inventories we have found the actual count of certain items of stock to be quite a bit lower than our stock records showed that we should have.

We did not follow this up at the time, as we felt the shortages were possibly due to clerical differences in our stock records. Recently, however, we have checked several of these items that have been consistently short, and we find that shortages also exist in the first eight months of this year.

Of course, our stock material is no different than cash. We have periodic audits made of our books and records in the office, which is good business practice, but up to now we have not followed a similar audit approach in the warehouse.

The continued existence of the above condition, added to information received from the outside that our material is being sold by some employees at ridiculously low prices, brings us to the point where we must take action.

We have, therefore, engaged Security Advisers Associates, investigative consultants, to make a security survey.

By November of 1966, the consultants concluded their study. Some of the changes which they recommended to management to stop the illegal disappearance of materials were as follows:

1. Start checking the truck loading process on a random basis;
2. Install a guard house at the gates and a procedure for checking materials entering and leaving;
3. Institute prehiring checks on all prospective employees;
4. Arrange for a larger loading area on the shipping platform so that when goods are left on the platform to await loading there is no confusion about which truck they are for, and so that supervisors can be sure no extra materials are being placed on trucks;
5. Check the shipping operations during the lunch hour break;
6. Make it an ironclad rule that a trucker may not load his truck.

Company officials put the first three of these suggestions into effect but decided not to implement the rest. They agreed that the loading area was too small and confused and thus comparatively easy for pilferage but felt it would be too costly to enlarge it significantly. Similarly, they chose not to prohibit any driver from loading his own truck, even though there were no available shippers, although they recognized certain security problems. Management also decided against checking the shipping area during the noon hour. They did not consider this a serious security problem since there was usually a lot of activity at the warehouse during the lunch hour, and someone trying to steal materials was likely to be seen by another employee or a commercial visitor.

THE RUSSO DISCHARGE

In September 1967, company officials uncovered a serious shortage of one of their products. This product was one which had also been disappearing in large quantities in the two previous years, so management believed that the pilferage problem was continuing. Early in October, the manager of one of the company's lumberyard customers notified the Wilson management that one of its drivers, Anthony Russo, had delivered some company materials to one of the lumberyard employees. This lumberyard was on Russo's regular route, but he had not been scheduled to make any stops there that day. The materials were transferred to a private garage in another part of the city the next day, Saturday. Shortly thereafter, local police entered the garage with a search warrant and recovered stolen company material worth approximately $1,000. Company officials examined the stolen material and found that the boxes had been marked for a company customer on another route, but the order numbers which had been written beside the customer's name were fictitious. A local handwriting specialist, who had frequently given expert testimony in court, was retained by the company, and she was able to match handwriting on the box with that of one of the company's warehousemen, Jack Blake.

While company officials immediately discharged Russo, they decided not to take any immediate action against Blake. They wanted to be positive before they confronted him, and they also hoped to discover first whether others in the warehouse had colluded to steal company property.

No court action was initiated against Russo. The lumberyard manager did not want to be identified as the informer. He indicated that although one of his employees had agreed to take material stolen from Wilson the employee was a trusted one of the lumberyard, and one they did not wish to antagonize. Management believed civil action against Russo would be fruitless without the lumberyard manager's testimony.

About two weeks later, Blake purchased some company materials for his own use and then told his supervisor he was leaving work early to take his wife and baby to the hospital. Management asked their security consultants to follow him, and they traced him to a bar where he was observed transferring the materials to another man's car. After remaining at the bar for several hours, Blake left and went to another bar where he worked evenings. He remained there for his night job. Management suspended Blake for three days for lying as to the reason he had to leave work and for breaking company rules by giving to another person the material that he had purchased at low rates for his own use.

When they told him of his suspension, company officials also questioned him about the stolen material they had uncovered and said that they had good reason to believe that he was involved. They told him about the results of the handwriting analysis they had performed and urged him to admit he had colluded to steal the materials. He denied stealing the material and refused to implicate others. When Blake did not report back to work after his three-day suspension, he was fired. Neither Russo, Blake, nor the union entered a grievance.

THE CASE AGAINST BOLINO

Throughout the early part of October 1967, John Wilson, vice president of sales, had been receiving information from the salesmen of other companies that Wilson drivers were again selling company goods at unusually low prices. On the morning of October 14, a customer told him that the company's truck driver, Thomas Bolino, had offered to sell company merchandise below cost to one of the employees of the customer. Accompanied by a representative of SAA, Wilson visited the customer's place of business. Both the customer and his employee told them that Bolino had offered to sell the employee merchandise at about half price.

Also on October 14, Alan Conway, treasurer and credit manager of the company, received a call from another customer claiming that the company's regular driver, Bolino, had offered to sell him company merchandise at a substantial discount. Three days later, another SAA investigator interviewed this customer. The customer positively identified Bolino from a photograph taken by SAA consultants and repeated that Bolino had approached him with an offer of merchandise at half price. In his report of this interview to the Wilson management, the SAA consultant stated that he was sure the customer was telling the truth.

On the morning of October 24, Donald Wilson was becoming increasingly concerned about Bolino's actions. Although Wilson believed that some of the other drivers had been stealing company property for some time, he thought that Bolino's approaches to customers had been very amateurish and probably were his first attempts. Wilson realized also that the company had no direct evidence that Bolino had actually stolen company property but only that he had attempted to find buyers for such material. On the other hand, Wilson felt that strong action against Bolino, if successful, would serve as a forceful deterrent against the other drivers who were engaging in dishonest activities but against whom the company had been unable to secure any substantial evidence. Wilson read the section of the labor agreement on discipline and discharge (see Exhibit 1) and wondered what action he should take.

EXHIBIT 1

ARTICLE VI MISCELLANEOUS

It is agreed that the employer has retained the usual management rights and that the right to manage the employer's business and direct the working force is vested exclusively in the management of the employer, which right shall include, but shall not be limited to, the right (except insofar as limited herein) to suspend, discharge, or otherwise discipline for just cause; to transfer or layoff because of lack of work or for other legitimate reasons; to plan, direct and control its operations; and to change methods, processes, equipment, or facilities; provided, however, that this will not be used for the purposes of discrimination against any employee or to avoid any of the provisions of this agreement or the obligation to bargain collectively concerning wages, hours, or working conditions.

Wilson Distributors Company(B)*

At 8:45 A.M. on the morning of October 24, Donald Wilson called Bolino to the office of Jerry Cooper, superintendent of the plant. [See Wilson Distributors Company (A) for earlier details.] In Cooper's presence, Wilson told Bolino that he had received reports from customers that he, Bolino, had approached them and had offered to sell the company's merchandise at much lower than standard prices. Bolino strongly denied that he had made such solicitations, asked who was responsible for the accusations, and demanded the right to confront them. Wilson refused to divulge the customers' names but said that he was convinced the reports were true and that, therefore, he had no choice but to discharge Bolino immediately.

Bolino then contacted the shop steward who called the union's business agent, Hank Rich. Rich, the steward, and Bolino went to Cooper's office, and Rich talked with Cooper. No agreement was reached at this meeting.

---

* This case was prepared by Michael Jay Jedel, research assistant, under the supervision of Professor Thomas M. Kennedy, as a basis for class discussion rather than to illustrate either effective or ineffective handling of an administrative situation.

Copyright © 1968 by the President and Fellows of Harvard College.

The company insisted that it had sufficient evidence to prove that Bolino had solicited customers to sell merchandise at far below regular prices and that it considered his action cause for discharge. The union vigorously dissented and argued that the evidence against Bolino was hearsay inasmuch as it involved unnamed persons, unnamed places, and unnamed times. Furthermore, they pointed out that Bolino denied all charges against him and that prior to his discharge he had never been disciplined or reprimanded. Management agreed that Bolino's previous record was good but repeated that he had offered to sell merchandise below cost and that this action constituted "just cause" for discharge. When further attempts to settle the issue were unsuccessful, the union demanded arbitration.

Following the union's demand for arbitration the company contacted the two customers who had made the accusations against Bolino and asked them if they would be willing to appear and testify at the arbitration hearing. Both customers refused to do so, saying that they would not have informed the company if they thought it would handle the matter so as to get them involved in arbitration or court proceedings. They appeared genuinely fearful and resentful. The company knew that it could ask the arbitrator to subpoena the two customers and thus force them to appear and to testify. It hesitated to take such action, however, because it valued the business of these customers and feared also that forcing them to testify might result in loss of goodwill among other customers as it became known throughout the trade. The company officials and the SAA consultants who had talked with the two customers remained convinced that the latter had told the truth. These company officials and the SAA representatives were prepared to testify regarding what the customers had said. Wilson wondered what action he should take.

Discussion questions

1. You are Jack Cooper, would you proceed with the case to arbitration? Justify your answer.
2. How should management present its case? How should the union present its case?
3. How do you think the arbitrator will rule in the case? Give specific reasons.

Incident cases and role-playing exercises in personnel

A. INCIDENT CASES AND ROLE-PLAYING EXERCISES: A DISCUSSION

Paul and Faith Pigors observed that sometimes cases do not simulate reality as well as they might.[1] They believed that this was so because cases can give the impression that all the material necessary to deal with a situation is given at one time. In fact, they argue, usually problems unfold over time and require the problem solver to act to gather more information than is first given.

Thus the Pigors advocated the use of the *incident* case method. The method works like this:[2]

Step 1: A short statement or incident (usually 100 words or so) is presented to the participants.

Step 2: Each participant examines the incident and asks, "What's going on here?" The participant tries to decide the main issues at stake.

Step 3: The participant formulates a series of questions which are essential or useful in solving or coming to grips with the case. Usually these questions focus on the who, what, when, where, and how of the incident.

Step 4: The focus becomes: What is the most important issue here, and what needs to be decided and done right now?

Step 5: The case as a whole is examined and all major issues are dealt with.

Thus, the incident method is similar to cases, but in some ways different. Typically, this is how an incident case is handled:

Step 1: Each participant reads the incident alone and makes notes about his or her reaction to it. He or she also answers the questions in Step 2. Then the participant discusses the conclusions of Step 1 and 2 with a small group in the class or seminar. Typically, this is a group of

---

[1] Paul Pigors and Faith Pigors, *Case Method in Human Relations: The Incident Process* (New York: McGraw-Hill Book Co., 1961).

[2] Ibid., pp. 142–45.

three to five persons. Together they come to agree on Steps 1 and 2, at least initially, and formulate the questions in Step 3.

When Step 3 is completed, the discussion leader for the group is chosen by the group. It is suggested that this role rotate among the members from time to time. This leader calls over the person conducting the session. The discussion leader asks the questions the group formulated of the person conducting the session. He or she has additional information available about the incident, and thus this simulates the search for information in the real problem-solving experience.

At this point, the groups formulate the responses to Steps 4 and 5. Finally, there is a group discussion of all the groups in which all the ideas developed are examined. This process involves more active participation by all present and is a useful learning experience in most cases. The incidents given in this text involve a variety of problems and settings, as was true with the case situations.

B. INCIDENTS

1. Pierce Construction

Pierce is a small firm which operates out of Waterton, New York. It constructs industrial buildings primarily as a subcontractor for major firms from New York City. At present, the company is building a nursing home for a nursing home chain under subcontract from the large contracting firm from the chain's headquarters in Los Angeles.

The job is too big for Pierce alone. So the contractor has two other subcontractors doing the same work as Pierce to get the job done. Recently, Ray Stinson, one of Pierce's foremen came to see Stuart Pierce and discuss the matter.

Stinson: We've got problems on that nursing home job.

Pierce: How's that?

Stinson: Our people are having to work with Oxley Construction's people. They aren't doing exactly the same work, but they are working in the area. Our people say that the Oxley people are doing a lousy job. Our people are afraid they'll be blamed for it, since some days it's hard to remember who did what part. Our people are having to work hard to do their own work and fix up the Oxley work, too. I'm afraid there's going to be a fight in the field one of these nights and it'll be nasty.

2. Mengel Clinic

Mary Gray is employed as a secretary for Dr. Darrell Pike at the Mengel Clinic in Fairbanks, Alaska.

Recently Dr. Pike found Ms. Gray very upset when he returned from lunch. Dr. William Waggener had just chewed her out unmercifully. She had helped out Dr. Waggener because his secretary was home ill. Ms. Gray had typed a report for Dr. Waggener.

He told her that she was incompetent and lazy and that the report needed a complete retyping. He added that he'd wait until his own secretary returned before he'd get that done.

Dr. Waggener had not consulted Dr. Pike before asking Ms. Gray to do the job or before criticizing her.

3. Meyer's Frozen Foods

Meyer's is a small frozen food company which processes frozen fish. Its main plant is in Pensacola, Florida. Meyer's organization chart is given in Exhibit 1.

EXHIBIT 1
MEYERS'S FROZEN FOODS: ORGANIZATION CHART

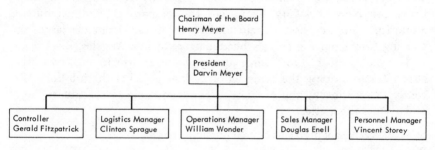

Recently, Darvin Meyer called Vince Storey and said: "Vince, I'm getting a lot of complaints lately about messups in shipping. I want you to check it out and see if it's Clint Sprague's fault. If it is, I want you to know what we can do about it."

Sprague was one of Henry Meyer's first employees. He is 48 years old. He attended Pensacola High for two years. He has been with Meyer's for 18 years. He started on the boats with Henry. Then he helped pack the goods, even delivered the merchandise. As the firm grew, he wound up in charge of shipping.

Storey checked with Douglas Enell, the sales manager. He also checked with some customers. Deliveries were coming in late and customers were complaining. Sprague's employees indicate he issues contradictory orders, and that he won't delegate authority. He insists on making all the decisions himself. He is not using all the newest shipping techniques. The warehouse, for which he is also responsible, is considered quite inefficient.

Storey thinks he knows what his report should say.

4. Maxine Mandeville

Maxine Mandeville is a graduate of the college of Engineering, Georgia Tech University. She has applied for a job at the LeBreton Electrical Company in Tampa, Florida.

Ms. Mandeville's parents have retired to St. Petersburg, and she would like to be near them. She sought an interview with John Jucius, the company president. The firm employs about 1,800 persons. Jucius was too busy to see her, so she talked to Van Utterback, the personnel manager.

Mandeville: Mr. Utterback, I saw an ad in this morning's paper for an engineer at your firm. So I rushed over here as soon as I could [It's 9:00 A.M.].

Utterback: Too late, I filled the job already.

Mandeville: But the ad just ran this morning. It wasn't in the evening paper or yesterday morning's paper.

Utterback: I know, but the job is filled.

5. Coffee Cart

Mary Werther is responsible for the coffee cart in her job with the department of housing and urban development. She works at the department's regional office in Kalamazoo, Michigan.

Taking care of the coffee cart is only one of the things she does. Twice a day, she takes the cart through each of the offices. The cart has coffee and tea on it. She also serves the donuts and rolls or cookies. Because so many people come up at one time, it has been the practice that each person puts 10¢ per cup into a change bowl for coffee or tea and 10¢ for each donut, roll, or cookie. This has worked well until recently.

The money Ms. Werther receives is used to buy the materials she needs. She must report carefully on its use. Recently, the coffee money has been short. She checked it out. Twice a day when she leaves one particular office she comes out with less money than she should. She asked this office's supervisor to help her with this.

The supervisor, Ray Burak, brought it up at his weekly department meeting. He said: "I know it may seem like a small thing, but Mary Werther tells me the coffee cart is coming up short of money from our department. It's not a lot of money, but it causes her trouble. Let's be especially sure we put the right change into the bowl."

Later that day, one of the department employees, Ed Jones, sought out Burak. Jones said: "I wondered when the coffee cart problem would be brought up. I know what the cause is. Sally Wood is your culprit. As hard as it is to believe, she puts a nickel into the bowl twice a day and pretends it's a quarter. Then she takes out 15¢ change. How petty can you get! I've seen her do it time after time."

6. Mark Robinson

· Mark Robinson is an account executive at Lacho, Heysinger, and Vogel, a medium-sized advertising agency with its office in New York City. Recently, Lisa Boyce, his supervisor, was explaining expectations about a new account and how each of the team fitted in.

When she came to Robinson's part, he stood up in front of the 20 people present and said, "I won't do it. Find someone else for that job." Then he left the room.

Later, Boyce confronted Robinson in his office.

Boyce: Why did you refuse to do your assigned task?

Robinson: Because it's beneath my abilities and you know it. Besides, you are too "military" and act like a dictator. We should form our own teams to get the job done. You seem to think that advertising people are like army privates and can be ordered around!

7. Gregory Business Forms

Gregory is a small distributor of business forms in Paducah, Kentucky. Recently, Max Gregory has been getting complaints about how long it takes to get orders processed and delivered.

Max spends about two thirds of each day "on the trade," taking orders and soliciting new business. His pattern has been to call on the trade mornings and afternoons until 3:00 P.M. or so.

Today, he decided to check on what was going on while he was away. About 10:00 A.M. he went in the back door and through the warehouse and entered his office through a back door. Then he listened to what was going on in the outer office.

Two of the three employees talked for a long while about personal matters. Gregory sat in his office and fumed. Then he called the two in and berated them for not attending to customer complaints instead of loafing on company time. He wondered what he should do to prevent this in the future.

8. Carson, Inc.

Carson is a large forest products company. It has a plant in Idaho Falls, Idaho, which produces wood shipping containers. Recently, as Everett Vickery, the plant manager, walked through the plant unannounced, he observed a group of men chasing a ball around. When they saw him coming, they quickly got back to work.

Vickery told one of the men that he wanted to see George Goshen, their foreman, in his office at once. When Goshen arrived, Vickery said: "Listen, Goshen you've seen our production record lately and our safety record too. What were you doing out there letting this horseplay go on? Maybe I need a new supervisor!"

9. FRX Pollution Control

FRX manufactures pollution control equipment for the mining and other industries in Bluefield, West Virginia, where spirits run high over football. The fans strongly favor the "Mountaineers" of the University of West Virginia.

It is Monday. Saturday is the big game with the University of Pittsburgh. This year both teams have good records and even more than the usual interest has been generated over it. It has been the chief conversation of most people in Bluefield for weeks.

Joe Firth, one of the FRX employees, is taking bets on the game. He is giving three points to Pittsburgh. A number of workers are standing around Firth ready to make a bet when Robert Manion, the personnel manager, walks by. He stops and asks Firth to see him in his office.

Manion: Firth, you know our rule against gambling on the premises. You know what it says in the employee handbook about that. I'm going to recommend a disciplinary layoff in your case to your foreman and the plant manager.

10. Post Office

Robert Fischer is employed in a post office in a medium-sized city in the northwestern United States. His supervisor, Harriet Chase, is having great difficulties with him.

He gets behind in his work and never seems willing to catch up. When she calls this to his attention, he listens and says he'll improve, but he never does. He will not work overtime. Some mornings he is late to work. Often he is late coming back from lunch. He never lunches with other postal employees. He often looks tired.

Fischer is 26 years old. He has been with the post office two years. He is a high school graduate. He and his wife have one child.

Chase is 35 years old. She is married and has two children who are in school. She is proud of her supervisory job and is not going to jeopardize it for Fischer.

11. Margaret Campagna

Margaret Campagna works for the Jackson Michigan Credit Bureau in Jackson, Michigan. She is 51 years old and has been an outstanding employee for ten years. In the last year, her work has dropped off substantially in quantity and quality.

She knows the job, and it hasn't changed so it can't be a technical problem. There has been no turnover in the office personnel, and she gets along well with her co-workers. She says she needs the job. So Carrie Victor, her supervisor, doesn't know what the problem is and is wondering what she can do. Ms. Campagna's co-workers are beginning to grumble some about having to do some of her work.

C. ROLE-PLAYING EXERCISES

This section also contains a series of descriptive settings that can be used as a basis for role playing. Role playing has some similarity to case studies and incident cases; that is, the individual or group assesses the data presented in the exercise. The problem is isolated, possible causes are considered, and attempts are made to solve the problem.

At this point, however, individuals are chosen to represent each of the key persons in the exercise. Each role player absorbs all he or she knows about the role to be played. The person attempts to determine how the role occupant would respond to problem solutions.

Then the role players come together. They react to each other as the persons in the exercise would likely react to the approaches made by the focal persons. Role playing allows the participants and observers to simulate how various solutions to problems might be concluded. The involvement of the role players provides a new dimension to learning experiences in personnel administration.

1. Dorothy Spencer

Dorothy Spencer is 21 years old. She is a typist at the EC Metal Stamping Company (EC) in Halifax, Nova Scotia. She is newly married. She is working to help build up savings, so she and her husband Vladimir can buy a house. They hope to have a family some day.

Spencer is a good worker. She has had several years' experience. She worked in Winnipeg before coming to Halifax. She met Vladimir there.

Spencer's supervisor is Kathy Fairbanks, who is 27 and has worked for EC for six years. Fairbanks feels she has a problem with Spencer. She explained it to the personnel manager, Melvin Zoller.

Fairbanks: We have some trouble with young hourly workers. They believe they have a specific job to do. They might be speedy and efficient like Dorothy. But when they finish their specific job, they want to quit before quitting time. They are unwilling to do more than this specific job. Even if there is other work to do and they are paid for eight hours, girls like Dorothy feel that if they do their job in seven hours, that should be it. How do I handle this motivation problem?

Zoller: That is a terribly difficult problem, Kathy, no doubt about it. At present, we have no incentive program to help at all. But remember she is a good worker. Don't be too hard on her like you were on Janice. She quit over your handling of this problem last year, remember?

Fairbanks: Yes, I remember. But I just can't send them home and what would the boss say if he saw them sitting around and just chatting at 4:05?

Zoller: He'd throw a fit and we both know it. Well, you better have a go at Dorothy. But be careful.

Fairbanks dropped over to see Spencer at 4:15 P.M.

2. Peter Glassman

Peter Glassman is a supervisor of data processing and computer programmers for a large city government in eastern Canada.

After completing his annual performance appraisals and appraisal interviews of his employees recently, he was called into his supervisor's office. Glassman's supervisor is Gregory Schwimmer.

Schwimmer: Peter, I just had a visit from one of your programmers, Carmen Larusso. He is very upset over his performance evaluation. He feels he is the best programmer you have, yet you didn't rate him as best. You use ranking to supplement the rating scale I know. In your rankings, where did you place him?

Glassman: About third, I believe, but with 15 programmers, I'd have to check my records, Mr. Schwimmer. You know, I supervise 22 people, and I don't always have all those ratings in my head.

Schwimmer: I know, but Carmen is a good man. I don't want to lose him over this. You know programmers are prima donnas. He's an excitable Italian, and let's make sure you are right about this. Let's go through your section.

Schwimmer required that Glassman discuss the ratings of his people as best he could from memory. Then he requested that Glassman document his ratings with Schwimmer and Larusso. He wanted objective data to support this. Glassman gathered this and he was ready to discuss it with both Larusso and Schwimmer. He found that Larusso was third best, based on such objective criteria as number of programs written, amount of debugging required in his programs, computer time used to process the data, Larusso's way versus others programs, and so forth.

He was ready to discuss this with them both.

Larusso is 24 years old. He's had three years' experience in programming after graduating from a school which specialized in computers. He is quiet, hard working, and at times, excitable.

Schwimmer is 47 years old, a lifetime civil servant. He is known for his ability to keep a happy department, with low turnover of employees. He is fair but firm. He knows very little first-hand about computers.

Glassman is 32 years old. He was hired by the city for his experience in programming supervision in Buffalo. He gives the appearance of being very busy, and he tries to minimize the time spent on paperwork and "people problems." He tends to be brusque. He does not tolerate slow learners very well. He has many job offers and has changed several times in the last five years. Each time he improved his position dramatically.

3. George Jessup

George Jessup is a design engineer for a large manufacturer of aircraft parts in the Los Angeles area. He is a graduate of the University of Michigan's college of engineering and has had six years' experience at the company.

Jessup's supervisor, Dewey Turrill, recently instituted the use of self-evaluations at performance evaluation time. He asked Jessup to come in on Monday to explain this new procedure.

Turrill: George, on Friday, I must turn in your performance evaluation form for the past six months. I've found it useful to ask each employee to complete a form, too, while I am doing so. I'll fill mine out in pencil, and Friday we'll get together, compare ratings, and have the evaluation interview.

Jessup: Fine, Dewey, I'll be ready.

Turrill is an experienced supervisor. Jessup was transferred to his section about six months ago. He considered Jessup to be an above-average employee. The company used a graphic-rating scale method, and he completed the form regarding Jessup as shown in Table 1. Jessup completed the form, too. His self-scores also are shown on Table 1.

Turrill had used self-evaluation as a supplement to supervisor's evaluation. Normally, what happened was that employees evaluated themselves lower than he did. In the interview Turrill and the employee could then discuss how Turrill could help them improve future performance. He had never had a case like Jessup's where the employee's self-evaluation was higher than the one made by Turrill. Turrill would agree that Jessup is good, but is he that good?

Jessup and Turrill are sitting across the table, and it is Turrill's turn to talk.

TABLE 1
EVALUATION SCORES ON JESSUP BY TURRILL AND JESSUP

	Maximum	Minimum	Turrill's score	Jessup's self-score
Quantity of work	25	5	20	25
Quality of work	25	5	20	25
Job knowledge	20	0	20	20
Initiative	15	0	12	15
Cooperation with others	15	0	12	15
Dependability	10	0	10	7
Agreeable personality	10	0	7	7
Total	120	10	101	114

4. Armstrong Power Tools, Inc.

Armstrong Power Tools (APT) is a medium-sized manufacturer of power tools and allied equipment. Its corporate headquarters are in Provo, Utah, with plants located at Provo; Springfield, Missouri; and Oswego, New York.

The company has been in business for some years. It evolved from a family-run firm. The last of the Armstrongs interested in the business, Clif Armstrong is now chairman of the board.

Until now, executive development has been an informal process. In general, persons were promoted up through a functional area, for example, personnel, finance, sales, operations. Then, whichever function seemed to be the predominant challenge of the next few years provided the top management.

But the board chairman feels the company has outgrown that method. He'd like to see all executives with real futures have multiple functional experience, if at all possible.

The manager at the Springfield plant is retiring. It is necessary to choose a replacement. The plant is a profit center with full responsibility for sales and production of the power tools in a region. It keeps its own financial records of these operations. The plant, which employs 474 persons, has a reputation of being the best run plant of the company.

Three candidates are being considered for the position.

1. Howard Morrison—age 48, assistant plant manager at Springfield. Morrison is a CPA and has been responsible for the finance and accounting function at Springfield for ten years prior to his promotion to assistant manager six months ago. Morrison is a quiet man, regarded primarily as a bookkeeper by some of his cohorts. Prior to working for APT, he was employed in the local CPA office of one of the "big eight" accounting firms.
2. Bob Schuster—age 34, assistant plant manager of a competitor's

power tool plant in St. Louis. Schuster is a graduate of Tuskegee Institute. He played professional basketball for the now defunct Cincinnati Royals. Schuster has worked at various management jobs for one of APT's competitors for the last five years as (1) assistant personnel manager, one-and-a-half years; (2) production planning, three years; and (3) assistant plant manager, his present assignment. He could be helpful with APT's Affirmative Action Program. He is well regarded by his colleagues.

3. Ross Fortuna—age 43, district sales manager for the Springfield plant. He reports to the plant manager. He would like to get some additional operations experience. He has worked for APT for 20 years. Fortuna's first five years' experience was in operations as foreman and quality-control supervisor. At the Springfield plant, he switched to sales. Ross graduated from the school of engineering of the University of Missouri–Rolla with a degree in industrial engineering. He is known as being energetic, outgoing, and competent. He has received many offers to work for competitors.

These men will be interviewed by L. S. Jones, executive vice president. Of course, they will make the best case for themselves. Jones has full responsibility for the decision. Jones is 59 years old. He holds a B.S. in engineering from U.C.L.A. and an M.B.A. from the University of Utah. His experience has been in operations. He is quiet, efficient, fair, and a "company man."

5. Howard K. Doutt

Howard Doutt is the manager of a municipally owned electric power plant in a small city in the eastern United States. He is 58 years old. He has worked his way up to be manager of the plant over 30 years. Doutt is a high school graduate. He also took a few college courses at night school 20 years ago.

Doutt runs a tight ship, uses authoritarian leadership, and is considered "crusty" by his co-department heads. He is a widower with two grown children. He is well fixed financially and could retire on a city pension at age 63 wth one half of his last salary or at age 60 with one third.

Doutt reports to the city manager and is responsible to the board of aldermen and ultimately to the mayor. Doutt has been under fire for some years for being out of date and too tied to traditional methods of operations. The board of aldermen recently received a consultant's report that recommended one of several steps be taken immediately.

1. Build on to coal-fired generators to expand current capacity, and add on pollution control equipment to meet state specifications.

2. Tie into the nuclear power plant being built 30 miles away by a private firm, thereby taking care of future needs.
3. Close the present plant when the nuclear plant opens up, and purchase electricity from it.

Doutt was asked how he felt about these issues during a campaign to get the voters to approve a bond issue to improve city services, including public transportation, streets, and the power plant. He was also reacting to national effort to conserve fuel.

The newspaper quoted Doutt: "This city is in no present danger of having to curtail generation of electricity because of the energy shortage. We are in good shape. The way I see it, we don't have a problem. The idea is to get the consumers to heed the conservation appeals. We'd be all right if it weren't for a number of nonprofessionals running around screaming about pollution all of the time."

City Manager Robert Carr received several phone calls after that. The mayor, the board of aldermen, the bonds committee chairman, the local ecology group chairman, and other called, wondering what was the trouble with Doutt. The mayor asked, "Has senility finally caught up with Howard? He has really undercut us at a time when the 'no-more-taxes-or-bonds' committee has been running great amounts of advertising against the issue."

Carr is 39 years old. He was appointed ten years ago as assistant city manager and became city manager five years ago. He is divorced. The city is his whole life. He has a master's degree in public administration from a nearby state university.

A recently elected board ran on a platform of "time for a change." The mayor had indicated that "one more misstep and you'll be managing a city somewhere else!"

The mayor has suggested that Carr take care of the power plant situation. Doutt's operation was run more or less efficiently, but it was not outstanding. Turnover was high. He had no assistant manager to fall back on—"unnecessary waste," he called it. He had a poor opinion of politicians and aldermen. Carr, on the other hand, felt that this board was intelligent, and he had to do something about the problem. Carr has been characterized as being level-headed and smooth in handling personnel issues. Doutt had sounded off once too often!

6. Industrial Gases, Inc.

Industrial Gases (IGI) is a small producer and distributor of industrial gases in Flagstaff, Arizona. (The firm's organization chart is given in Exhibit 1.) Recently, Fred Schwartz was overheard talking with Don

Pinto and Hal Taylor about salary administration at IGI. Schwartz feels that IGI has not developed a good program. There are no cost-of-living adjustments. Typically, salaried employees receive adjustments each 11 months which are designed to cover cost-of-living adjustments, merit raises, seniority adjustments, and so forth.

EXHIBIT 1
ORGANIZATION CHART, IGI

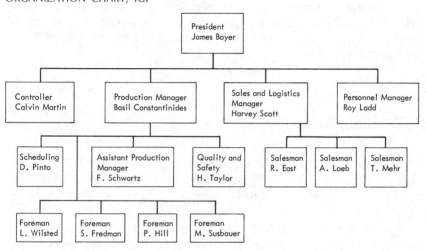

Recently, Schwartz has felt that the cost of living has been going up much faster than wage increases. New employees are hired at very close to the salaries of experienced employees. Schwartz feels this is very unfair.

For example, Schwartz is paid $17,500 per year plus a $1,500 bonus. But, Taylor, who was recently hired, who has much less experience than Schwartz, and who is only 29 years old, was hired at $16,000. Schwartz asks: "Isn't my extra ten years' experience worth something?"

Schwartz is 39 years old. He is a graduate of Arizona State University and has 15 years' experience in the industry, 11 of them with IGI. He is a bachelor, but he supports his widowed mother and is putting his younger sister through college. Schwartz is a direct person and believes that it is best to get things off his chest and out in the open. He wants to discuss his salary and the salary program in general with Roy Ladd, the personnel manager, and Basil Constantinides, the production manager.

Constantinides is 51 years old. He helped found IGI. He is not a college graduate. He learned the business from the bottom up. He came to the firm in 1946, after leaving the army as a master sergeant in the chemist corps.

Constantinides is quiet and believes that one should keep his salary secret. His salary is $27,000, and he received a bonus of $3,500 last year. He feels the company has been quite fair in salary administration.

Ladd is 48 years old. He has been an employee of IGI for 24 years. He has a degree in personnel administration from the University of Southern California. He feels the salary program is well administered. The company uses the point system of job evaluation. They take yearly wage and salary surveys in Flagstaff and the industry. Since Ladd does not believe that cost-of-living adjustments motivate higher productivity, he has always opposed them. The president, James Boyer, has always emphasized to Ladd that salaries are an important portion of IGI's costs and should be kept as low as possible.

7. Drinking on the Job

In an electric lighting fixture plant in Flint, Michigan, a confrontation took place recently. Steven Bossort, a worker who had a history of disciplinary layoffs for being drunk on the job, was accused of drinking on the job again.

Bossort had been "on the wagon" for three months. His work had been good. He had not missed a minute of work. Bossort always was a good worker when he was sober. He was well-liked by his fellow workers. He was jovial and always helped out where he was needed.

On this particular Friday afternoon, Bossort's foreman, Vic Pike, said Bossort was drunk. He sent him home and said he was going to dock his pay and perhaps institute another layoff. Bossort's shop steward from the Electrical Workers, Walt Young, was sick that day with flu. When he came back to work Monday, everyone knew there was going to be trouble. Young was Bossort's best friend. A reformed alcoholic himself, Young had gotten Bossort into Alcoholics Anonymous. Young took Bossort to meetings and in general tried to help him get back on his feet.

No one had seen Bossort in a drunken condition that Friday when Pike sent him home. Bossort said he didn't want to make trouble, and without his steward to advise him, he didn't know what to do. However, he vehemently denied that he was drunk.

On Monday morning everyone in the section was waiting for the action. It was rumored that a grievance would be filed. The contract was going to expire in two weeks, too.

Pike is 21 years old and has been with the company about four months. He was hired as a management trainee, and after a week's orientation to the plant was made foreman. He is a mechanical engineering graduate of Louisiana State University.

Pike is 5'7" and weighs 150 pounds. Pike is not well-liked generally.

He is conservative and has strong feelings about management rights and the worker's place. He feels that employees should do what they are told and follow the company rules. He believes that employees are paid well to do just that.

Bossort is 36 years old, a high school graduate. He has been with the company five years. He is 6'1" and weighs 210 pounds. He is a strong union man and feels that he should be treated with dignity by management. Generally, Bossort is quiet and doesn't make trouble.

Young is 47 years old, a high school graduate. He has been elected steward for 12 one-year terms thus far. He is aggressive and won't put up with any nonsense from management. Young is 6'6" and weighs 275 pounds. He played tackle on a semipro football team for some years after high school.

Bossort and Young approach Pike at 8:30 A.M. Monday.

8. Rhonda Latta

Rhonda Latta is an employee of the University of Virginia in Charlottesville. She has worked at the university for two years and, until recently, did excellent work. All of a sudden, her work began to deteriorate. The quality and quantity of her typing dropped.

Latta's supervisor, Earl Schnoor, decided to talk the problem over with one of the university's personnel specialists, Irving Heizer.

Schnoor: As I understand it both from my chats with her and from her coworkers and friends, Rhonda had been happily married. Her husband Chris was in law school. He started running around. She caught him once in the apartment with a coed. They were living off her salary, his scholarship, and help from his parents. Eventually, they were divorced. This caused her to have financial difficulties. She had been living better than she could on her salary only, and she couldn't or she wouldn't cut back.

Thus far, there were few problems. Latta's personal life affected her morale and thus her job some, but not markedly. Then she decided to moonlight. She became a cocktail waitress at night. She started missing days at her university job or came to work late. Several of the other women said she had gone through a series of love affairs—often with older married men. Some of the girls occasionally dropped in at the Swinger's Bar, where she worked. They suspected that she was drinking a lot or taking dope. Then her work really started dropping off. At times, I had to ask the others to help out on her work. One person flatly refused. She said: "I'm not about to do her work. If she wants to have her good time, that's her business. But I'm not going to pay for her good times!"

Heizer: I see from her personnel folder that she is 23. She graduated from Stephens College in art history, got married, took a typing course, got an average score. Not much else in her folder. What's her personality like?

Schnoor: Well, she used to be a quiet, happy type. Made no trouble for us, did well. Lately, she has been snapping at people and when the other women complain about her absenteeism and late days, she practically snarls at them. One day, I heard her say: "Sandra, you're so jealous of the good times I'm having you can't stand it!"

Schnoor has called Latta to come to his office at 4:30 P.M. today.

9. Cohack Manufacturing Corporation*

The Washburn division of the Cohack Manufacturing Corporation came into existence in August 1963 when Cohack completed building a new production plant at Crooked Tree, Montana. Crooked Tree is a small town in a rural resort area approximately 125 miles from Butte, Montana, the home office of Cohack Manufacturing.

The work force had grown to approximately 900 employees by July 1, 1969. They were recruited from Crooked Tree and the surrounding ten counties. Almost all new employees were completely without past industrial experience. However, employment standards were high, and all persons hired appeared to have considerable potential. With only five exceptions, on July 1, 1969, all production supervisors in the lower three echelons of management had been promoted from within.

Washburn division had the usual problems of all new plants plus the technological problem of a manufacturing process completely new to industry.

In January 1966, the plant was organized by the Amalgamated Workers of America after a long and costly strike. Employee-management relations were never recovered. There were numerous changes in top management and union leadership. The union refused to follow grievance procedure and demanded instant affirmative answers to all problems. The wildcat strike was frequent. Lower echelons of management suffered repeated abuses and threats from a limited number of employees. Sleeping, loafing, gambling, and even sabotage of production was not unusual. Higher management had, at times, failed to back lower management when it attempted to take disciplinary action.

---

* This case was made possible by the cooperation of a business firm which remains anonymous. It was prepared by Dr. James C. Hodgetts of Memphis State University as a basis for class discussion rather than to illustrate either effective or ineffective administrative practices. The letter from the president appears as it did in the original except for changes in names and places that would reveal the company's true identity.

By the end of 1968 the Washburn division had forced the Cohack Manufacturing Corporation to the verge of bankruptcy. Early in 1969 the company was able to borrow $4 million on the physical facilities at Washburn, and local top management was again changed. By July 1969 the technical problems were decreasing, but the human problems remained unchanged.

On July 29, 1969, the president of the company wrote the following letter to all Washburn employees with the hope that it might help to correct the situation.

Cohack Manufacturing Corporation
Butte, Montanna
July 29,1969

To all Washburn division employees:

As you know we have recently made many changes in the top management group at Butte. There were also some changes made at Washburn. These were made because mistakes in the past had taken us to the point of bankruptcy. It was recognized that there were two (2) basic problems. One was the deterioration and lack of proper operating facilities, and the other was the small percentage of our employees who were seriously affecting our operating efficiency.

With regard to the first problem, this new management team immediately appropriated approximately four million dollars ($4,000,000) to improve facilities over the next three (3) years. Some improvements can already be seen; others will take time because of engineering and delivery delays.

Concerning the second problem, there are some employees who loaf, sleep, play cards, abuse and threaten our management, or just plain don't do the job they are being paid to do. We know, as you do, that no business can operate for long under these conditions. Their actions have caused us to reach the point where our operations are being seriously affected. When this happens, the security of everyone is threatened—we will not allow this to continue. Some feel that we are afraid to correct these problems. Nothing could be further from the truth. We honestly believed that since the future of so many employees and their families were at stake we, as management, had to first try persuasion and cooperation before resorting to disciplinary action. This approach has not been successful; in fact, matters have gotten worse.

In the interest of the job security of everyone concerned, we are hereby serving notice that we will no longer tolerate such things as sleeping, loafing, gambling, or game playing on company property, threats or abuse to management, or other interferences which affect production. Our management has the authority to take the necessary corrective measures to stop these practices.

We feel confident that most of our employees will do the job that has to be done. They performed magnificently in our recent production crisis. The only thing which good employees have to worry about is what the few bad ones can do to their job security. We ask for your cooperation in helping us make this a better, safer, more secure place to work. We are doing everything humanly possible and within reason to reach this goal.

C. J. Cohack, President

10. Selection by Interview and Application Blank*

BACKGROUND FOR THE BUSINESS FORMS SALESMAN

The salesman's job

Moore Business Forms, Inc., manufactures and sells business forms. Their products range from marginal punched forms used in data processing to restaurant checks and sales books. The company does business throughout the United States.

The basic assignment of the salesman is to sell business forms designed to solve his customers' systems problems. His territory is a defined geographical area, the size of which depends upon the density of population. In rural areas the territories may include a number of towns and require overnight travel.

The new salesman's territory has a nucleus of established company accounts from which he builds and grows. He must service these existing customers efficiently in order to secure their repeat orders. He can also create new business by selling additional products to established accounts and by developing new customers from the unsold accounts in his territory.

The salesman is expected to conduct himself at all times in such a manner as to reflect credit on himself and on his company. He is encouraged to participate in worthwhile community affairs and to become a member of leading community organizations.

Basically, the success of the salesman depends upon hard work, the practice of sound techniques of salesmanship, and the maintenance of a high standard of customer service. The salesman works to keep his customers thoroughly satisfied. His success depends on keeping the company and its salesmen well and favorably known.

Training for the job

The job of the Moore salesman requires thorough indoctrination and systematic training. Prior to his assignment to a territory, the new salesman completes a field training program in the district sales office to which he is assigned. Upon assignment to his territory, his training continues in the form of close supervision and guidance by his immediate supervisor.

In addition, regular sales meetings, special sales clients, weekly mailings of selling aids, and personal coaching form a continuous training program.

---

* Reprinted with the permission of the publishers, the Graduate School of Business. Copyright by the board of trustees of Leland Stanford Junior University.

Income

The salesman determines his income by his sales volume. A salary payment provides stability of income. Incentive is offered by a direct commission payment on sales volume and the automatic upward revision of the salary payment as sales increase. Starting salaries for new salesmen are determined by their individual experience and qualifications.

The salesman furnishes his own automobile, and his expense account is determined by the nature of his territory.

Opportunities for growth

The company adheres to the policy of promoting within the organization. As the new salesman gains experience, he is placed in more responsible sales assignments. His income grows with each added year of experience.

For men with management abilities, there are opportunities to progress into field sales management positions of supervisor, district manager, and regional manager. Every major executive has graduated from the ranks.

ROLE FOR COLLEGE RECRUITER

You are a sales supervisor for Moore Business Forms, Inc. You have been with the company six years and have made good progress. But since you were promoted into your present job you have found that you cannot progress further without some improvement of your five-man sales crew. The major weakness is in the servicing of the big accounts. These accounts require more technical service than others, and only one of the three salesmen assigned them is fully qualified for his job. As a result, you have to spend about half your time with the other two. To make matters worse, your one good man is up for promotion out of your area. For various reasons, none of the other salesmen can be reassigned to the coming vacancy; so you have to hire a new man for this position.

You think that if you can find a mature college graduate with a good accounting background and some part-time selling experience you can break him in before your best man leaves.

You have prepared a job description and sent it to the placement office of a nearby college. The starting rate is about the same as other companies are offering, but you think this is an unusually good opportunity for the right man. The three men referred to you by the college were all good fellows, but there was no evidence, either in their college records or in their conversation, of the technical accounting background that this particular sales job required.

Another applicant from the college has an appointment with you this morning. Your secretary just told you that he has come in, and you have asked her to send him in right away.

RECRUITER'S INTERVIEW GUIDE

Points you want to cover include the following. Make notes during the interview in appropriate spaces.

1. *Voice, manner, and appearance.* Are these suitable?

2. *Work history.* What work has he done? Why did he do it? Did he like it? Why did he leave? Has he had any paid work in sales or office work, especially accounting?

3. *School history.* Which subjects did he like most, least? Which subjects did he get the best grades in? What was his grade average? What were his extra-curricular activities?

4. *Personal.* What is he looking for in a job? Why does he want this job?

ROLE FOR COLLEGE MAN

You are graduating next month and are very glad to get out of school. The last year has been pretty tough. Although your grades have been very good, you have become upset about your course of study. You have specialized in accounting but now you are sure that you dislike the work and want to get into something else. This year you took courses in merchandising and advertising and liked them. But, after talking to an employment man for a steel company, you feel like a misfit; he indicated that interest and training in the same area would be desirable.

What you really want is to make some money. A lot of sales jobs pay on some commission basis, and this one for which you are going to be interviewed looks good to you. What worries you most is that the interviewer man will expect you to have had experience in sales. This is exactly where you are weak. The only thing you ever did for money was deliver morning papers. But, if the company's training program is any good, you think you should be able to make up for this weakness.

Anyway, you have asked for an interview, gone to the company office, and now are waiting to see the recruiter.

Exercises in personnel

PART THREE

The following is a series of exercises to be completed by the user of this book. Some of them are cost-and-benefit exercises. They require the participant to calculate specific costs of a personnel function, to calculate or infer its benefits, and to recommend whether or not to continue the activity. If it is to be continued, the participant must specify the future form or approach.

The other exercises require the participant to take part in data gathering before analysis takes place. In some of the exercises, the participant enters the field, observes, gathers data, and analyzes it. In others, the participant interacts with other participants in the classroom or other settings. The exercise takes place and analysis and recommendations follow. Both of these approaches have in common participant input to the exercise before analysis can take place.

The purpose of these exercises is to provide the participant the opportunity to put his or her knowledge of personnel activities to work. Not only are participants building their decision-making skills in these exercises, but they are also developing some more specific skills in designing and evaluating such activities as human resource planning, recruitment and selection programs, performance evaluation systems, work scheduling, and compensation and benefit plans. The participant will realize there is still much work to be done after the decisions are made and also will realize some of the problems involved in implementing the decisions. Participants find these specific skills useful as most managerial positions are involved in implementing and evaluating personnel policies and programs.

A. COST-BENEFIT AND FIELD EXERCISES

1. Human Assets and Accounting Exercise

Exhibit 1 is a recent balance sheet and income statement from the R. G. Barry Company. This company has 1,300 employees and manufactures such items as chair pads, robes, foam cushioned slippers, and other

EXHIBIT 1

Balance Sheet		
Assets	*December 31, 1967*	*December 31, 1968*
Currents assets (cash, etc.)	$ 1,000,000	$ 1,500,000
Plant and equipment	8,000,000	8,000,000
Investment in individual employees (recruiting, training, development, etc.)	750,000	850,000
Organizational investments (start-up, planning, development, etc.)	900,000	700,000
Total Assets	$10,650,000	$11,050,000
Equities		
Liabilities	$ 2,000,000	$ 2,000,000
Owner's equity: stock	6,000,000	6,000,000
Retained earnings (including investment in human resources) ..	2,650,000	3,050,000
Total Equities	$10,650,000	$10,050,000

Income Statement Year Ending December 31, 1968		
Sales		$ 2,000,000
Expenses		1,500,000
Net income		$ 500,000
Adjustment for change in investment in human resources:		
Individual employee adjustment ...	+$100,000	
Organizational adjustment	−$200,000	−100,000
Adjusted Net Income		$ 400,000

Source: R. Lee Brummet, et al., "Human Resource Accounting in Industry," *Personnel Administration*, July-August 1969, pp. 34–46.

EXHIBIT 2
A HUMAN RESOURCE ACCOUNTING MODEL (with examples of variables)

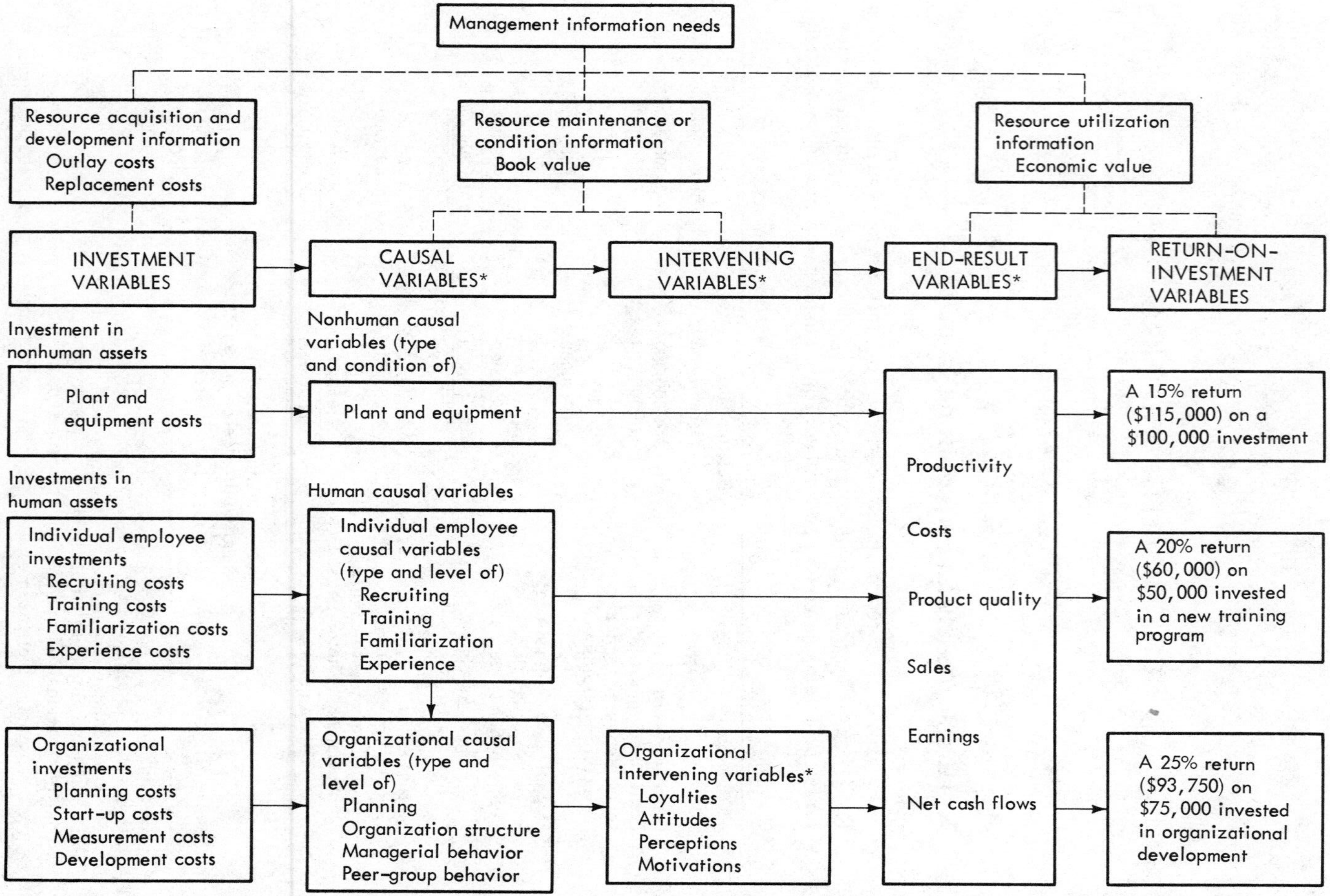

Source: R. Lee Brummet, et al., "Human Resource Accounting in Industry," *Personnel Administration*, July–August 1969, pp. 34–46.

leisure wear. The firm is located in Columbus, Ohio. It had sales of $20 million in 1968, up from $5.5 million in 1962. The model it uses to assess what factors should be computed in human assets is given in Exhibits 2 and 3.

EXHIBIT 3
MODEL OF AN OUTLAY COST MEASUREMENT SYSTEM

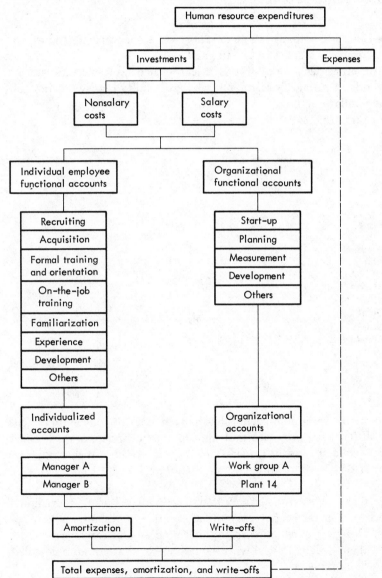

Source: R. Lee Brummet, et al., "Human Resource Accounting in Industry," *Personnel Administration*, July-August 1969, pp. 34–46.

Requirement. Examine this model and expand it to include other personnel expenditures normally present in a firm of this size.

2. White Leather Company

White Leather Company is a moderate-sized leather tanning and manufacturing company located in Oklahoma City.

The firm processes about half of the leather needed to manufacture its leather goods. It primarily manufactures high-quality luggage, belts, golf bags, and similar goods.

Some characteristics of its work force are:

Age distribution	Number of employees	Percent of employees
<25	73	
26–35	61	
36–45	84	
46–55	116	
>56	127	
Skill distribution		
Blue collar		
Skilled		18
Semiskilled		32
Unskilled		27
Total		77
Grey collar		
(maintenance)		8
White collar		12
Managerial		3

The company is not unionized. It has had a history of good employment relations. It has been proposed that the company change from a five-day eight-hour-per-day two-shift operation. It is proposed that the company go to a four-day week or to flexitime scheduling.

Requirement. Design a strategy to determine if White Leather should make such a change. Prepare several alternative combinations and approaches. Design a questionnaire to determine employee response. Prepare contingency plans to deal with the possibility that not all blue-collar workers will approve.

Prepare flexible plans so that if a group of employees prefers to stay on a five-day week, it can. Finally, design a strategy to measure results after a trial period.

3. Planning for Executives

Recently the state of California's government has been trying to anticipate its future needs to improve its long-range planning. The state department of labor has also been participating in this endeavor.

Ralph Hoover is the bureau chief in Sacramento. He was asked to prepare an executive replacement chart and anticipate what his future needs would be for executives and when he would need them. He has been asked to project 5-, 10-, and 15-year needs.

Exhibit 1 is his current organization chart. Table 1 is his data on turnover records. The bureau has been pressed to increase its percentage of minority employees and female executives.

Requirement. Prepare 5-, 10-, and 15-year needs for the bureau and prepare preliminary recruiting plans, considering that on the average it may take one year on the job to replace an effective executive. The agency is not expecting major increases in the number of employees during these periods.

EXHIBIT 1
ORGANIZATION CHART OF THE BUREAU

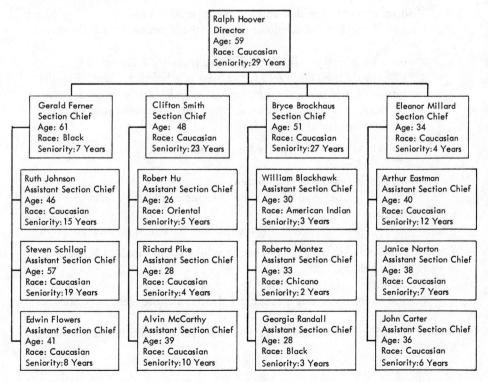

TABLE 1
TURNOVER DATA FOR THE BUREAU, PAST FIVE YEARS

Year 5....2 section chiefs	(1)	age 45; race: Black; seniority: 5 years.
	(2)	age 43; race: Caucasian; seniority: 20 years.
Year 4....None		
Year 3....1 section chief		age 39; race: Caucasian; seniority: 12 years (female).
1 assistant section chief		age 28; race: Black; seniority: 3 years.
Year 2....1 assistant section chief		age 33; race: Caucasian; seniority: 8 years.
Year 1....1 section chief		age 41; race: American Indian; seniority: 12 years.
2 assistant section chiefs	(1)	age 33; race: Caucasian; seniority: 10 years (female).
	(2)	age 41; race: Oriental; seniority: 10 years (female).

4. Job Analysis and Job Description Exercise

Job descriptions have many uses in personnel practice today. Yet many positions do not have up-to-date or written job descriptions or job specifications.

Requirements

A. Visit an enterprise which employs at least 50 persons.
B. Choose three jobs which have at least three persons with the same job title.
C. Prepare a job analysis for each of these three jobs. Do this by
    1. Observing the employees for at least one half hour, during which you will interview the employees as individuals or as a group.
    2. Reviewing available records, prior job analyses, and so forth. Data to be analyzed include:

       a. Work activities (procedures used, physical motions, human interactions).

       b. Machines, tools, equipment used.

       c. Job related materials used, products made, or services performed.

       d. Job context—working conditions, inventories, and so forth.

D. The job analysis for each of the three jobs should include at least the following items:
    1. Job title.
    2. Job summary: one paragraph describing the general duties of the job.
    3. Descriptions of tasks: detailed description—step by step—of the

physical duties performed by the employee using the data described in C above.

E. Prepare a job description for each of the three jobs. These should include:

1. Description of job content: job content factors which can be used include:

   a. Information input needed on the job.
   b. Mental processes used on the job.
   c. Work output (physical activities required).
   d. Relationships on the job (contacts required, and so forth).
   e. Job context (safety; pleasantness/unpleasantness).
   f. Other characteristics.

F. Return to the workplace. Show the Job descriptions and analyses to the following:

1. Personnel officials.
2. The supervisors of the employees studied.
3. The employees studied.

Record the reactions of each involved person to your analyses and descriptions.

G. Prepare final job analyses and job descriptions acceptable to personnel, supervisors, and employees involved.[1]

5. St. Basil's Hospital

St. Basil's is a community general hospital in Winston-Salem, North Carolina. It is operated by a group of Catholic sisters, although its board of trustees is composed of community leaders. In fact, as a policy of the religious order, the sisters have withdrawn from active administration of the hospital. All key administrators are now lay persons. The ten sisters serve as nurses or in similar professional-technical roles. Sister Rosemary is a psychiatric social worker, for example.

The hospital has 400 beds and about 1,000 full-time equivalent employees. There are actually 1,240 employees. Mr. Harold Henri is the personnel manager at St. Basil's, and he was recently discussing a problem with the hospital administrator, Mr. R. W. Ludmer.

---

[1] For more information on this subject, see Ernest McCormick, "Job and Task Analysis," in Marvin Dunnette, *Handbook of Industrial and Organizational Psychology* (Chicago: Rand McNally, 1976), pp. 651–96.

Henri: Ron, one special problem hospitals in general and St. Basil's in particular have is motivating some of our professional-technical employees after a few years.

Ludmer: What do you mean, Hal?

Henri: Well, you take a field like medical technology. A person enters it. He or she does lab tests a while; then if she is good, she can become head of department. Then that's it. There's no place to go. I had my training in industry, and they don't stifle people like that. They have no drive to go up in the world.

Ludmer: Well, most of these fields require specialized training. They must be good or people can die. They must pass tests administered by state boards before they can get their jobs.

Henri: I know that, but why can't these people become assistant administrators or administrators? At present, they cant't.

Ludmer: Oh, I guess they could be, but most are too specialized. Tell you what, why don't you try to develop a career plan for converting some of these specialists into generalists such as hospital administrators?

Mr. Henri is looking at St. Basil's organization chart (Exhibit 1, page 229) and wondering if this can be done.

Requirement. Develop a career plan to convert specialist managers into generalists.

6. Temporary Help

Goebel Barge Line is a moderate-sized firm with headquarters in Cairo, Illinois. The firm ships goods primarily on the Mississippi, Ohio, and other inland waterways.

Traditionally, barges have been used for bulky cargo which does not need to arrive quickly, which is not damaged by water, and which requires very inexpensive transportation.

Business has been good, and with continuing improvements on locks and dams on the rivers by the Army Corps of Engineers and others, it is getting better.

Harding Goebel, the company president, feels that business will get even better with the energy crisis. The crisis makes the barge lines even more competitive with truck lines and railroads.

Goebel believes his business will increase so much that he will need to hire three more clerical employees. These persons should be able to type 40 to 50 words per minute, file records, take dictation occasionally, and have the ability to use their initiative.

EXHIBIT 1
ORGANIZATION CHART OF ST. BASIL'S HOSPITAL

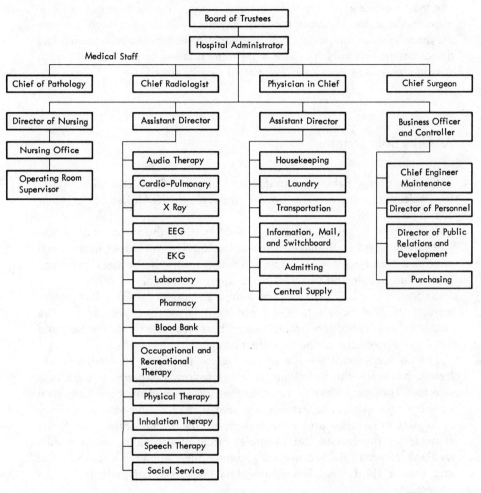

Because he is conservative, Goebel is considering hiring temporary help. If the business does not hold, he feels he can let temporary employees go more easily than permanent help. Goebel is willing to pay the going wages. After three months on the payroll, permanent help receive benefits such as insurance, health insurance, vacations, and so forth, which cost the company $20 per week. After one year, the cost increases to $30 per week.

He understands that temporary help costs more per week, and that there is greater turnover. This leads to greater training cost and time. He wonders what he should do.

Requirement. You are the personnel advisor to Goebel. Investigate what it costs in your area to hire three such persons each with at least one year's experience. Then, investigate what it would cost per week to acquire them from temporary-help agencies. Then, interview an employer who uses temporary help regularly to determine advantages and disadvantages. Finally, prepare a recommendation to Goebel with your reasons for and against each alternative clearly stated.

7. Gil's Soft Drinks

Gil's is a large national manufacturer of soft drinks. It markets syrup for its drinks to independent bottlers throughout the United States, Canada, and overseas.

In addition to selling the independent bottlers the syrup, it also provides many services to make them successful. This includes international advertising and market planning. Gil's also trains the bottlers' sales and production people and provides the bottlers with legal advice.

Recently, Frank Dick, vice president of personnel for Gil's, has recommended to Mel Schwartz, Gil's president, that they provide for the company and its bottlers projections of business growth (or decline) and consequent need for hiring or reductions.

He has read about the use of the Delphi technique to predict future trends. Basically, the technique works as follows: A panel of experts is selected. They are asked to estimate the future trend of something such as soft-drink sales. The experts are sent a mailed questionnaire. They make their estimates and return them to the home office. The office summarizes the results (for example, range of estimates, mean, mode, median), returns this information and new questionnaires a second time, and then a third time. From these final data, the company makes its projections.

Dick received a positive response from Schwartz and so now has the job of designing the system. He is wondering if he should try first for national and international trends or include major regions as well, for example, northeastern United States or western Canada.

He also is wondering whom he should include as experts: home office people, bottlers, economists, stock analysts, marketing professors, ad-agency executives. He wonders if he'll get outsider's cooperation without pay. And he wonders what information he should include on the questionnaire, remembering that this is primarily designed as a predictor of employee demand for the company and the bottlers.

Requirement. Draw up a plan to implement the employment fore-casting scheme using Delphi. Include the number of experts, number from each sector (for example, home office), the questionnaire, how fre-quently it should be done (for example, two, three, or four rounds), and whether this should be performed yearly, more often, or less often.

8. Northern Airlines

Northern Airlines is a regional airline company whose corporate head-quarters is near Rochester, Minnesota. The firm has been growing, but it has not been attracting a sufficient number of college graduates to staff its management training program.

Like many other airlines, for some years Northern has paid somewhat less than other industries because it believed the glamour of the airline industry would attract a sufficient number of trainees. With recent prob-lems regarding crashes and news about lack of profitability, Northern has not met its recruiting goals. The territory which Northern serves includes the Canadian provinces of Saskatchewan, Alberta, and Manitoba and the states of Minnesota, North Dakota, South Dakota, Montana, Wyoming, Nebraska, Iowa, and Wisconsin.

You are Ron Dyer, personnel manager at Northern. You have been assigned to a project designed to improve college recruiting. Specifically, you have been asked to:

1. Prepare a list of colleges that should be visited by Northern and arrange a time schedule.
2. Prepare recruiting brochures which include the major points you feel should be stressed at Northern. If properly designed, they could also be used for present employees.
3. Design a training course for executives who will be helping do the recruiting.

Top management has given you the following guidelines. Your recruit-in goal for next year is 20 college graduates in business, engineering, or liberal arts, preferably in the top 25 percent of their graduating classes. Their pay will be about 10 percent below the market. You should spend no more than 25 days in the field recruiting, and ten executives will each spend two days recruiting. The brochures should be inexpensive.

Requirement. Prepare an effective recruiting campaign for Northern.

9. Public Works Department

A large eastern city's public works department needs to hire 25 new employees. If past practice is followed, 50 employees will have to be hired to have 25 effective ones. The training cost has been $750 per employee.

It has been proposed that testing might improve this employment record. For administrating and using the test, the cost will be $2.50 per applicant. Table 1 on page 233 presents data on the percentage of applicants who score various levels on the test and the percentage of applicants likely to be successful at various predictor-score levels.

Requirement. Calculate the best predictor scores designed to minimize costs and maximize the number of best applicants to get 25 successful employees.

10. Fox Appliances, Inc.

Fox (FA) is a medium-sized manufacturer of small appliances located in Fresno, California. The firm employs 1,500 persons. Fox also has a plant in Fort Smith, Arkansas, and Youngstown, Ohio.

Recently, the firm has been trying to hire a new plant manager for the Youngstown plant. Because of the importance of the position, the firm has used multiple selection techniques. The techniques include: (1) interviews, (2) tests, (3) polygraphs, (4) graphology, and (5) references. A brief description of the candidates is given in Exhibit 1, page 234.

Fox has had about an average profit and growth record for the industry. But Youngstown has been the real problem plant. Costs are high and there has been a history of labor strife there.

Each of the applicants was interviewed by five executives at FA. Then the executives were asked to rank the applicants in their order of preference. The results of these rankings are given in Table 1. The results of the intelligence tests are given in Table 2, page 234.

In terms of personality analysis drawn from interpretation of thematic apperception tests, the psychologist ranked the individuals as follows: (1) Klam, (2) Eggers, (3) Radick, (4) Williams, and (5) Taylor. One of the psychologist's comments was that "Klam and Eggers are quite competitive and ought to take charge well especially when faced with a real challenge."

The polygraph analyses indicated that most were thought to be honest, although the analyst had some questions about Klam.

TABLE 1
EMPLOYEE SELECTION AND PERSONNEL COSTS

Frequency	10	20	30	40	50	60	70	80	90	100	110
						20					
20						X					
19						X					
18						X					
17					*16*	X	*16*				
16					X	X	X				
15					X	X	X				
14					X	X	X				
13				*12*	X	X	X	*12*			
12				X	X	X	X	X			
11				X	X	X	X	X			
10				X	X	X	X	X			
9				X	X	X	X	X			
8				X	X	X	X	X			
7			*6*	X	X	X	X	X	*6*		
6			X	X	X	X	X	X	X		
5		*4*	X	X	X	X	X	X	X	*4*	
4		X	X	X	X	X	X	X	X	X	
3	*2*	X	X	X	X	X	X	X	X	X	*2*
2	X	X	X	X	X	X	X	X	X	X	X
1	X	X	X	X	X	X	X	X	X	X	X
Score	10	20	30	40	50	60	70	80	90	100	110
Percent	2	6	12	24	40	60	76	88	94	98	100

High

Criterion measure	10	20	30	40	50	60	70	80	90	100	110	
							16	*12*	*6*	*4*	*2*	
							X	X	X	X	X	
						20	X	X	X	X	X	
						X	X	X	X	X		
						X	X	X	X	X		
						X	X	X	X			
					16	X	X	X				
					X	X	X	X				
					X	X	X	X				
					X	X	X	X				X (50) *successful*
				12	X	X	X	X				
				X	X	X	X					
				X	X	X	X					(50) *unsuccessful*
				X	X	X	X					
			6	X	X	X	X					
			X	X	X	X						
			X	X	X	X						
			X	X	X	X						
		4	X	X	X	X						
		X	X	X	X							
		X	X	X	X							
	2	X	X	X	X							
	X	X	X	X								
Low	X											
Percent	2	6	12	24	40	60	76	88	94	98	100	

Predictor

EXHIBIT 1
BIOGRAPHICAL DATA ON THE CANDIDATES

1. Charles Radick, assistant plant manager at Youngstown. Age 48. Education:
    B.S.B.A., Ohio State University; M.B.A., Youngstown State University. Has always
    worked for FA except during military service.
2. James Williams, assistant plant manager at Forth Smith. Age 51. Education: high
    school graduate. Has worked for FA for ten years. Prior to that, worked for two
    other appliance manufacturers (six and four years, respectively), and before that
    a variety of other jobs.
3. Ron Taylor, assistant plant manager at Fresno. Age 41. Education: B.A. in political
    science, Yale University. Has four years military experience. Worked in appliance
    sales for competitors for three years and had production experience for competitor
    for five years. Has worked for FA for six years.
4. George Klam, plant manager of small plant for a very aggressive competitor. Age
    36. Education: B.S. in engineering, University of Florida. Has been employed at
    present company for ten years, three of which as plant manager. Has four years
    military experience.
5. Daniel Eggers, former plant manager of electrical equipment firm which went
    brankrupt in Youngstown. Age 58. Education: high school graduate. Worked for
    prior employer all of his working life. Ran a successful plant for this company,
    which failed for other reasons.

TABLE 1
PREFERENCES FOR CANDIDATES BY FIVE FOX APPLIANCES EXECUTIVES

| | Candidates | | | | |
Interviewers' rankings	Radick	Williams	Taylor	Klam	Eggers
President					
James Cox	5	3	1	2	4
Vice president–personnel					
Dale Young	3	2	1	5	4
Vice president–production					
Kenneth O'Connor	2	5	3	4	1
Plant manager–Ft. Smith					
Stanley Hepler	4	3	5	1	2
Plant manager–Fresno					
Ernest Butler	5	1	3	2	4

TABLE 2
INTELLIGENCE TESTS RESULTS AT FOX APPLIANCES

Candidate	Test (1) score	Test (2) score
Radick	127	133
Williams	118	121
Taylor	123	128
Klam	130	131
Eggers	110	115

The graphologist was asked to analyze an essay written by each in long-
hand entitled "The Challenges in Appliance Manufacturing Today." She
was asked to select a person most likely to initiate change in a difficult
established situation. Her recommendations were:

Outstanding . . . . Klam
                               Eggers
                               Williams
Acceptable . . . . Taylor
Not acceptable . . . . Radick

Reference letters were favorable to all candidates.

Requirement. You are Dale Young. Prepare a recommendation for decision by Kenneth O'Connor and James Cox. Document your choice with systematic analysis.

11. Sellmore Insurance Co.*

On October 1, 1975, the Sellmore Insurance Company announced plans to open a regional headquarters office in Lincoln, Nebraska. The firm expects to begin hiring for its office positions in early January and anticipates reaching a full complement of 400 employees by mid-summer 1976. This figure does not include insurance agents or other employees working in regional branch offices or in the field. Of the total, approximately 320 would be classified as white-collar "nonexempt" salaried personnel and would be employed in such positions as clerk, clerk-typist, receptionist, secretary, administrative assistant, key punch operator, computer operator, and similar office classifications.

The firm is quite concerned about procuring an efficient work force and expects to offer pay, benefits, and working conditions that are at least comparable—and probably superior—to those offered by similar companies in the Lincoln area. Because they are starting from scratch with only a small nucleus of managerial and technical personnel being transferred in to form the initial staff, the company plans to launch a large advertising campaign for recruiting purposes. The firm would like to establish a selection ratio of 1/10—and anticipates an even more favorable ratio after it is established.

Hirman Goode, newly appointed general manager of the firm's Lincoln office, is especially concerned about developing an effective selection procedure. No one has been appointed to the position of personnel manager for the firm, but Hiram still wants to establish the basic hiring policies and procedures rather than wait for this key position to be filled. (The firm hopes to hire a person with at least three years experience in personnel for this position and would prefer to hire someone already living in the Lincoln area.)

---

* This case was prepared by Professor Cary Thorp, University of Nebraska, Lincoln, Nebraska as a basis for class discussion.

Hiram, after consulting with others on his staff, has decided to follow this procedure in selecting personnel for nonexempt salaried positions:

Step 1:   Completion of application blank.
Step 2:   *a*. Brief interview with those applicants whose application indicates that they lack basic qualifications for available positions.
          b. Comprehensive interview by someone on the personnel staff for all other applicants. (Approximately 30–40 minutes in length.)
Step 3:   Battery of tests for most of those who have been interviewed. (Less qualified people will not be tested) The specific tests will be dependent upon the job(s) for which the applicant is being considered but will include a mental ability test for *all* applicants. Personality tests and interests tests will *not* be used. Other tests will include (but not necessarily be limited to):
          a. Minnesota Clerical Test (for all clerks, receptionists, clerk-typists and related office positions).
          b. General Clerical Aptitude Test—including filing, spelling, grammar, general math, reading comprehension, and vocabulary (for all clerks, receptionists, clerk-typists, secretaries, administrative assistants, and related office positions).
          c. Typing test (for all typists, clerk-typists, secretaries, and related office positions).
          d. Key punch operators test (for all key punch operators).
          e. Key punch operator aptitude test (for all key punch operator trainees).
          f. Computer operators test (for computer operators).
          With the exception of the typing test and the keypunch operator test which will both test actual proficiency on company equipment, all tests are to be of the paper-and-pencil variety and will be purchased from companies specializing in standardized tests.
Step 4:   *a*. Reference check by telephone with all previous employers in the last five years for those applicants still being given serious consideration for employment.
          b. Reference check by telephone with the applicant's high school for those applicants with no previous work history and who are being given serious consideration for employment.
Step 5:   Employment interview by (the) department head(s) who have job vacancies matching the interests and qualifications of the best applicants. The department head will be empowered to extend an offer of employment, contingent upon satisfactory medical

report, of any applicant completing Step 5—consistent with any overriding employment policies that may be established by the firm.

While Mr. Goode has expressed a great deal of confidence in this selection procedure, there are some aspects of selection that bother him. Consequently, he has called upon *your* services and advice as an expert in personnel selection. In your first meeting with Mr. Goode, he has expressed his concern as follows:

Before we interview our first applicant we've got to have some useful employment forms. I could use some of the forms from the other regional offices, but frankly I'm not the least bit impressed with them. They've been asking the same questions for over 25 years, and except for some minor changes to accommodate the EEOC people, there hasn't been any change in the forms at all. What I am looking for are some forms which are concise but which at the same time give us all the information we need to make employment decisions. There are too many irrelevant questions being asked in employment offices, and I'd like to put a stop to that before it gets started here. Also, I want to make sure that the forms are consistent with EEO guidelines. Specifically, there are three forms I would like to have you design. These are to be used in processing applicants for nonexempt salaried personnel only. We'll develop forms for the other classifications later. The three forms I would like for you to provide me are:

1. An application blank.
2. An interview schedule including all the important questions—and in an appropriate sequence—to be raised by the personnel interviewer for those applicants who will be given a comprehensive interview.
3. A telephone reference check form to be used in gathering information from previous employers.

I'm also concerned about our testing program and would like your advice. Here's our dilemma. We feel very strongly that employment testing is an important step in the selection process—particularly for the nonexempt salaried positions we will be filling in our office. On the other hand, the EEOC testing guidelines and recent court decisions, such as the *Albermarle* v. *Moody* case, point up how difficult it is to administer test validation procedures that will satisfy the courts and the EEOC. Did you know that less than 3 percent of the population of Lincoln is black? It doesn't make sense to be as a businessman to drop a procedure that I have confidence in to guard against a possible charge of unintentional discrimination. I can assure you we have no intention of discriminating against women, blacks, Chicanos, Indianas, older applicants, persons who are disabled, or any other group protected by law. In fact, we plan to initiate a vigorous affirmative action program in all of these areas. But as far as dropping testing from our selection procedure—well, I just don't know. I'm hoping you can give us a fresh perspective on this dilemma.

Your assignment, should you decide to accept it, is to:

1. Design the three forms requested (don't worry about "art" work—
   that part won't be graded).
2. Develop a detailed analysis of the testing dilemma facing Mr. Goode,
   and make specific recommendations as to what his firm should—
   or should not—do.
3. Be prepared orally to defend your forms and recommendations to
   your instructor should he so request.

12. Dickinson Ceramics, Inc.

Dickinson (DCI) is a large manufacturer of ceramic materials primarily
for industrial uses. Its headquarters is located in New York City. It employs 6,200 persons in the following categories:

Operative and clerical	5,041
Supervisory and technical	744
Middle management and professional	372
Top management	43

As part of its most recent personnel audit, one of the major objectives
was to evaluate the effectiveness of their formal performance evaluation
system. Arthur Neifert, vice president of personnel and organizational
development, has requested his department to begin this evaluation. The
department decided to try to determine the costs and benefits as part of
its assessment. The costs were calculated first.

At DCI, the supervisor evaluates the person and then spends at least
30 minutes discussing it with him or her. Thus, 3,100 hours in employee
time were expended each year. This was roughly estimated to be worth
$22,000–$25,000 in employee time.

The cost in managerial time was based on 30 minutes to prepare each
evaluation and 30-minute discussions with each employee. The cost is
estimated as follows:

Supervisory managers	5,041 hours @ $ 7 hour	$35,287
Middle managers	744 hours @ $10 hour	7,440
Top managers	372 hours @ $25 hour	9,300
		$52,027

Personnel's time for filing the reports, developing them, consulting,
and so forth is estimated to be $12,000 yearly. Total direct cost to DCI is
about $90,000 yearly, or about $15 per employee per year.

TABLE 1
RESULTS OF PERFORMANCE EVALUATION ITEMS ON THE ATTITUDE SURVEY (in percent)

Question	Company as a whole					Employees					Supervisors					Top and middle management				
	SA	A	N	D	SD	SA	A	N	D	SD	SA	A	N	D	SD	SA	A	N	D	SD
1	19	39	9	8	2	23	38	11	4	1	26	42	8	9	3	15	23	21	16	12
2	3	8	31	23	12	4	9	28	21	9	2	7	30	24	14	1	2	34	26	15
3	23	43	6	5	1	26	39	6	7	2	23	38	10	8	6	9	18	27	19	14
4	21	41	5	6	1	25	41	8	3	2	27	41	10	8	2	16	21	23	18	9
Supervisor's questions																				
1											35	43	14	7	1	17	26	22	21	14
2											28	32	21	5	4	20	21	28	23	18
3											14	23	40	12	9	9	17	18	29	27

Rod Boyer, vice president of operations, remarked when he heard that figure: "What a waste! That should be paid out in additional dividends." Neifert disagreed and said he was sure most of the employees would disagree too. So the personnel department added several items to the annual attitude survey of employees (see Exhibit 1). The results of the survey are given in Table 1, page 239. The less than 100 percent response by employees was checked out. It was found that about 23 percent had never received formal evaluations.

EXHIBIT 1
ATTITUDE SURVEY AT DICKINSON CERAMICS

Part III   Performance evaluation
Yearly, we ask supervisors to spend about half an hour with each employee to evaluate them. Please tell us how you feel about this process.

	Strongly agree	Agree	Neutral	Disagree	Strongly disagree
1. I feel I will do a better job next year because of what I learned from the performance evaluation.					
2. I feel the form used to evaluate me is a good one.					
3. I feel my supervisor's comments during the interview are helpful.					
4. I would like to see these evaluations continued.					

For supervisors, the following questions were added:

1. My employees are better workers because of performance evaluation.
2. It is a good use of my time to do performance evaluations.
3. I think our performance evaluation system is a good one.

Requirement.   You are Neifert. Evaluate the costs and benefits of the performance evaluation system at DCI. Should it be continued, changed, and how could it be improved?

13. Acme Paperboard, Inc.

Acme Paperboard (API) is a large manufacturer of forest products, especially paperboard. Its main office is located in Salem, Oregon. The firm has 11 branch headquarters in the following cities: El Paso, Texas; Hutchinson, Kansas; Rockford, Illinois; Bay City, Michigan; New Bedford, Massachusetts; Elmira, New York; Durham, North Carolina; Gadsden, Alabama; St. Boniface, Manitoba; Hamilton, Ontario; and Trois-Rivieres, Quebec.

The personnel department at API has been examining the performance evaluation interviews of the supervisors at the various locations. Vice President of Personnel Gordon Ingenohl said: "We've tried a variety of approaches to performance evaluation. There are many good ones, but I'm convinced that the most important part of the performance appraisal process is what goes on between the supervisor and employee when they discuss what happened last year and what should happen next year."

API has been experimenting with a variety of approaches to evaluation. These approaches are graphic-rating scale, ranking, critical-incident technique, and forced distribution. The different techniques were tried in the branch offices shown below.

1. Graphic-rating scale—El Paso, Rockford, and New Bedford.
2. Ranking—Hutchinson, Hamilton, and Elmira.
3. Critical-incident technique—Bay City, Gadsden, and Trois-Rivieres.
4. Forced distribution—St. Boniface and Durham.

Table 1 summarizes the responses to attitude questionnaires given to supervisors and employees on the uses of the techniques over the three-year experimental period.

TABLE 1
EMPLOYEE REACTION TO PERFORMANCE EVALUATIONS AT API (in percent)

		Year 1				Year 2		
	VF*	F†	U‡	VU§	VF*	F†	U‡	VU§
1. Graphic-rating scale								
El Paso	30	34	19	17	31	38	20	11
Rockford	28	39	21	12	30	34	16	20
New Bedford	32	41	24	3	33	35	23	9
2. Ranking								
Hutchinson	49	29	16	6	45	21	20	14
Hamilton	46	27	13	14	39	19	21	21
Elmira	51	32	17	0	38	26	23	13
3. Critical-incident technique								
Bay City	37	36	17	10	41	34	16	9
Gadsden	30	38	18	14	39	35	15	11
Trois-Rivieres	34	39	11	6	48	38	9	5
4. Forced distribution								
St. Boniface	14	29	33	24	26	31	24	19
Durham	28	33	21	18	18	22	32	28

* Very favorable.
† Favorable.
‡ Unfavorable.
§ Very unfavorable.

TABLE 1 (*continued*)

		Year 3			
		VF*	F†	U‡	VU§
1.	Graphic-rating scale				
	El Paso	30	37	16	17
	Rockford	29	41	20	10
	New Bedford	30	36	24	10
2.	Ranking				
	Hutchinson	31	17	24	28
	Hamilton	29	14	32	25
	Elmira	26	18	25	31
3.	Critical-incident technique				
	Bay City	45	36	11	8
	Gadsden	48	37	9	7
	Trois-Rivieres	49	40	7	4
4.	Forced distribution				
	St. Boniface	17	25	31	27
	Durham	17	20	39	24

    * Very favorable.
    † Favorable.
    ‡ Unfavorable.
    § Very unfavorable.

In addition to experimenting with specific techniques, the firm experimented with training supervisors in interviewing employees during the third year. There were several points covered in this training.

1. Discuss the employee's past behavior in this order—positive, negative, positive.
2. Balance the amount of positive and negative comments with the overall evaluation. That is, if the employee has scored 80 on a scale of 100, 80 percent of the interview should be spent reinforcing positive behavior, only 20 percent on criticism.
3. Put major emphasis on the future behavior and how the supervisor can help the employee improve.

In addition to the experimental groups of supervisors who received this training, a subset of these were urged to have their employees supplement their own evaluations with self-evaluations. Then the supervisor and employee compared the evaluations as a point of departure in the interview. Table 2 presents some data on the results of this experiment. If the employee was encouraged to use self-evaluation, he or she was twice as likely to regard performance evaluation "very favorably" or "favorably."

Requirement. You are Jim Curry, assistant to Ingenohl. You have been asked to review these data and recommend companywide performance evaluation policies.

TABLE 2
PERCENTAGE OF EMPLOYEES WHO REGARDED PERFORMANCE
EVALUATION VERY FAVORABLY OR FAVORABLY

Plant	Experimental group*	Control group
Rockford	45	25
Bay City	57	24
Trois-Rivieres	66	23
Durham	32	5

    * Supervisors received training.

14. Training Costs

A major unit of the U.S. Army recently was considering the costs of training enlisted men to use communications equipment properly. The goal was the most effective use of these telephones and radios with the least training cost.

The experimental goup was trained with programmed instruction manuals. The control group was trained with classroom lectures and exercises.

The relative costs of the experience are shown in Table 1.

TABLE 1

Groups	Costs
Control group (30 students)	
Training aids	$100
Cost of lecturers	600
Administrative costs (including counseling)	500
Experimental group (30 students)	
Preparation and printing of manual	$750
Counselors*†	100
Administrative costs	300

    * Prorated over the expected number of students for the course that year.

    † Students needed some persons to explain points they didn't understand.

The test scores achieved on identical tests were as follows—the control group had a mean score of 75 with a range of 67 to 96 and the experimental group had a mean score of 73 with a range of 48 to 98. An attitude survey administered to the students at the end of the course asked the students to evaluate it as follows: "I feel that this course was one of the best I have ever had in my life." The results are given according to percentage of agreement (Table 2).

TABLE 2

	Strongly agree	Agree	Disagree	Strongly disagree
Control group	20	55	15	10
Experimental group	10	20	35	25

Requirement. You are Harold Bushway, a training specialist for the army. Recommend whether or not the experiment should be extended and how you might change future evaluations and assessments.

15. Pay Secrecy Exercise

Studies about whether employees prefer to have their compensation known have had conflicting findings. At present, many experts feel that some categories of employees prefer total secrecy, some want full knowledge, and some accept a middle ground: Everyone knows everyone's pay range but not the specific pay within the range.

Requirements
1. Choose an enterprise that follows one of these three policies. Determine if the employees are satisfied with the present enterprise policy on this issue[1] [2A; 2B; 2C; 2I; 2J; 2K in Exhibit 1] and recommend
   a. No change.
   b. Partial change.
   c. Full change.
2. To implement this, choose a sample of about one third of all large employee categories (operation, clerical) and total sample of all smaller categories (groups of ten or less).
3. Interview these employees using the schedule attached as Exhibit 1.
4. Analyze the results as follows:
   a. Total sample.
   b. Female responses versus male responses [1A].
   c. Racial/cultural responses—[use Caucasians, blacks, Hispanic, American Indians, Orientals in the United States; in Canada: English speaking versus French speaking] [1B].
   d. Age [1C].
   e. Education [use less than high school graduate; high school graduate; some college; college degree; more than college degree] [1D].

---

[1] Note: The reference in brackets at the end of each item [for example, 1A] refers to the item in the interview schedule which follows which gathers these data.

EXHIBIT 1
PAY SECRECY INTERVIEW SCHEDULE

1. First let's ask some questions about you. [If answers are obvious such as
    French speaking, just record.]
    A. Sex: ___ Male   ___ Female.
    B. Race/culture _____.
    C. Age: Are you: ___under 20; ___20–29; ___30–39; ___40–49; ___50–
        59; ___60 or older.
    D. Highest education level completed: _____.
    E. Are you a union member? ___ Yes   ___ No.
    F. You work for _____ supervisor.
    G. Your section is _____.
        Your department is _____.
    H. Experience:
        ___Number of years working full time since last left school.
        ___Number of years working full time for the enterprise.
        ___Number of years working full time in this work unit.

2. Please respond to these items by telling me whether you strongly agree
    (SA); agree *(A)*; not sure *(N)*; disagree *(D)*; strongly disagree *(SD)*.

Item	SA	A	N	D	SD
A. I believe the policy here is to keep employees' pay secret from others.					
B. I believe the policy here is to allow the pay range of a person's job to be known but not the actual pay itself.					
C. I believe the policy here is for people to know what others are paid.					
D. I believe that I am paid a *fair* wage (salary).					
E. I believe that I am overpaid.					
F. I believe that I am underpaid.					
G. I believe that the pay system as a whole is fair.					
H. I believe that on the whole the pay system is well administered.					
I. I believe that my pay should be kept from other employees more than it is now.					
J. I don't care if my actual pay is known by everyone I work with.					
K. I don't care if my pay range is known by everyone I work with.					
L. In general, I'd say I'm very well satisfied in my job here.					
M. In general, I'd say I'm very well satisfied with my pay here.					

f. Experience: [1H].
   (1) Total years.
   (2) Total years with enterprise.
   (3) Total years in this section.
g. Union membership [1E].
h. Departments, sections, and other subgroups [1F; 1G].
i. Perception that the person is fairly or unfairly paid now. [2D; 2E; 2F].
j. Employee satisfaction [2L; 2M].
k. The perceived effectiveness of the pay system [2G; 2H].

5. Recommend a policy of secrecy, openness, or middle for
   a. The total enterprise.
   b. Certain departments.
   c. Categories of employees.

16. Profit Sharing at CSR

CSR is a medium-sized manufacturer of synthetic rubber and similar materials. The home office is Sherbrooke, Quebec.

Recently CSR's president, George Stickney, was searching for a means of increasing the motivation, output, and morale of his employees. One day he hit upon profit sharing as the ideal mechanism.

The next day he dictated a letter to personnel consultant, Harold Nordstrom. Nordstrom had written the article which stimulated Stickney's interest. The consultant recommended the following plan:

The payment of 30 percent of profit after taxes and dividends to employees. The percentage is used because 70 percent of productivity increases have been due to capital improvements, 30 percent due to labor in the last few years.

These payments are to be made quarterly and are to be based on employee's contribution to the company success. Since this is difficult to measure, it will be based on their salary. Thus, if the person's salary represents 1 percent of total wages and salaries, he will receive 1 percent of the profit-sharing fund.

Because of major variations in profits quarterly, Stickney decided to make the payment yearly. CSR's year ran July 1 to June 30th. His goal was to pay the profit-sharing bonus on Dominion Day, July 1.

He announced the new plan with a real fanfare after receiving the board's approval. Letters were sent to each employee. The plan was played up in the monthly CSR newsletter.

The results attributed to the plan by the personnel department were as follows:

1. Better turnover record. It was reduced from 28 percent to 26 percent the first year and at the end of the third year stands at 24 percent. This was estimated to have saved the company $100 per employee. The firm employs 250 persons.
2. Lower absenteeism. "Voluntary" absenteeism was reduced from six days per year per employee to four-and-a-half days after three years. This is estimated to save the firm $12.50 per employee per year.
3. High morale. The morale score per employee rose from a median of 76 on a multiple-item scale to 80.
4. Slightly higher productivity per employee. It rose 8 percent the first year (up from 6 percent the year before) and has risen 1 percent per year above that which was expected before the plan was instituted.

Profit-sharing payments to employees have been as follows: first year—$25,000, second year—$40,000, and third year—$28,000.

The past year has been a difficult one for the industry. The board is expecting a very difficult few years coming up. They have instructed Stickney to cut all possible costs or they might have to pass up giving a dividend.

Requirement. You are Albert Gray, personnel manager at CSR. Stickney has asked you to evaluate the effectiveness of profit sharing. He is considering eliminating it.

17. Pay, Benefits, and Services Exercise

Compensation and benefits is the personnel activity which costs the most money. In most cases, enterprises are not able to expend the funds to give employees all the pay and benefits they would like.

This exercise suggests that one way an enterprise can decide how to solve the allocation problem is to ask the employees what they would like.

Requirements
1. Select an enterprise with at least 200 employees. Interview or give questionnaires to the following employees:
    a. A 30 percent sample of all large groups of employees (more than ten in a category such as operation, clerical, and so forth) and the total sample of groups composed of less than ten persons.
    b. Use attached interview schedule/questionnaire.
2. Recommend how the management should spend the expected $40 per week increase that has been agreed upon. Base this on an analysis of the responses of some of the following groups:

  a. Total sample.

  b. Employee groups [managerial; professional; technical; service; sales; clerical; operation] [1A].[1]

  c. *Age* [1B].

  d. Sex [1C].

  e. Marital status [1D].

  f. Education [1E].

  g. Experience [1F].

  h. Race/culture [1G].

  i. Union membership [1H].

  j. Pay category [1L].

  k. Department worked in [1I; 1J; 1K].

  l. Employee satisfaction [2F].

  m. Employee satisfaction with pay [2A; 2B; 2C; 2G].

  n. Employee satisfaction with benefits [2I, 2J, 2K].

  o. Employee satisfaction with pay and benefits' effectiveness [2E; 2D].

  p. Analysis of which benefits should be increased, if any; if pay alone should be raised; or which combination of pay and benefits should be offered. [3].

EXHIBIT 1
PAY, BENEFIT, AND SERVICES INTERVIEW SCHEDULE/QUESTIONNAIRE

---

 1. Some questions about you.
  [If the answer is obvious such as sex of respondent, just note.]

  A. How would you characterize yourself as: ___manager; ___professional; ___technician; ___service; ___sales; ___clerical; ___operations; ___blue-collar.

  B. Your age is ___19 or under; ___20–29; ___30–39; ___40–49; ___50–59; ___60 and over.

  C. ___Male ___Female.

  D. Are you ___single; ___single with a child or children; ___divorced; ___divorced with a child or children; ___married; ___married with a child or children.

  E. Your highest educational achievement was ___high school; ___high school graduate; ___some college; ___college graduate; ___more than college degree.

  F. With regard to your work experience,
   ___Number of years working full time since last left school.
   ___Number of years working full time for this enterprise.
   ___Number of years working full time for this work unit.

  G. Would you say you are [U.S.] ___Caucasian; ___Black; ___Spanish surnamed; ___Oriental; ___American Indian.
   [Canada] ___English speaking; ___French speaking; ___Native born.

---

 [1] [1A] and similar number/letter combinations refer to items in the interview schedule.

EXHIBIT 1 (continued)

H. Are you a member of a union? ___Yes ___No.
I. You work for _____ supervisor.
J. Your section is _____.
K. Your department is _____.
L. At present what is your pay range: ___below minimum wage; ___minimum wage; ___under 3.50 per hour; ___3.51–4.00 per hour; ___4.01–5.00 per hour; ___5.01–6.00 per hour; ___6.01–10.00 per hour; ___10.01–15.00 per hour; ___more than 15.00 per hour.

2. Please respond to these items by telling whether you strongly agree [SA]; agree [A]; not sure [N]; disagree [D]; strongly disagree [SD] to each:

Item	SA	A	N	D	SD
A. In general, I believe that I am paid a fair wage or salary.					
B. I believe that I am somewhat overpaid.					
C. I believe that I am somewhat underpaid.					
D. I believe that the pay and benefits system is well administered.					
E. I believe that the pay and benefit system as a whole is fair.					
F. In general, I'd say I'm very well satisfied with my job here.					
G. In general, I'd say I'm well satisfied with my pay here.					
H. In general, I'd say I'm well satisfied with the benefit-services program here.					
I. In general, I believe the benefit-services program here is fair.					

	SA	A	N	D	SD
J. In general, I believe the benefit-services program here is too generous.					
K. In general, the benefit-services program is inadequate.					

3. Suppose your employer is able to offer you a 10-percent raise for next year. Please indicate how you'd spend it. *The raise must not exceed 10 percent.*

Increase in pay	___%
Increase in health and medical insurance	___%
Increase in life insurance	___%
Increase in accident insurance	___%
Increase in holidays	___%
Increase in break times during the day	___%
Increase in vacation time	___%
Increase in social security	___%
Increase in workers' compensation	___%
Increase in unemployment insurance	___%
Increase in employers' pension plan	___%
Total	10%

18. OSHA Exercise

OSHA is under attack as a poorly run agency whose program has miscarried. Others feel that health and safety is too important a personnel activity to be left up to employees alone, for some employers may do a good job; others may ignore it. A third group feel government legislation is necessary, but OSHA is not good legislation.

One way for students to make up their own minds on this issue is for them to go into the field, question firms, and gather data on the health and safety issue.

Requirement. Create a three-person team. Ask each team member to interview ten firms on their reactions to OSHA. Then they should write a report which:

a. Assesses the present value of OSHA. Compare and contrast the attitudes and feelings of the company.
b. Prepares suggestions for OSHA improvements.
c. Prepares suggestions for how the firms might live with OSHA better.

Exhibit 1, page 251 is the interview schedule to be used for the field research.

19. Field Exercise: Equal Employment Opportunity and Human Rights

The vice president-personnel is concerned about how adequately the enterprise is dealing with EEO/HR. The vice president wishes to take preventative action in case the enterprise is not achieving a balance of employees by sex, race, color, ethnic background, and similar categories. As a beginning point, the vice president wishes to analyze the employment by race (in the United States; in Canada: language and minority groups) and sex.

Exhibit 1 is designed for use in the United States; Exhibit 2, for Canada.

Requirement
1. Visit an enterprise with at least 75 employees. This enterprise can be a total organization, such as a firm, or a subunit of the enterprise. Collect data on the questionnaire.
2. Then identify "imbalances" in employee distribution. For example, if the racial composition of the area is 60 percent black and the enterprise's black employees comprise 1 percent of the total employment, some might infer discrimination is being practiced. Or suppose total

EXHIBIT 1

OSHA Questionnaire

Company _____

Number of employees _____

1. Do you feel that OSHA's stated purpose, "to provide a safe and healthful working place for every working man and woman in the nation," is an important one?

2. How well do you feel you understand the OSHA regulations?

3. How do you find out about changes in the regulations?

4. Has OSHA done a good job designing accident-reporting reports and systems?

5. How much time does it take you to complete these reports?

6. Have you ever been inspected by an OSHA inspector? Which of these reasons for inspection did he give—imminent danger, catastrophe, complaint, target industry, or random selection?

7. Were you fined by OSHA? How much? What for?

8. Do you believe that OSHA inspectors and their inspections are helpful? To you? To your employees?

9. Are you aware that OSHA is trying to help with voluntary compliance? Would you be interested? Do you use any outside assistance such as an insurance company to help with compliance?

10. What has been OSHA's impact upon management-labor relations at your company?

11. Would you estimate your cost of compliance since OSHA was enacted in 1970?

12. Which health and safety activities did you perform before OSHA was enacted?

    _____Inspections. How often? _____ By whom? _____

    _____Accident records maintained.

    _____Safety contests.

    _____Safety training.

    _____Safety posters and communication.

    _____Health clinic.

    _____Health inspections.

13. Do you feel OSHA has been effective in producing safer working places? Why or why not?

14. Do you feel there is a better way to provide safer working conditions than through OSHA? How?

15. Instead of OSHA's approach, would taxing employers who have accidents and deaths through workers' compensation have worked better?

[Where appropriate]
16. Would you favor a state plan over the federal plan although _____ _____ does not offer one at present?

EXHIBIT 1
EQUAL EMPLOYMENT OPPORTUNITY QUESTIONNAIRE (U.S.)

| Job categories | Total employees | Total male employees | Total female employees | Minority group employees | | | | | | | | |
| | | | | Male | | | | Female | | | |
				Black	Oriental	American Indian	Hispanic	Black	Oriental	American Indian	Hispanic
Officials and managers											
Professionals											
Technicians/ technical employees											
Sales workers											
Office and clerical											
Service workers											
Operations employees											

EXHIBIT 2
HUMAN RIGHTS QUESTIONNAIRE (CANADA)

Job categories	Total employees	Total male employees	Total female employees	Distribution of employees					
				Male			Female		
				English speaking	French speaking	Indians and natives	English speaking	French speaking	Indians and natives
Officials and managers									
Professionals									
Technicians/ technical employees									
Sales workers									
Office and clerical									
Service workers									
Operations employees									

employment is 75 percent female, but no sales, technical, professional, or managerial employees are female; some may contend that discrimination is being practiced. Set realistic EEO/HR goals for each sex and employee group category.

3. Then:

a. *Assuming* the enterprise wishes to have a "balanced" employee group,

b. *Assuming* that attrition is as follows:

Operations .... 20% yearly overtime
Service .... 15% yearly overtime
Office .... 20% yearly overtime
Sales .... 10% yearly overtime
Technical .... 5% yearly overtime
Professionals .... 5% yearly overtime
Managerial .... 5% yearly overtime

The attrition percentage should be used this way. If there are 30 operations employees, 20 percent yearly means 6 leave. Where the numbers are small (let's say one manager), use the 5 percent this way: A manager changes every 20 years [5% × 20 = 100%].

c. *Assuming* the enterprise is growing and net hirings (in addition to attrition) are as follows: operations, service, office, and sales: 5 percent each, yearly; technical, professional: one person each, yearly; managerial: one per 75 employees about two years from now.

d. *Given* assumptions a, b, and c, design an EEO/HR program that includes:

Recruiting approaches and goals,
Selection approaches and goals,
Promotion approaches and goals,
Training/management development goals and approaches,

that will help achieve an effective preventative EEO/HR program.

20. Enforcing the Rules: How Do Managers Differ?

The company has a plant rule: "An employee shall be fined five dollars ($5) for being tardy a third time, as well as for any subsequent dates, within any given six-month period.

In each of these instances the employee is late for the third time within the six-month period.

Adams, a highly respected employee, is a key man on a subassembly. When he is late, four other men are idle. He is to retire in less than two years, and following a new policy, the company has helped him buy a small farm located 30 miles from town. There are no telephone lines, and after a heavy snow the snowplow doesn't reach his home until late in the morning. He has been late three times because of heavy snows.

Baker, a very conscientious and better-than-average worker, was late for the third time because his wife was giving birth to a son, who arrived at 8:05 A.M. After seeing that his wife and baby were well, he came immediately to work.

Carter, an average worker and a shop steward, reporting late to work for the third time, tells you that although leaving home at a reasonable time he had a flat tire. Not wanting to be late, he had a service-station attendant change the wheel for him, although he could have done it himself. He produces the charge slip in proof of his story.

Edmonds, the "joker" of the crew, arrives late for the third time. His excuse is that as he was leaving the house his wife said she wanted to ride downtown with him. He waited quite a while for her to get ready. Moreover, it was raining, so he had to take her out of his way to work.

1. Would you dock Adams? .... Yes   No
2. Would you dock Baker? .... Yes   No
3. Would you dock Carter? .... Yes   No
4. Would you dock Edmonds? .... Yes   No

Requirement. You are the supervisor for the above employees, what action will you take against each individual employee? Justify your answers.

In-basket exercises

A. IN-BASKET EXERCISES: A DISCUSSION

INTRODUCTION TO THE USE OF IN-BASKETS

This section introduces the last group of exercises: in-basket exercises. An in-basket is a series of items such as letters and telephone calls. This group of materials is designed to simulate the kind of material a manager such as a personnel manager would receive in a work day.

The first part of the exercise consists of a description of the managerial setting and the role the participant will play. Next, the actual material waiting for the manager on his or her desk is provided.

These items are presented in the order in which they were received. It is your responsibility to sort out those which are the most pressing from those which can wait a bit. You will be given a time limit within which you must complete the work.

The instructional leader will describe how he or she wants you to proceed with the data. In addition to the letters and phone calls provided, it is possible that during the exercise you will receive additional phone calls and memos. For, when you are on a job, no one hands you all your work for the day and then leaves you uninterrupted until you are finished.

Remember that you must place yourself in the situation described. When you have completed what you would do and in which order of importance, this can be compared with norms developed for the exercise. You should learn how you react to time pressures and how well you make decisions in the usual less-than-full-information environment in which most managers work.

B. IN-BASKET EXERCISES

1. Russell Manufacturing Co., Ltd.

Russell Manufacturing is a medium-sized firm in Toronto, Ontario, Canada. Founded in the 1920s the firm has manufactured a variety of products in its history. It has never been directly involved in manufacturing for the consumer market. It has always directed its attention to making subassemblies or parts for other firms to their specifications. At present and for the last ten years, the major focus has been on parts for the auto industry.

It's not clear why Russell has not been involved with consumer goods. It could be that the top management has traditionally been trained in engineering. The organization chart for Russell is given in Exhibit 1.

The board is composed of the following: seven members of the Sheridan family; two lawyers from the firm Russell uses; an officer of the Toronto Dominion Bank; the CEO, and the executive vice president.

The backgrounds on the focal persons are as follows:

Giles Sheridan, age 61, is the son-in-law of Peter Russell—the man who made RMC. Giles is a graduate in engineering from a major British engineering school. He has spent his entire career with RMC and plans to retire in two years.

Landon Sheridan, age 57, is Giles Sheridan's brother. Landon is a graduate of M.I.T. in mechanical engineering. He worked in the United States for ten years prior to joining RMC when Peter Russell died.

Hugo Sheridan, age 38, is Giles Sheridan's son. He is a graduate engineer from a major Canadian engineering school with an M.B.A. from the University of Toronto. He also is a chartered accountant. Hugo spent five years with a major Canadian C.P.A. firm before joining RMC.

J.R.S. Lewis, age 36, is the son-in-law of Landon Sheridan. Mr. Lewis has an engineering degree from the University of Michigan and joined RMC shortly after marrying Patricia Sheridan 15 years ago.

Felix Sheridan, age 40, is Giles Sheridan's son. Felix received his engineering degree (with honours) from a major Canadian university. He is very active in professional engineering circles in Canada. He has spent his entire career with RMC.

EXHIBIT 1
RUSSELL MANUFACTURING CO., LTD., ORGANIZATION CHART

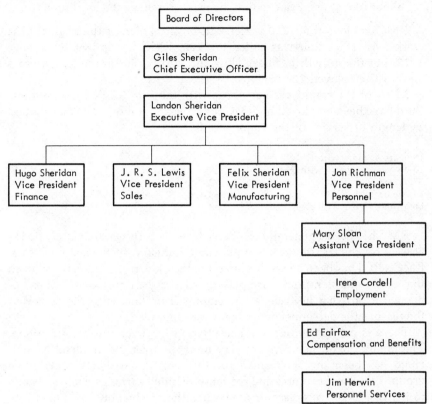

Jon Richman, age 32, is a graduate in business/commerce of the University of Western Ontario. He has been with RMC for one year. Prior to that, he spent eight years with the personnel department of the Canadian division of a major U.S. auto firm.

Mary Sloan, age 50, is a high school graduate. She headed the personnel unit of RMC, reporting to Felix Sheridan, until last year. At that time, Giles Sheridan decided to "upgrade" the personnel function. He created a vice president level position and hired Jon Richman at that time. Mary has worked for RMC for 31 years.

Irene Cordell, age 48, has been with RMC for 21 years. She is a high school graduate. She has done employment work for most of those 21 years.

Ed Fairfax, age 22, has a commerce degree from York University in Toronto. This is Ed's first job, and he joined RMC when he left college six months ago.

Jim Herwin, age 28, is working on a commerce degree at night at York. He's completed about two thirds of it. He's been employed by RMC for about four years. Prior to that, he was a foreman at a local foundry.

RMC employs about 760 persons. Its physical plant is the original 1922 works. An office unit was added in 1928. RMC has grown some since 1928. But the growth has been slow and steady. For example, ten years ago RMC employed 727 persons.

Many of the employees have been with the firm for years. About one third have been employed by RMC for 15 years or more. The distribution by length of service of the employees is:

15 years or more with RMC	253
10–14 years or more with RMC	127
5–9 years with RMC . . . . : . .	72
1–4 years with RMC	64
Less than a year with RMC	244

RMC has been a generally profitable firm. Its fortunes are closely tied—at least for the last ten years—to the auto industry. In the last five years, RMC's ROI has been one of the lowest in the industry. Landon has blamed that on an old plant and price pressures from their customers. Giles has blamed it on what he feels is low employee productivity. That's one of the reasons the personnel department was upgraded.

There is conflict within the executive group over profit distribution. The family board members are very unhappy over the dividend payout. Hugo has been the spokesman for this position within the executive group. Felix has been pressing for more retained earnings. He also wants to increase debt to replace or modernize the production facilities. J.R.S. Lewis has not involved himself in this dispute. Jon Richman has been trying to increase personnel's budget and upgrade pay, benefits, and the personnel program in general. RMC is the largest nonunionized unit in the industry, and Jon worries what will happen if a union appears on the scene.

Exhibit 2 is the time of the exercise. Jon has been ill for several days and took a few days' leave to include Dominion Day (July 1) and July 2.

He returns to work July 5. The items which follow are in the in-basket on his desk at 8:30 A.M. July 5.

```
July
S   M   T   W   T   F   S
                1   2   3
4   5   6   7   8   9  10
11  12  13  14  15  16  17
18  19  20  21  22  23  24
25  26  27  28  29  30
```

ITEM 1

Russell Manufacturing Co., Ltd.

INTEROFFICE MEMORANDUM   July 2

TO: Jon Richman
FROM: Giles Sheridan
SUBJECT: Proposed Personnel Budget

I am in receipt of your proposed budget for next year.

It calls for substanial increases in funds and the adding of another personnel professional.

The budget includes increases of 10 percent or more in the training area and safety areas. You propose increased activity in selection, orientation, counseling, performance evaluation, human rights, and personnel audit areas as well as substantial pay and benefit increases.

In these stringent economic times, all of these are just not possible. Several RMC executives are proposing cuts to your last budget, not increases.

The executive committee will meet at 2 P.M. July 7.

Please come prepared with detailed documentation to defend the proposed budget. You might also prepare a contingency plan of which of the proposals you'll give up and or where you would entertain cuts to your proposed budget.

Participant action

1.   How important is this item?

---

2.   What should be done about this item?

ITEM 2

American Society for Personnel Administration
Berea, Ohio

June 28

Dear Mr. Richman,

As you may know, ASPA has a program for professionalizing person-nel executives in North America.

Attached please find our program for accreditation.

We invite you to apply and participate. From what we've heard about you, with proper energy on your part you should be able to complete the diplomat program.

Sincerely,

R. J. Jones

Participant action

1. How important is this item?

---

2. What should be done about this item?

ITEM 3

Russell Manufacturing Co., Ltd.

INTEROFFICE MEMORANDUM   July 2

TO: Jon Richman
FROM: Felix Sheridan
SUBJECT: Training Budget

I have before me your training budget request for my department's employees.

Apparently you believe the manufacturing employees are poorly trained. I see that you requested a 25-percent increase.

Perhaps you've forgotten that we need to increase the dividend. I'm not sure training does much good anyway. I feel you hire a good man, put him to work for a tough foreman, and he'll produce.

I'm recommending the cutting of last year's training budget for my unit by 50 percent of last year's figures.

cc: Giles Sheridan
      Hugo Sheridan

Participant action

1. How important is this item?

2. What should be done about this item?

ITEM 4

Russell Manufacturing Co., Ltd.

INTEROFFICE MEMORANDUM   July 2

TO: Jon Richman
FROM: Ed Fairfax
SUBJECT: Mandatory Retirement Policy

Noises are being made in the Ontario House about passing a law against required retirement at an age before 70. I don't know how serious they are, but as you know, our policy requires retirement at 65.

And as you know, in last year's recession we forced out 15 men at the early retirement age of 62.

Do you wish to talk with your superiors about a change in retirement policy?

The reason I ask is we have two men who become 65 the week of July 15: Both have come to me asking if they can stay on. What should I tell them? They both are outstanding employees, who have been with us more than 20 years each.

Participant action

1. How important is this item?

---

2. What should be done about this item?

ITEM 5

Russell Manufacturing Co., Ltd.

INTEROFFICE MEMORANDUM   June 28

TO: Jon Richman
FROM: Arlo Miru, Supervisor, Finance Department
SUBJECT: Raise Request for Happy Weylin

Mr. Hugo Sheridan suggested that I write you directly on this. Happy Weylin is a very unusual person. She has a college degree in accounting. She is very close to becoming a chartered accountant. Are you aware of how few women meet those requirements at age 24?

I have heard unofficially that she has a very generous offer from a large insurance company. To keep her, I must give her a raise. Yet your salary structure will not allow it. Besides, the salary policy you set allows only one raise per year. She got the maximum raise allowed by your guidelines two months ago.

I know there have been accusations of salary inequities in my unit. But I made pay recommendations on the basis of education and merit, not just years on the job.

Happy's job offer expires July 6. Please let me know if I can give her a raise of $200 per month. Attached are Happy's performance evaluations by me. Note she scored the top ratings possible.

Participant action

1. How important is this item?

---

2. What should be done about this item?

ITEM 6

Russell Manufacturing Co., Ltd.

INTEROFFICE MEMORANDUM   June 28

TO: Jon Richman
FROM: Jim Herwin
SUBJECT: Health and Safety

Attached is the quarterly health and safety report. Please note that accidents are up 10 percent from last quarter and 20 percent from last year. What's worse, the severity rate is way up.

Page 2 of the report is the trend line for the last five years. Note that the trend line is upward. The safety posters aren't enough. We have no operating safety committees. We haven't had real safety training for as many years as anyone can remember.

Our workers' compensation rate has been increasing. We *must* do something soon. A friend of mine is the government safety inspector. He came through last week and found numerous violations of the safety code.

I propose that we institute a thorough safety training program soon. I can't do it. We'll need to bring in an outside expert. Estimated cost: $15,000.

We'll need a safety contest. Prize costs are estimated at $3,000 a year.

We'll need to hire a consultant to prepare some safety engineering, guards on machines, and so forth. Cost: unknown. My friend, the inspector tipped me off that the warnings he gave me requires him to reinspect within two weeks to see if we complied. He'll be back before July 9.

_____

Participant action

1. How important is this item?

_____

_____

_____

2. What should be done about this item?

_____

_____

_____

ITEM 7

Dear Mr. Richman

Jane 30

I believe that I have not been promoted in the finance department because my primary language is French

In addition, Mr Sheridan has promoted two less experienced, less well educated, & less senior but English speaking women over me.

I am considering filing a complaint with the Ontario Human Rights Commission, going to Mr Giles, about it, or quitting.

Sincerly —

Laurant M. Trudeau

ITEM 7 (continued)

Participant action

1. How important is this item?

2. What should be done about this item?

ITEM 8

Russell Manufacturing Co., Ltd.

INTEROFFICE MEMORANDUM   July 2

TO: Jon Richman
FROM: Felix Sheridan
SUBJECT: Union Organizing

Both Landon and I have heard reports that a union organizer or several are meeting (at various time) with some of the younger, more disgruntled employees about unionizing RMC. You know we couldn't survive with our old plant and equipment if we had to pay union wages and benefits, Jon. And you know the pressures the board is putting on us to increase dividends.

Check to see if these rumors are true. Then let's have lunch—the three of us—to design a compaign to combat the union—whether it's here now or not. Please get back to me soon.

Participant action

1. How important is this item?

2. What should be done about this item?

ITEM 9

Russell Manufacturing Co., Ltd.

INTEROFFICE MEMORANDUM   July 2

TO: Jon Richman
FROM: Giles Sheridan
SUBJECT: Pay Problems

Sorry you were sick, Jon. Hope you are better.

While you were ill, a sales employee came to see me. You know how I've always had an open door policy, so I wasn't concerned that he jumped channels.

He's an old, trusted employee, been with us 22 years. I've known of his contributions all along and he has felt free to come to see me since the days I supervised the sales department.

It seems they may have their pay practices mixed up there. Here he is with 22 years experience being paid less than a man here less than 5. Look into that.

But equally important, you know how *strongly* I feel about keeping salaries and wages quiet to prevent this kind of issue. Call me and I'll give you the employees' names. Look into the pay structure there (coordinating with JRS, of course) and let me know about it—and some new policies for security on pay scales, too—as soon as you can, Jon. This upsets me greatly.

Participant action

1.   How important is this item?

---

2.   What should be done about this item?

ITEM 10

DATE _7/2_ _____ HOUR _____

TO _____

WHILE YOU WERE OUT

M _Arthur Lewis_ _____

OF _____

PHONE _____ _767- 4897_ _____
          AREA CODE   PHONE NUMBER

TELEPHONED		RETURNED CALL		LEFT PACKAGE	
PLEASE CALL		WAS IN		PLEASE SEE ME	
WILL CALL AGAIN		WILL RETURN		IMPORTANT	

MESSAGE _Please call back by_
July 2nd _____

SIGNED _ABK_ _____

Participant action

1. How important is this item?

_____

_____

_____

2. What should be done about this item?

_____

_____

_____

ITEM 11

Russell Manufacturing Co., Ltd.

INTEROFFICE MEMORANDUM   June 26

TO: Jon Richman
FROM: Irene Cordell

While you were gone, I received a visit from Harold Shelby, an old friend. Harold has left his old firm to found a new firm, H.S. Polygraph Security, Ltd. Harold is offering regular screening of present employees and potential hires for security, theft, and so on.

Harold took a three-month course on how to use the polygraph. Over the years, Landon and I have talked about our serious theft problem. So Harold, Landon, and I went to lunch.

Harold made a very thorough proposal at very reasonable fee [attached]. Landon and I both think we should move ahead on this.

Please call Landon for verification if you like. Harold would like an appointment with you early the week of July 2 to finalize the plans.

Participant action

1. How important is this item?

---

2. What should be done about this item?

ITEM 12

Russell Manufacturing Co., Ltd.

DATE _July 2_ HOUR ___

TO _Jon Richmon_

WHILE YOU WERE OUT

M S _R. Brown_

OF ___

PHONE ___
AREA CODE   PHONE NUMBER

TELEPHONED		RETURNED CALL		LEFT PACKAGE	
PLEASE CALL		WAS IN		PLEASE SEE ME	
WILL CALL AGAIN		WILL RETURN		IMPORTANT	

MESSAGE _Please call me at once. Urgent_

SIGNED _ABK_

Participant action

1. How important is this item?

_____

_____

_____

2. What should be done about this item?

_____

_____

_____

ITEM 13

Russell Manufacturing Co., Ltd.

INTEROFFICE MEMORANDUM   June 30

TO: Jon Richman
FROM: Greg Joyce (Department Head, Manufacturing Division)
SUBJECT: Pay Policy

My section just ordered a new machine which simplifies the operator's job. It also produces about twice as much output in the same time. We plan to order more of these machines if they work as well as the supplier says they will.

The present operator of the old machine came to his foreman yesterday. He says he'll quit if he's forced to run the new machine without a raise. As he sees it, the company will get twice the output out of him. So he wants a raise; or he wants to put out the same output, or he says he'll quit. He talked it up among the other operators, and they seem to agree with the operator.

The machines are very expensive. We can't afford to pay the kind of raise he wants. The machine is not cost effective at the old output rate, of course. Yet we hate to lose an experienced work crew. What can we do?

The new machine will be delivered July 8.

Participant action

1. How important is this item?

---

2. What should be done about this item?

ITEM 14

Russell Manufacturing Co., Ltd.

INTEROFFICE MEMORANDUM June 25

TO: Jon Richman
FROM: Felix Sheridan
SUBJECT: Coordination

On this date one of my foremen, Harry Paine, had a dispute with one of his employees, Joe Stanford. As Harry tells it to me, Joe has been repeatedly late for work. He says he told Joe that if he were late once more, he'd be laid off for a week for disciplinary purposes.

When Harry tried to do this and took him to personnel to arrange it, Jim Herwin told him he couldn't. He claimed our policy was to give Joe warnings in writing before a man can be laid off. Before you came here, we didn't have all this red tape. The foremen's job has been eroded of its authority enough! I personally ordered Joe Stanford for a week's disciplinary layoff. You and Jim can fix up the paperwork as far as I am concerned.

Participant action

1. How important is this item?

---

2. What should be done about this item?

ITEM 15

June 29, 19

Dear Mr Richman,

I am writing you because Mr Felix would never understand. Three Months ago, he reached into the ranks & promoted me! He says I'm doing a great job. But I dont see it that way. I enjoyed my three years as Machinist here more.

Its not the same with the guys anymore. They dont ask me out for drinks on Friday nite. I got dropped from their bowling invitations. The pay + responsibility difference doesn't seem worth it. also my replacement is slow & its hard to stand by & watch her do in ten minutes what I did in 5. I'm tempted to criticize instead of helping her.

Most of my workers are older & have more years on me So I can see how they resent me + call me "straw boss" - All in "fun" of course. I spent my three years here learning from them.

I know the job is tough - Mr Felix fired the three previous foremen last year. But I want out - or advice. Please call soon. Ben Bulcer

ITEM 15 (continued)

Participant action

1. How important is this item?

---

2. What should be done about this item?

---

2. Health Agency

Near Atlanta, Georgia, there is a regional office of the Department of Health, Education, and Welfare (HEW), a federal agency of the U.S. government.

HEW is the largest agency in the government other than the defense department. It has been under budgetary pressure for several years, and at the present time the health agency in Atlanta is having a hard time reaching its goals, given its current budget in these inflationary times. It has been reducing the size of its work force by attrition and has a freeze on hiring.

The Atlanta agency has about 500 employees in its offices (in Atlanta and field offices responsible to Atlanta). The agency has multiple goals and is a complex organization.

Some aspects of the agency's work have been changing very fast in the last few years, but, in general, the agency has had a rather stable environment to work in.

About 15 percent of the employees in the agency—in several subunits —have unionized. These subunits are now bargaining units. They belong to the AFL-CIO Government Workers Union. The administrators are quite worried about further union inroads, fearing the union will interfere in areas they consider their areas of responsibility.

The agency has been in Atlanta since 1956. Government agencies are circumscribed by many laws and congressional regulations. Because of pressures—often at cross purposes—from Congress, the public, and other bodies, the agency tends to be centralized in its decision making, with written procedures which standardize operations, clear lines of authority and responsibility, precise job descriptions, clear compensation policies (GS pay grades). In short, it is a conservative, bureaucratic organization.

The official in charge of personnel function at the health agency is Elizabeth Higginson. She is a career civil service employee. She has been with the civil service since graduating from Swarthmore with a degree in psychology 22 years ago. She has specialized in personnel work for the last ten years and has held her current job for four years.

She has just returned from her month's vacation. She has visited her widowed mother who lives near Phoenix, Arizona. Higginson was an only child and is unmarried. She returns to work on January 3. The calendar for that month is shown below. The items await her when she arrives at work.

```
January
S  M  T  W  T  F  S
                  1
2  3  4  5  6  7  8
9  10 11 12 13 14 15
16 17 18 19 20 21 22
23 24 25 26 27 28 29
30 31
```

Exhibit 1 is an organization chart for the agency. There are ten field offices responsible to Atlanta. Each is headed by a deputy director. The four largest have personnel directors. Higginson is responsible directly for the personnel functions at the other field offices and gives advice to the personnel directors at the field units.

About half the employees of the agency work in the field units, half at the home office. Because of the geographic dispersion, Higginson has worked out a system where the field office personnel directors help the nearest field office in personnel, subject to her general supervision.

She has two assistants at the agency headquarters who help her in her work. Earl Gamby is new to the agency and government work. He is a recent graduate in business and economics from Atlanta University. He has been on the job about six months.

Donald Pickle is 51 years old. He attended Georgia State University. He has had many years of administrative and personnel experience with a large pharmaceutical firm. He returned to Atlanta five years ago to be near his aging parents. He has been with the agency since then.

EXHIBIT 1

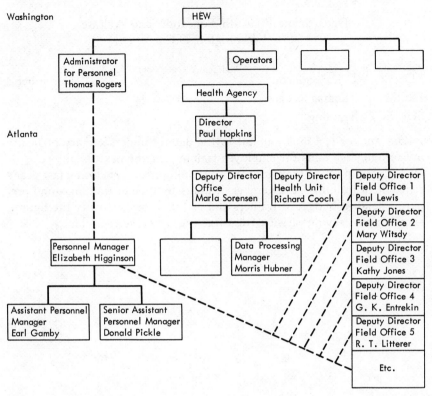

ITEM 1

Department of Health, Education, and Welfare
Washington, D.C.

TO: E. J. Higginson   December 4
FROM: Thomas Rogers
SUBJECT: Training

On January 6, I must submit to the deputy undersecretary of health my recommendations for employee training for the next fiscal year.

You should estimate your agency's training needs, enclosing last year's schedule of training—the number of hours by type of training—and prepare a detailed budget of trainers and materials costs. Justify the figures, showing past savings arising from training, wherever possible.

Participant action

1. How important is this item?

_____

_____

_____

2. What I will do.

_____

_____

_____

ITEM 2

Health Agency
HEW
Atlanta

INTEROFFICE MEMO   December 4

TO: E. J. Higginson
FROM: Earl Gamby
SUBJECT: Vacation

I would like to take a week's vacation beginning January 17 to visit my grandmother in Daytonna Beach. Please let me know as soon as possible since I need to make travel plans.

Participant action

1. How important is this item?

_____

_____

_____

2. What I will do.

_____

_____

_____

ITEM 3

Health Agency
HEW
Atlanta

INTEROFFICE MEMO

TO: Elizabeth Higginson   December 11
FROM: Zelda Cox
SUBJECT: Advice: Personal

As a newly appointed unit supervisor, I am 11 years younger than any of the employees in my unit. These employees are unpromotable. In fact, they did not want to be promoted to supervisor because of the responsibility.

Yet all resent a young, less experienced person being their supervisor. I need to see you to see what I can do to improve my situation. I wonder if I should resign this job.

Participant action

1. How important is this item?

_____

_____

_____

2. What I will do.

_____

_____

_____

ITEM 4

Health Agency
HEW
Atlanta

INTEROFFICE MEMO

TO: Ms. Elizabeth Higginson   December 27
FROM: John Cutler
SUBJECT: New Employee Orientation Program

As a section leader, I regularly have rap sessions with my crew. We were talking about how the agency could improve this as a workplace and cut the increasing turnover we're experiencing.

Several employees said they thought our orientation program was very poor and that a lot of new people quit because they didn't know their way around. Could you look into this?

cc: Marla Sorenson

Participant action

1. How important is this item?

---

2. What I will do.

ITEM 5

Health Agency
HEW
Atlanta

INTEROFFICE MEMO

TO: Elizabeth Higginson   January 3
FROM: Marla Sorensen
SUBJECT: Objectives for Your Department

As you know, Mr. Hopkins has decided that this agency should be guided by a Management by Objectives approach in the new year of 19—.

Explanatory material is attached. You will need to prepare preliminary *quantitative* objectives for consolidation and review by Mr. Hopkins and me by January 14.

Please make every effort to make this powerful new system work so we can serve our clients better.

Participant action

1. How important is this item?

---

2. What I will do.

ITEM 6

Health Agency
HEW
Atlanta

INTEROFFICE MEMO

TO: E. J. Higginson   December 28
FROM: Earl Gamby
SUBJECT: New Recruiting Plan

As you know, we have been reducing overall employment by attrition. Still, there are categories of employment which we need to replace, especially in the professional and technical categories.

Attached you will find the recruiting plan I will use. The list of schools and institutes where I will recruit is given. Affirmative Action has been considered in schools and has established priorities for employment.

Please give me your comments on this at your earliest convenience, so I can set up my schedule for late January to April 15.

Participant action

1. How important is this item?

---

2. What I will do.

ITEM 7

Department of Health, Education, and Welfare
Washington, D.C.

TO: Elizabeth Higginson   December 27
FROM: John Jacoby, Assistant to
           Thomas Rogers
SUBJECT: Job Descriptions Update

As you will no doubt recall, Regulation 168.7 calls for a complete updating of all job descriptions of all positions in HEW every three years.

January 1 is the day which completes the third year. Thus the update is now due.

Please do a thorough job of it, consulting with those in each job, doing job analyses, and so forth. These are due in our office March 1.

Participant action

1. How important is this item?

_____

_____

_____

2. What I will do.

_____

_____

_____

ITEM 8

U.S. Civil Service Commission
Washington, D.C.

TO: Ms. E. J. Higginson   January 1
FROM: Buellah Mae Smith
SUBJECT: Equal Employment Opportunity Program

As you know, you are participating in an equal employment opportunity program to increase your participation of blacks and women in better jobs.

At the last reporting job, your employment distribution was as follows:

Job category	Percentage			
	Male	Female	White	Black
Clerical	5	95	63	37
Operative	90	10	20	80
Technical/professional ...	40	60	75	25
Managerial	77	23	95	5

Please report the progress you have made to meet your goals to increase the percentage of females and blacks in managerial positions and blacks in professional and technical positions.

Participant action

1. How important is this item?

2. What I will do.

ITEM 9

Health Agency
HEW
Atlanta

INTEROFFICE MEMO

TO: E. J. Higginson   December 23
FROM: G. K. Entrekin
SUBJECT: Promotion of George Tate

After thorough consideration, I have decided that George should be promoted to be my assistant. This calls for his being moved from GS10 to GS11.

Attached please find supporting documents, including his last four years' performance evaluations. I hope you will expedite this. I have heard through the grapevine that a large hospital in Atlanta is trying to hire him away. I would appreciate immediate approval, if possible. Welcome back from vacation!

Participant action

1. How important is this item?

2. What I will do.

ITEM 10

Health Agency
HEW
Atlanta

INTEROFFICE MEMO

TO: Elizabeth Higginson   December 28
FROM: Paul Lewis
SUBJECT: New Employees

My section has had a very large increase in our services in the last six months. We've got to have three more GS4s, or we'll have to turn people away. We are desperate!

Participant action

1. How important is this item?

---

2. What I will do.

ITEM 11

To _E. J. Higginson_

WHILE YOU WERE OUT

Date _12/28_   Time _3:00 PM_

Name _Thomas Rogers_

of _HEW - Washington_

Phone _____

☑ TELEPHONED	☐ RETURNED YOUR CALL
☐ WILL CALL AGAIN	☐ WANTED TO SEE YOU
☑ PLEASE RETURN CALL	☐ WAS HERE TO SEE YOU

Message: _Call as soon as possible. He seemed angry_

Signed _S.L._

Participant action

1.   How important is this item?

2.   What I will do.

ITEM 12

Health Agency
HEW
Atlanta

INTEROFFICE MEMO

TO: Elizabeth Higginson   December 28
FROM: Donald Pickle
SUBJECT: Recruiting Report

Attached please find this year's report on walk-ins. We record the number of people who come in looking for a job. This is partly due to the economy and the rest to our image as a good employer.

As you know, Atlanta's economy has been excellent. Our walk-ins are down 10 percent in all categories except clerical.

Participant action

1. How important is this item?

---

2. What I will do.

ITEM 13

Health Agency
HEW
Atlanta

INTEROFFICE MEMO

TO: E. J. Higginson   December 23
FROM: R. T. Litterer
SUBJECT: Overtime request

     Paragraph 12 of regulation 172.6 requires that you approve all over-time requests, especially in view of our budget situation.

     Our workload has increased 12 percent in the last year. Up until now, we have absorbed it all with current personnel. We are now beyond that point. Since there is a freeze on hiring, the only way I can handle this is by adding some overtime. It is my estimate that this will involve $1,875 over the next 90 days.

     Surely you do not want us to turn clients away, and that is what we had to do yesterday. Please let me know as soon as possible on this.

Participant action

1.   How important is this item?

_____

_____

_____

2.   What I will do.

_____

_____

_____

ITEM 14

The Testing Corporation
Houston, Texas

December 19

Personnel Director
The Health Agency
Atlanta, Georgia

Dear Sir or Madam:

Have you been having a turnover problem? Productivity declines? One reason for both of these is inadequate selection of people and matching of them to the right jobs.

TTC has a test battery that has been used all over the country by employers of people similar to yours.

The attached brochure describes some of the tests and their track record. We will call you on January 19 to discuss this with you further. Until then, we hope you'll have a chance to read the material and tell us which test battery appeals to you.

We look forward to talking with you on January 19.

Sincerely,

Leonard Fox

Leonard Fox

Participant action

1. How important is this item?

_____

_____

_____

2. What I will do.

_____

_____

ITEM 15

Union Headquarters
Local . . .

Ms. Elizabeth Higginson   December 14
Health Agency
Atlanta, Georgia

Dear Liz:

Recently we've had complaints from some of our members about how boring and routine their jobs are at the agency.

I asked them if they were interested in a job enlargement program (after explaining what it was), and they enthusiastically agreed. I'd like to meet with you shortly to see how we can work together on this.

Sincerely,

Bill

Bill Maxwell
Business Agent

Participant action

1. How important is this item?

---

2. What I will do.

ITEM 16

Health Agency
HEW
Atlanta

INTEROFFICE MEMO   January 1

TO: E. J. Higginson
FROM: Henry Watkins, Chairman of Recreation
          Committee
SUBJECT: Support of Baseball Team

As you know, the agency has in the past picked up half the cost of the four employee ball teams and sponsored a Little League team.

Our recent survey indicates there is a need for two more employee teams for this spring. Will the agency be able to support these as they have in the past? It's a real morale builder for the money. By the way, Liz, why don't you join us this year or come to the games anyway.

Participant action

1. How important is this item?

2. What I will do.

ITEM 17

To _E. J. Higginson_

WHILE YOU WERE OUT

Date _Dec 29_ Time _3:00_

Name _Mr. Paul Hopkins_

of _This agency_

Phone _X 21_

☑ TELEPHONED   ☐ RETURNED YOUR CALL

☐ WILL CALL AGAIN   ☐ WANTED TO SEE YOU

☑ PLEASE RETURN CALL   ☐ WAS HERE TO SEE YOU

Message: _____

_____

_____

_____

_____

Signed _S. L._

Participant action

1. How important is this item?

_____

_____

_____

2. What I will do.

_____

_____

_____

ITEM 18

The Health Agency
HEW
Detroit, Michigan

TO: E. J. Higginson   December 29
FROM: Arthur Boyer, Personnel Director
SUBJECT: Earl Gamby

We have heard a good deal about the qualifications of Earl Gamby. We are in need of a person with his qualifications. This position would be a promotion, and his pay grade would increase one GS.

    Naturally, we would not solicit him for this job without your consent. But would you please send us copies of his performance evaluations and a letter of appraisal of his abilities, personality, and so forth. Since we need to fill this position at once and have already interviewed other candidates who might not wait, please send this to us within ten days.

Participant action

1. How important is this item?

_____

_____

_____

2. What I will do.

_____

_____

_____

ITEM 19

Health Agency
HEW
Atlanta

INTEROFFICE MEMO   December 29

TO: Elizabeth Higginson
FROM: Paul Hopkins
SUBJECT: Donald Pickle

While you were on vacation, Don Pickle received a call from Paul Lewis requesting personnel's help in requisitioning some added personnel for his section. Paul called me afterward. Don was very uncooperative, Paul said. Not wishing to interfere without your being here, I said nothing. Please call me at your earliest convenience about the facts of this interaction and your recommendations on more people for Paul Lewis.

Participant action

1. How important is this item?

---

2. What I will do.

ITEM 20

Health Agency
HEW
Atlanta

INTEROFFICE MEMO   December 27

TO: E. J. Higginson
FROM: Earl Gamby
SUBJECT: Pay Survey Results

As you know, we are required to conduct a pay survey yearly by regulation #_____ as a consequence of _____ Law. Its purpose is to make sure that our pay scales are in line with the private and third sector.

Enclosed is the most recent survey. In most categories, our pay scale is in line.

A.   Note that in the following jobs [E–12; J–17; R–70] our pay is slightly below the local market.

B.   Note further that in the three circled jobs, we are 20 percent above the local market. Local hospitals and labs are complaining that we are pirating their employees. I've attached letters they've written the local congressman about our "unfair and excessive" pay scales.

What do you want me to do about these findings?

___

Participant action

1.   How important is this item?

_____

_____

_____

2.   What I will do.

_____

_____

_____

ITEM 21

Health Agency
HEW
Atlanta

INTEROFFICE MEMO

TO: Elizabeth Higginson   December 27
FROM: Martha Crawford
SUBJECT: Cafeteria Costs

I called you, but you were on vacation, you lucky girl.

Elizabeth, we just can't make it in the cafeteria any more. As you know, the agency subsidizes each person's meal 30 cents per day. With the explosion in food costs, we cannot sell the food at the prices you approved and pay our bills. Either prices will have to go up, or you'll have to increase the subsidy by 15–20 cents per person per day. I can't stretch the budget anymore.

Please call me about this as soon as you can. We're losing money down here.

Participant action

1.   How important is this item?

_____

_____

_____

2.   What I will do.

_____

_____

_____

ITEM 22

Health Agency
HEW
Atlanta

INTEROFFICE MEMO

TO: E. J. Higginson   December 31
FROM: Morris Hubner
SUBJECT: Computer Usage Report

Attached please find your quarterly usage report for last quarter. You'll note your usage has been increasing slowly. Last quarter it was up 3 percent.

In order for me to get a computer budget increase approved, which I need to serve you and the others of the agency, please send me your estimate of your January through March computer needs by January 5.

Participant action

1. How important is this item?

---

2. What I will do.

ITEM 23

Health Agency
HEW
Atlanta

INTEROFFICE MEMO   December 29

TO: E. J. Higginson
FROM: Donald Pickle
SUBJECT: Preretirement Counseling Program

Recently, in chatting with some of our older employees, I've had some requests for a preretirement counseling program. Several other employers in the area have them.

An examination of the age distribution of our employees indicated the following number of potential users of the proposed program.

$$
\begin{array}{ll}
\text{Year 1 (this year)} \ldots\ldots & 15 \\
\text{Year 2} \ldots\ldots\ldots\ldots & 12 \\
\text{Year 3} \ldots\ldots\ldots\ldots & 17 \\
\text{Year 4} \ldots\ldots\ldots\ldots & 19 \\
\text{Year 5} \ldots\ldots\ldots\ldots & 21 \\
\end{array}
$$

Please advise me if you wish me to proceed on this since ASPA is offering a training program in early February in Miami. I'd like to attend if we are going ahead on this.

Participant action

1. How important is this item?

---

2. What I will do.

ITEM 24

Health Agency
HEW
Atlanta

INTEROFFICE MEMO   January 1

TO: Elizabeth Higginson
FROM: Earl Gamby
SUBJECT: Safety and Health at the Agency

As you know, one of the first responsibilities you assigned me to when
I arrived was safety and health. Attached please find my biyearly report
on safety and health programs at the agency. This cover letter summarizes
some of the highlights for your information.

1.   Since I had no experience in safety and health, I familiarized myself
with the regulations, read all I could on the subject, and became as prepared as I could.

2.   Safety and health inventories—One of the first programs I established was a safety consciousness program. I acquired all the posters I
could and placed them on all bulletin boards. I prepared safety slogans
for the house organ.

3.   I conducted safety training sessions in all offices with the help of the
supervisors. Many employees were surprised to learn of all the hazards in
the office situation. All 500 employees were exposed to the training.

4.   In conjunction with the supervisors, I conducted safety inspections
of all offices and labs.

5.   I sought a hygienist from Washington to inspect for occupational
health inspections since I'm not trained to do these inspections. She has
made unannounced inspections quarterly.

6.   Results—The number of accidents has not changed. Occupational
health statistics are stable.

7.   I am disappointed in these results. What recommendations do you
have for me? I must report to Washington by January 15 and don't know
how to explain our statistics which are 10 percent higher than HEW's
average figures.

ITEM 24 (*continued*)

Participant action

1. How important is this item?

_____

_____

_____

2. What I will do.

_____

_____

_____

ITEM 25

Health Agency
HEW
Atlanta

INTEROFFICE MEMO   December 2
TO: Elizabeth Higginson
FROM: Don Pickle
SUBJECT: Performance Evaluation Results

Attached please find the yearly performance evaluation forms for all employees in the agency. As you know, we conducted these on October 15 for all employees.

We have been using a graphic-rating scale for all nonsupervisory positions and critical-incident techniques for managerial personnel.

The following action items are needed:

1.   Authority to include an item on the attitude survey to determine if the employees are receiving the required interview for feedback after the evaluation is completed.

2.   Authority to plan some training sessions to train new supervisors in the use of evaluation techniques. Expected time: four hours.

3.   Authority to design critical-incident approach for clerical employees on an experimental basis. Washington is encouraging experimentation since at present more than 50 percent of employees are receiving top ratings and the expected percentage is about 15 percent.

In our agency, 60 percent are receiving the top ratings.

I need to report to Mr. Rogers by February 1 on what we're going to do to make our evaluations more meaningful in view of that 60 percent figure.

Participant action

1.   How important is this item?

2.   What I will do.

ITEM 26

Department of Health, Education, and Welfare
Washington, D.C.

TO: Atlanta Unit   December 31
FROM. Thomas Rogers
SUBJECT: Employee Turnover Report

Attached please find the printout on your employee turnover. As usual, we also include the past performance of your unit and the average overall of HEW.

As you note, your turnover in all categories is still lower than HEW as a whole. But, the turnover at lower GS levels is creeping up on the average at Atlanta.

Please let me know by January 30 what steps you plan to take to reverse this trend.

Participant action

1. How important is this item?

_____

_____

_____

2. What I will do.

_____

_____

_____

ITEM 27

United Fund of Atlanta, Inc.
Atlanta, Georgia

Ms. Elizabeth Higginson   December 27
The Health Agency
Atlanta, Georgia

Dear Ms. Higginson,

The greetings of the season to you and all the employees of your fine agency.

In the past, the agency has given our fund drive outstanding support. This year we are trying to raise 12 percent more than last year. This is because the cost of operating our many agencies has increased because of inflation. We also have two new agencies to support.

Under separate cover, we have sent you material for each of your employees, including preprinted donation forms and return envelopes.

Please send them a letter urging specific gifts (hopefully 12 percent greater than last year). Your director, Paul Hopkins, is on our advisory board, and I'm sure he'll give you his fullest support. Last year the agency was a 100 percenter. Hope you come through this year, too.

Please return the pledges to us by January 31.

Thank you.

Sincerely,

John P. Smith
Large Employer Gifts
Committee Chairman

Participant action

1. How important is this item?

_____

_____

_____

2. What I will do.

_____

_____

_____

ITEM 28

Atlanta Job Fair
Atlanta, Georgia

Personnel Director   December 27
The Health Agency
Atlanta, Georgia

Dear Sir or Madam:

During the Easter holiday (April — to —) we are holding our Atlanta Job Fair at the Convention Center. It will last three days this year. The fair will be widely promoted in electronic and print media to invite area youth to take jobs in this area.

Many employers have found these fairs an inexpensive yet effective method of recruiting new employees.

We note that you had a booth for several years but then did not participate last year. The cost of a booth of the same size as your last one will be $300. Please reserve as soon as possible. Last year, we were booked solid by January 20.

See you at the fair.

Sincerely,

Richard Brahms
Director

Participant action

1.   How important is this item?

---

2.   What I will do.

ITEM 29

Department of Health, Education, and Welfare
Washington, D.C.

TO: Elizabeth Higginson   December 23
FROM: Arthur Wilson
SUBJECT: Performance Evaluation Experiment

Mr. Rogers and I have been discussing the possibility of trying an experiment at one of our agencies to shift from our present classification to the widely used point system of job evaluation.

Your agency was recommended as a likely experimental unit. Please respond in writing to me, carboning Mr. Rogers by January 7 on:

1. Your willingness to participate in the experiment.
2. The extent of the expertise at your unit to design and conduct the experiment.
3. The expected reaction of your employees to such an experiment.

Participant action

1. How important is this item?

---

2. What I will do.

---

3. U.S. Airlines

U.S. Airlines is a large national carrier of passengers and freight with headquarters in New York City.

Vice President of Personnel and Public Relations Lawrence Penney has just returned from two weeks in the hospital for surgery. The time of this exercise is 9 a.m., October 2. The calendar for the month is shown in the accompanying illustration.

```
October
S   M   T   W   T   F   S
    2   3   4   5   6   7
8   9  10  11  12  13  14
15  16  17  18  19  20  21
22  23  24  25  26  27  28
29  30  31
```

Penney has been a personnel specialist most of his 28 years with U.S. Airlines. He received a B.A. in economics from Cornell and an M.B.A. from the Harvard School of Business. He is married and has two grown children. His wife is a lawyer with a prominent firm. He worked his way up the personnel side of the department. He has an assistant vice president who is largely responsible for the formal public relations side of his department.

In general, Penney is thought to be a very correct person, but a good fellow. He is well liked by his peers, superiors, and subordinates. Exhibit 1 shows how U.S. Airlines is organized.

The personnel department has functional responsibility over all personnel employees at all locations around the United States, though of course these individuals owe their primary loyalty to their local unit manager. The home office personnel department performs the personnel functions for the home office and New York operations. It sets all personnel policies. Home office is responsible for benefits throughout the company. It has major responsibilities in safety, has the only personnel research unit, handles all company management development, and does much of the college recruiting. Local personnel officers implement noncollege recruiting, most selection orientation, compensation policies, and technical training. They implement corporate programs in the other areas.

Jerome Chew is a professional engineer, a graduate of Pennsylvania State University. He is 35 years old and has been with U.S. Airlines for three years. Prior to that, he had a similar position at a smaller airline.

EXHIBIT 1
ORGANIZATION CHART: U.S. AIRLINES

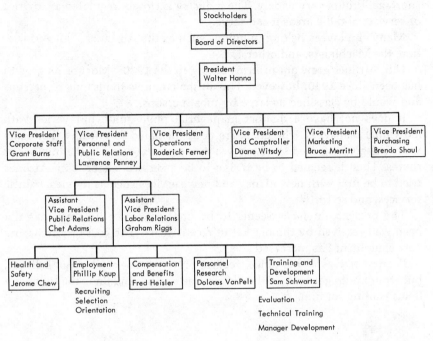

Phillip Kaup is 41 years old. He has a degree in psychology from the University of Rhode Island and a M.B.A. from New York University. He has been with U.S. Airlines for 12 years, all of them in personnel. Prior to that, he was in sales for a major packaging firm.

Fred Heisler is 39 years old, a graduate of Yale. He has been in personnel for four years. Prior to that, he had been in public relations for U.S. Airlines and another airline.

Delores Van Pelt is 27 years old. She has a bachelors in personnel administration from the University of Pittsburgh, a M.A. in psychology from Brocon, and a D.B.A. in business administration (personnel) from Indiana University. She established the personnel research program at U.S. Airlines after working in that function for a few years at Texaco, Inc.

Sam Schwartz is 36 years old. He holds a bachelor's degree from Teachers College, Columbia University, and a M.B.A. from Bernard Baruch. Schwartz joined U.S. Airlines two years ago. He had been employed in personnel and training by three other companies before he joined U.S. Airlines: General Motors, Westinghouse, and Armstrong.

The airline industry is quite volatile. Whenever a new type of plane is developed, the industry tends to replace its equipment, which is very expensive. It is difficult to predict demand, for it is quite susceptible to the swings of the business cycle and external changes such as the energy shortage. Profits vary widely. The industry is closely regulated as to price of services and the areas it can serve.

Many employees belong to unions such as the Air Lines Pilot Association, the Machinists, and others.

U.S. Airlines grew out of firms dating to the 1920s. Most of its growth has been since 1940, however. The airline employs thousands of persons and would be classified as large by most persons.

It does not have a distinct managerial philosophy, but varies with individual managers. The goals are not articulated specifically. For some years the goals seemed to be growth in areas served and in the number of routes. Then it seemed to be trying to be a service leader. U.S. Airlines tried to be first with new planes and new services such as movies, shuttle services, and so forth.

The present emphasis seems to be financial, since its stock has not been well received by the market in recent years. The cost of purchasing new equipment has increased.

Penney arrives at his office, feeling pretty well—not his old self yet, but straining to get back in the old routine again—and finds the following items waiting for him.

ITEM 1

Leadership Dynamics, Inc.
Columbia, Mo. 65201

September 28

Mr. L. Penney
Vice President, Personnel and Public Relations
New York, N.Y. 10001

Dear Mr. Penney,

In these days of *Future Shock*, explosive changes politically, techno-logically, and morally, only those firms with dynamic leaders will survive.

Yet too few firms do anything positive to develop their future leaders. What is U.S. AIRLINES doing to develop, really DEVELOP LEADERS —YOUR MOST IMPORTANT RESOURCE.

Leadership Dynamics has just the leadership program for you: differ-ent, *research based*, hard hitting. Our former clients are our best sales-men. Please read the enclosed literature and do *something* today. Call us on our toll free line ——————————.

Sincerely,

Rod R. Grander
Managing Director

Participant action

1. How important is this item?

————————————————————————

————————————————————————

————————————————————————

2. What I will do.

————————————————————————

————————————————————————

ITEM 2

U.S. Airlines
Across America's Skies
New York, N.Y. 10001

INTEROFFICE MEMO

TO: L. Penney   September 28
FROM: P. Kaup
SUBJECT: Skills Inventory

We have never really done anything about that computerized skills inventory we talked about developing almost a year ago. It surely would help us in recruiting and selection. I know there would be a start-up cost, but it probably would pay for itself in three to five years. May I proceed on this?

Participant action

1. How important is this item?

_____

_____

_____

2. What I will do.

_____

_____

_____

ITEM 3

Sullivan, Calmes and Boozer
Attorneys at Law
Los Angeles, California

Mr. L. Penney   September 18
Vice President of Personnel
U.S. Airlines
New York, N.Y. 10001

Dear Mr. Penney:

Our firm represents the employees of Oregon Airlines, which as you
know is likely to be merged into U.S. Airlines if the government agencies
approve.

Our clients are quite concerned about the terms of the merger, especially as it affects their benefits such as pensions. Could you tell us please
just how you plan to merge the benefit plans (if you do) or if you plan to
keep the two pension trusts, and so forth, separate.

We'd appreciate a speedy reply.

Sincerely,

John R. Sullivan, J.D.

Participant action

1. How important is this item?

---

2. What I will do.

ITEM 4

U.S. Airlines
Across America's Skies
New York. N.Y. 10001

INTEROFFICE MEMO

TO: L. Penney   September 21
FROM: S. Schwartz
SUBJECT: Managerial Evaluation

As you know, we have not really done anything for the corporation to help the superiors of managers or potential managers choose the best subordinates.

Why not get into an assessment center? AT&T and others have had great success with these. Please let me know if I can go ahead on this and what the budget limits on it would be.

Participant action

1.   How important is this item?

---

2.   What I will do.

ITEM 5

U.S. Airlines
Across America's Skies
New York, N.Y. 10001

INTEROFFICE MEMO

TO: L. Penney   September 22

FROM: J. Chew

SUBJECT: Vacations

I have been under such pressure here lately that I'd like to take off two weeks the end of October and two weeks after Christmas vacation.

Please let me know if this is O.K. so I can make my travel plans. The airlines are so booked up at that time of year.

Participant action

1. How important is this item?

_____

_____

_____

2. What I will do.

_____

_____

_____

ITEM 6

To _L. Penney_

WHILE YOU WERE OUT

Date _4:10 PM_   Time _9/29_

Name _John Stone_

of _Marketing Dept_

Phone _X 273_

✓ TELEPHONED	☐ RETURNED YOUR CALL
☐ WILL CALL AGAIN	☐ WANTED TO SEE YOU
✓ PLEASE RETURN CALL	☐ WAS HERE TO SEE YOU

Message: _needs to see you soon about a personal problem._

Signed _S. N._

Participant action

1. How important is this item?

---

2. What I will do.

ITEM 7

College of Business Administration
University of Connecticut
Storrs, Connecticut

September 21

Mr. L. Penney
Vice President—Personnel
U.S. Airlines
New York, N.Y. 10001

Dear Mr. Penney:

We are planning to have the three-day short course designed for middle managers in personnel departments again in late November. Last year Sam Schwartz attended and said he found it quite worthwhile. In fact, he said he'd like to come again.

The course is intended to update persons who are usually busy on their jobs and have little time to catch up with the press of daily duties.

Please let us know if you wish to sponsor a person and which one. Last year we closed enrollments by October 8.

Sincerely,

Arthur K. Cleveland

Arthur K. Cleveland
Management Development Director

Participant action

1. How important is this item?

_____

_____

_____

2. What I will do.

_____

_____

_____

ITEM 8

U.S. Airlines
Across America's Skies
New York, N.Y. 10001

INTEROFFICE MEMO

TO: Mr. L. Penney   September 18
FROM: Debbie Silvoso
SUBJECT: Profit-Sharing Plan

The last issue of the U.S.ER had an article from Mr. W. Hanna out-lining the problems of our firm and the whole economy has in productivity. At the weekly meeting of my section, I brought the subject up.

Several of the women suggested that a profit-sharing plan would induce them to work harder. I thought that was a great idea. Since Hanna suggested we write our suggestions to you, I wrote it up as soon as I could.

We in unit 127 will be most anxious to hear what you think of our idea and when we can get rolling on profit sharing.

cc: Mr. W. Hanna

Participant action

1. How important is this item?

---

2. What I will do.

ITEM 9

U.S. Airlines
Across America's Skies
New York, N.Y. 10001

INTEROFFICE MEMO

TO: L. Penney   October 2
FROM: Walter Hanna
SUBJECT: Social Security Taxes

We have heard through the grapevine that because of increasing resistance on the part of taxpayers to pay increased social security taxes that the proposed increase to cover another boost in payout to the retired will be funded by the employer *alone*, rather than matched by the employee.

The proposed tax on the employer will be 6.5 percent on the first $15,000 of pay. What additional cost will this amount to for U.S. Airlines?

Participant action

1. How important is this item?

_____

_____

_____

2. What I will do.

_____

_____

_____

ITEM 10

U.S. Airlines
Across America's Skies
New York, N.Y. 10001

INTEROFFICE MEMO

TO: Lawrence Penney   September 21
FROM: Sinclair Jameston
SUBJECT: Personal

I am asking Jane Trinkaus, an employee in my unit, to come to see you. I'm new as her supervisor and she won't talk to me.

She recently went through a messy divorce, and since then she seems very preoccupied. Her work is falling off. Perhaps someone with your experience can help counsel her. She was one of my best technicians, and they are hard to get.

Participant action

1. How important is this item?

---

2. What I will do.

ITEM 11

Second National Bank
New York, N.Y.

Mr. Lawrence Penney   September 21
Vice President
U.S. Airlines
New York, N.Y. 10001

Dear Mr. Penney:

Ms. Jane Sinart of your department has applied for a personal loan of
$1,000 to purchase furniture for her apartment. She has listed you as a
reference. Would you please write us a letter of reference for her. Please
include in this letter whether you would be willing to cosign the note or
guarantee it in any way.

Sincerely,

Higginson R. Van Schyler

Higginson R. Van Schyler III
Vice President

Participant action

1. How important is this item?

---

2. What I will do.

ITEM 12

New York Insurance Company
New York, N.Y.

Mr. L. Penney   September 25
Vice President—Personnel
U.S. Airlines
New York, N.Y.

Dear Larry,

We have just come up with a new package of insurance benefits for programs such as yours. It will provide better coverage for your employees at lesser cost in the long run. I am anxious to see you about it. When may I call to make an appointment to see you?

Sincerely,

Rachel

Rachel Musbaum

Participant action

1. How important is this item?

_____

_____

_____

2. What I will do.

_____

_____

_____

ITEM 13

U.S. Airlines
Across America's Skies
New York, N.Y. 10001

INTEROFFICE MEMO

TO: Lawrence Penney   September 20
FROM: Graham Riggs
SUBJECT: Grievances

Enclosed is my annual survey of grievances at the firm. Note that the grievance rate is increasing at units one and seven, increasing significantly at units two and three, stabilized at six, and decreasing at four and five.

When examined for seriousness of the grievances, two and three appear to be problems as does six.

We need to meet soon to discuss what steps we should take about this. Also attached are grievances 14 and 72. These have not been resolved at lower levels, and I must now decide whether to try to resolve them at our level or turn them over to binding arbitration. The union has given us until October 6 to respond on these grievances. With contract negotiations coming up in November, I'd like to settle these as quickly as possible. What is your advice on these? Please call soon.

Participant action

1. How important is this item?

---

2. What I will do.

ITEM 14

U.S. Airlines
Across America's Skies
New York, N.Y. 10001

INTEROFFICE MEMO

TO: L. Penney   September 28
FROM: Bruce Merritt
SUBJECT: Incentive Plans

I was reading an article the other day about the fantastic possibilities of performance shares as an incentive plan for management.

We dropped our stock option plans some years ago when our stock had difficulties. I'd like to discuss this with you as soon as we could get together. No reason these couldn't be raised as district sales manager's incentives too.

Participant action

1. How important is this item?

---

2. What I will do.

ITEM 15

U.S. Airlines
Across America's Skies
New York, N.Y. 10001

INTEROFFICE MEMO

TO: L. Penney   September 22
FROM: G. Riggs
SUBJECT: Performance Ratings

As you directed September 5, I have completed the performance evaluations on my five-person staff.

The performance evaluation process is especially difficult in a staff service such as ours. Using the forced distribution system you suggested, my overall ratings are as follows:

> Above average .... Maynard Springfield
> Average .... Imelda Alfonso
> Average .... Neil Mosier
> Average .... Colin Buckenmyer
> Below average .... John Tellier

The detailed explanations are attached.

Participant action

1. How important is this item?

_____

_____

_____

2. What I will do.

_____

_____

_____

ITEM 16

To_____

WHILE YOU WERE OUT

Date _10/2_____ Time _8:30 AM_____
Name_Walter Hanna_____

of_____

Phone_____

✓ TELEPHONED   ☐ RETURNED YOUR CALL

☐ WILL CALL AGAIN   ☐ WANTED TO SEE YOU

✓ PLEASE RETURN CALL ☐ WAS HERE TO SEE YOU

Message:_____

_____

_____

_____

_____

Signed ___S. N._____

Participant action

1. How important is this item?

_____

_____

_____

2. What I will do.

_____

_____

_____

ITEM 17

U.S. Airlines
Across America's Skies
New York, N.Y. 10001

INTEROFFICE MEMO

TO: Mr. Lawrence Penney   September 28
FROM: Fred Heisler
SUBJECT: Compensation Policy

I've just had a call from Bruce Merritt. He as very unhappy. One of his department heads just found out what another department head makes. The unhappy person is John Maine. He's been with us ten years. He's working on an M.B.A. at N.Y.U. He's had average performance evaluation ratings for years. John's talents are not that unique and could easily be replaced. He's unhappy about Jane Barnes' salary. She's been with us about three years. She has an M.B.A. from Harvard. Her ratings have been better than John's. I don't know how much of the differential is due to the fact that a female Harvard M.B.A. starts out at a good salary. But John feels he should make much more than she since he has seven years' seniority and also has more experience in the industry.

I don't know how John found out Jane's salary, but Bruce wants us to find out. He also wants to know if we can't design a system that will guard pay secrecy more. As you know, at present it is against our policy to release salaries to anyone except the person's superior. Bruce says he's checked it out, and he didn't discuss the salary with John nor did Jane or any of her employees. That's why he blames us. My preliminary check with my section and payroll hasn't turned up anything. By the way, John wants to see you and me about this salary inequity, too.

Bruce's really angry at us and threatens to call Walter Hanna if we don't get back to him by October 4. Please advise.

Participant action

1. How important is this item?

---

2. What I will do.

ITEM 18

U.S. Airlines
Across America's Skies
New York, N.Y. 10001

INTEROFFICE MEMO

TO: Mr. Lawrence Penney   September 20
FROM: Fred Heisler
SUBJECT: Job Transfer

I feel that I have contributed all I can to my present job. I believe that as it is presently structured I can no longer grow as a person. I hereby request a transfer from this job or a major restructuring of the present job.

Participant action

1. How important is this item?

---

2. What I will do.

ITEM 19

Personnel Psychology
Durham, North Carolina

Mr. L. Penney   September 25
Vice President of Personnel
U.S. Airlines
New York, N.Y. 10001

Dear Mr. Penney:

We were surprised to learn that an industry personnel leader like you does not subscribe to *Personnel Psychology*. It is the journal for the sophisticated and well-informed personnel executive such as yourself.

Enclosed is a brochure describing some recent and upcoming issues. We hope you will join the ranks of our satisfied subscribers by completing the post card enclosed.

Sincerely,

R. W. Johnson
Subscription Consultant

Participant action

1. How important is this item?

_____

_____

_____

2. What I will do.

_____

_____

_____

ITEM 20

U.S. Airlines
Across America's Skies
New York, N.Y. 10001

INTEROFFICE MEMO

TO: Lawrence Penney   September 18
FROM: Sam Schwartz
SUBJECT: Tuition Reimbursement Plan

As you know, several years ago my predecessor started a tuition reimbursement plan for exempt employees. The plan has grown like Topsy. People are taking all kinds of courses. Many unrelated to their jobs. Others want reimbursement whether they finish the courses or not and whatever grade they get. And now the hourly people are asking if they are able to participate. The program is just too loosely run. Jane Mendelson put in for a course in flower arranging. What's that got to do with computer programming?

I think you should act on this quickly and stop this monster before it eats us all—at least eats my budget.

Participant action

1. How important is this item?

_____

_____

_____

2. What I will do.

_____

_____

_____

ITEM 21

U.S. Airlines
Across America's Skies
New York, N.Y. 10001

INTEROFFICE MEMO

TO: L. Penney   September 19
FROM: Jerome Chew
SUBJECT: Inadequate Staffing

As you may know, the Occupational Safety and Health Administration has become increasingly demanding in its enforcement of OSHA Act. We can no longer adequately inspect all our sites as thoroughly and frequently as we must do to fulfill their expectations.

Consequently, I am requesting authorization for one more safety specialist. My expectation is that beginning yearly salary will range from $15,000–$20,000 depending on the person's experience.

Please let me know on this at your earliest convenience. Our convention is coming up October 8 and 9, and that would be the best place to recruit such a person.

Participant action

1. How important is this item?

2. What I will do.

ITEM 22

To **L. Penney**

WHILE YOU WERE OUT

Date **930 AM** Time **Sept 20**

Name **Marylyn Becker**

of _____

Phone **798-6147**

✓ TELEPHONED	☐ RETURNED YOUR CALL
☐ WILL CALL AGAIN	☐ WANTED TO SEE YOU
✓ PLEASE RETURN CALL	☐ WAS HERE TO SEE YOU

Message:

Signed **S. N.**

Participant action

1. How important is this item?

2. What I will do.

ITEM 23

Dynamic Security Systems, Inc.
P. O. Box 7874
New York, N.Y. 10005

Mr. L. Penney   September 26
Vice President—Personnel
U.S. Airlines
New York, N.Y. 10001

Dear Mr. Penney:

We are a nationwide system of consultants who can cut your selection costs and theft by 50 percent or more. Hundreds of firms use our services yearly and are quite satisfied.

We utilize only thoroughly trained technicians, and the information is handled with great care. Please call us at 674–8968 for more information about the use of polygraph in selection to improve the quality of your decisions and to cut your theft rate.

Sincerely,

Carter G. Unterman

Carter G. Unterman
President

Participant action

1. How important is this item?

---

2. What I will do.

ITEM 24

U.S. Airlines
Across America's Skies
New York, N.Y. 10001

INTEROFFICE MEMO

TO: L. Penney   September 19
FROM: G. Riggs
SUBJECT: Union Demands

   I just heard through the grapevine that the machinists plan to ask for
46 cents per hour plus 10 percent increase in pensions and other fringes.
How are we going to handle that demand?

Participant action

1. How important is this item?

_____

_____

_____

2. What I will do.

_____

_____

_____

ITEM 25

U.S. Chamber of Commerce
Washington, D.C.

Mr. L. Penney   September 15
Vice President
Personnel and Public Relations
U.S. Airlines
New York, N.Y. 10001

Dear Larry:

You have been so helpful with our past national meetings that I have come back again. We'd like you to be part of a panel on Affirmative Action: Problems and Prospects.

You would be asked to speak for 20 minutes and field questions with the rest of the panel.

The meeting will be in Los Angeles, November 29. Please send a draft of your remarks to me by October 7.

Sincerely,

Fred

Fred Chapman
General Chairman

Participant action

1. How important is this item?

_____

_____

_____

2. What I will do.

_____

_____

_____

ITEM 26

Fourth National Bank
Long Island, N.Y.
Trust Department

Mr. L. Penney   September 19
Vice President Personnel
U.S. Airlines
New York, N.Y.

Dear Mr. Penney:

Attached please find our report on the effectiveness of our investing
your pension fund for 19—. For the last three years, our investments were
so effective that you had to contribute 7 percent less than you would have
had to pay out on a cash basis, thus saving this 7 percent.

But all years are not equally good. In the year ending August 31, the
stock market did not perform well as you know. As a result, you must
make an additional payment of 4 percent on the pension reserves.

Please forward payment as soon as possible so we can extend pension
checks to your retired employees on time.

Sincerely,

Wadsworth Yeats

Wadsworth Yeats
Vice President

Participant action

1. How important is this item?

---

2. What I will do.

ITEM 27

Equal Employment Opportunity Commission
New York, N.Y. 10001

Employment Relations Department   September 15
U.S. Airlines
New York, N.Y. 10001

Dear Sir or Madam:

Our records indicate that you are presently using the _____
Selection Test. Our data to date indicate that this test discriminates against
minority persons, especially Puerto Ricans, blacks and Cubans. Unless
you have established the scientific validity of the test showing that it
does not discriminate, we may have to institute proceedings against
you.

We plan to check back on the status of this test at your office October 5.

Sincerely,

Malcolm Brown

Malcolm Brown

Participant action

1. How important is this item?

_____

_____

_____

2. What I will do.

_____

_____

_____

ITEM 28

U.S. Airlines
Across America's Skies
New York, N.Y. 10001

INTEROFFICE MEMO

TO: L. Penney   September 29
FROM: D. VanPelt
SUBJECT: Reorganization of Personnel Department

You asked me to convene a committee of the department regarding a proposed reorganization of the department. As we understood it, Mr. W. Hanna asked all department heads to consider this.

The proposed changes are described in more detail in the attached document. Basically, we suggest splitting public relations off and adding it to marketing or corporate staff.

Within the department, we suggest splitting compensation and benefits into two units. Mr. Hanna called me September 27 and asked me to expedite the report since he needs to take his recommendations on this to the next board meeting.

Participant action

1. How important is this item?

---

2. What I will do.

ITEM 29

U.S. Airlines
Across America's Skies
Chicago, Illinois 60601

TO: Lawrence Penney   September 25
FROM: George Clark
SUBJECT: Incentive Plans

We have been playing with the idea of incentive wage and salary schemes for nonunion employees. We have written Fred Heisler several times for his suggestions and have not received a reply. Could you tell us what your experience has been with these plans? We've had no reply over a two-month period and would like to move ahead on this. We thought that was what the home office was for.

Participant action

1. How important is this item?

_____

_____

_____

2. What I will do.

_____

_____

_____

ITEM 30

U.S. Airlines
Across America's Skies
New York, N.Y. 10001

INTEROFFICE MEMO

TO: L. Penney   September 27
FROM: D. VanPelt
SUBJECT: Employee Attitude Survey

Attached please find a summary of the attitude survey which was conducted throughout the company September 5.

You will note that, overall, morale is lower this year compared to last. It is lowest in the employee's evaluation of leadership-supervisory attitudes and employee security.

The most dramatic drops were at divisions one, seven, and eight, the next largest drops were at two and four. Divisions three and five held even. Only division six increased.

I believe immediate action is called for to improve employee morale and productivity.

Participant action

1. How important is this item?

---

2. What I will do.

ITEM 31

U.S. Airlines
Across America's Skies
New York, N.Y. 10001

INTEROFFICE MEMO

TO: Larry Penney   September 27
FROM: Rod Ferner
SUBJECT: Coffee Breaks

It has come to my attention that many of our employees are abusing break time. They are taking too many breaks, or they take one third to double the allowable time.

I have asked my managers to crack down on this. We sure need an increase in productivity. I hope you will cooperate with me on this. Please alert your people to help out.

cc: Walter Hanna

Participant action

1. How important is this item?

_____

_____

_____

2. What I will do.

_____

_____

_____

ITEM 32

U.S. Airlines
Across America's Skies
New York, N.Y. 10001

INTEROFFICE MEMO

TO: L. Penney   September 15
FROM: Chet Adams
SUBJECT: U.S.ER

Attached please find the items for our next edition of U.S.ER. The employees seem to be liking the U.S.ER better since we brightened it up.

The attached articles are those which, because of their content, probably need your personal approval.

Because of publication deadlines, please return to me by October 3.

Participant action

1. How important is this item?

---

2. What I will do.

ITEM 33

U.S. Airlines
Across America's Skies
New York, N.Y. 10001

INTEROFFICE MEMO

TO: L. Penney   September 26
FROM: Sam Schwartz
SUBJECT: Evaluation of Nonmanagerial Employees

In an effort to develop something more acceptable to all employees at U.S. Airlines than the forced distribution system we currently use, I have been doing some reading and calling my peers in other corporations.

More and more frequently, it appears that I am hearing about the critical-incident technique. I've called a consultant, Dr. Henry Saxbe, who would like to come to talk to us both about this as soon as we can. I'd like to start it out on a test basis January 1. What do you think?

Participant action

1. How important is this item?

---

2. What I will do.

ITEM 34

```
To Lawrence Penney
        WHILE YOU WERE OUT
Date 10-2    Time 830 AM
Name Duane Wrtody

of _____

Phone _____
  ☑ TELEPHONED          ☐ RETURNED YOUR CALL
  ☐ WILL CALL AGAIN     ☐ WANTED TO SEE YOU
  ☑ PLEASE RETURN CALL  ☐ WAS HERE TO SEE YOU

Message: _____
_____
_____
_____
_____

Signed    SM.
```

Participant action

1. How important is this item?

_____

_____

_____

2. What I will do.

_____

_____

_____

ITEM 35

U.S. Airlines
Across America's Skies
New York, N.Y. 10001

INTEROFFICE MEMO

TO: Lawrence Penney September 21
FROM: Walter Hanna
SUBJECT: Reorganization of U.S. Airlines

Attached please find a plan to reorganize the company and recentralize it. As you know, about ten years ago we decentralized into profit centers.

With the advent of new high-speed computers, it appears possible that we can move many decisions which would have taken us too long at home office a few years ago back here.

I'd like your comments on the likely impact on productivity and employee morale. I'd like to discuss this with the board at our January 30 meeting. So your report should reach me by January 10.

Participant action

1. How important is this item?

_____

_____

_____

2. What I will do.

_____

_____

_____

ITEM 36

U.S. Airlines
Across America's Skies
New York, N.Y. 10001

INTEROFFICE MEMO

TO: Lawrence Penney   September 26
FROM: Fred Heisler
SUBJECT: Job Evaluation Program

We have been using the classification system of job evaluation for some years now. I believe we have outgrown it.

I would like to propose that we convert to the factor comparison system or preferably the point system.

This should improve our equity rating on the compensation questions on the attitude survey. I'd like to meet you at an early time to show you some of the results of a pretest we did at our Chicago facility.

Participant action

1. How important is this item?

---

2. What I will do.

Bibliography

The following items provide the reader with a preliminary list of references to aid the user in analysis of the cases and exercises in the book.

1. INTRODUCTION TO PERSONNEL

"Canada's Personnel People," *Labour Gazette*, December 1975, pp. 892–94.

Killian, Ray. *Human Resource Management: An ROI Approach*. New York: Amacon, 1976.

Kumar, Pradip. "Personnel Management in Canada: A Manpower Profile." *Canadian Personnel and Industrial Relations Journal*, January 1976, pp. 32–34.

Miner, John, and Miner, Mary. "Managerial Characteristics of Personnel Managers," *Industrial Relations* 15, 2 (May 1976): pp. 225–34.

"Personnel: Fast Track to the Top," *Duns Review*, April 1975, pp. 74–77.

White, H., and Boynton, R. "The Role of Personnel: A Management View," *Arizona Business* 21, 8 (1974): pp. 17–21.

2. EMPLOYMENT PLANNING

Bonham, T.W., et al. "A Gert Model to Meet Future Organizational Manpower Needs," *Personnel Journal*, July 1975, pp. 402–6.

Burack, Elmer, and Walker, James. *Manpower and Programming*. Boston: Allyn and Bacon, 1972.

Conference Board in Canada *Corporate Manpower Planning in Canada*. Scarborough, Ontario, 1976.

Elbert, Norbert, and Kehoe, William. "How to Bridge Fact and Theory in Manpower Planning," *Personnel*, November-December 1976, pp. 31–39.

Levesque, J. R. "Manpower Planning in Canada: Trends and Prospects," *The Canadian Business Review*, Spring 1976, pp. 30–33.

McCormick, Ernest. "Job and Task Analysis," in Marvin Dunnette (ed.), *Handbook of Industrial and Organizational Psychology*. Chicago: Rand McNally, 1976.

Mendelson, Jack. "Does Your Company Need Outplacement," *SAM Advanced Management Journal*, Winter 1975), pp. 4–12.

Milkovich, George, and Mahoney, Thomas. "Human Resources Planning and PAIR Policy." In Dale Yoder and Herbert Heneman (eds.), *PAIR Handbook*, vol. 4, Berea, Ohio: American Society of Personnel Administrators, 1976.

Staszak, F. James, and Mathys, Nicholas J. "Organization Gap: Implications for Manpower Planning," *California Management Review* 17, 3 (Spring 1975): pp. 32–39.

Vogel, Myles. "Manpower Forecasting with Linear Programming," *Industrial Engineering*, January 1976, pp. 43–45.

3. RECRUITING OF PERSONNEL

Dahl, Dave, and Pinto, Patrick. "Job Posting: An Industry Survey," *Personnel Journal*, January 1977, pp. 40–42.

Gaymer, Rosemary. "Preparing Students to Apply to You for a Position," *Canadian Personnel and Industrial Relations* 22, 6 (November 1975).

Greco, B. *How to Get a Job That's Right for You.* Chicago: Dow Jones—Irwin, 1975.

Taylor, H. Nathaniel. "Job Posting Update," *The Personnel Administrator*, January 1977, pp. 45–46.

4. SELECTION OF PERSONNEL

Alexander, Harold, et al. "Usefulness of the Assessment Center Process for Selection to Upward Mobility Programs," *Human Resource Management*, Spring 1975, pp. 10–13.

Ash, Phillip, and Krocker, Leonard. "Personnel Selection, Classification, and Placement," *Annual Review of Psychology.* Palo Alto, Calif.: Annual Reviews, 1975.

Executive Enterprises Publications. *Conducting the Lawful Employment Interview.* New York, 1974.

Kessler, Clemm C., III, and Gibbs, Georgia J. "Getting the Most from Application Blanks and References," *Personnel* 52, 1 (January-February 1975): pp. 53–62.

Lumsden, James. "Test Theory," *Annual Review of Psychology.* Palo Alto, Calif.: Annual Reviews, 1976.

Schneider, Benjamin. *Staffing Organizations.* Pacific Palisades, Calif.: Goodyear, 1976, cpr. 4.

Shaffer, David, et al. "Who Shall Be Hired: A Biasing Effect of the Buckley Amendment on Employment Practices," *Journal of Applied Psychology* 61, 5 (1976): pp. 571–75.

Wangler, Lawrence. "Employee Reference Request Revisited," *The Personnel Administrator*, November 1975, pp. 60–62.

5. ORIENTATION OF PERSONNEL

Gomersall, Early R., and Myers, M. Scott. "Breakthrough in On-the-Job Training" *Harvard Business Review* 44 (July-August 1966): pp. 62–71.

Holland, Joan, and Curtis Theodore. "Orientation of New Employees," In Joseph Famularo (ed.), *Handbook of Modern Administration*, chap. 23. New York: McGraw-Hill, 1972.

Ornstein, Michael. *Entry into the American Labor Force.* New York: Academic Press, 1976).

Van Maanen, John. "Breaking in: Socialization to Work," in Robert Dublin (ed.), *Handbook of Work, Organization, and Society*. Chicago: Rand McNally, 1976.

Wanous, John. "Organizational Entry: From Naive Expectations to Realistic Belief," *Journal of Applied Psychology* 61, 1 (February 1976): pp. 22–29.

6. CAREERS, CAREER DEVELOPMENT, AND COUNSELING

Bray, Dougles, et al. *Formative Years in Business.* New York: Wiley Interscience, 1974.

"When Career Couples Have Conflicts of Interest," *Business Week*, December 13, 1976.

Crites, John. "Work and Careers," in Robert Dubin (ed.), *Handbook of Work, Organization, and Society*. Chicago: Rand McNally, 1977.

Glueck, William F. "Career Management of Managerial, Professional, and Technical Personnel," in Elmer Baurack and James Walker (eds.), *Manpower Planning and Programming*. Boston: Allyn and Bacon, 1972, pp. 239–55.

Hall, Douglas. *Careers in Organizations.* Santa Monica: Goodyear, 1976.

Kaufman, Herbert. *Obsolescence and Professional Career Developments.* New York: Amacon, 1974.

Kay, Janice. "Career Development for Women: An Affirmative Action First," *Training and Development Journal*, May 1976, pp. 22–24.

Mahler, Walter, and Wrightnour, William. *Executive Continuity.* Homewood: Dow Jones—Irwin, 1963.

Van Maanen, John, and Schein, Edgar. "Career Development," in J. Richard Hackman and J. Lloyd Suttle (eds.), *Improving Life at Work*. Santa Monica: Goodyear, 1977.

Walker, James. "Let's Get Realistic about Career Paths," *Human Resources Management*, Fall 1976, pp. 2–7.

7. PERFORMANCE EVALUATION AND PROMOTION

Bureau of National Affairs. "Employee Performance: Evaluation and Control," *Personnel Policies Forum*, 108 (February 1975).

Cummings, Larry, and Schwab, Donald. *Performance in Organizations.* Chicago: Scott Foresmen, 1973, chap. 5.

Finkle, Robert. "Management Assessment Centers," in M. Dunnette, *Handbook of Industrial and Organizational Psychology.* Chicago: Rand McNally, 1976, pp. 861–88.

Levinson, Harry. "Appraisal of *What* Performance?" *Harvard Business Review,* July-August, 1976, pp. 30–34; 36; 40; 44; 46; 160 ff.

Maier, Norman R. "Three Types of Appraisal Interviews," *The Appraisal Interview.* New York: John Wiley and Sons, 1958.

Meyer, Herbert, et al. "Split Roles in Performance Appraisal," *Harvard Business Review,* 43, 1 (January-February 1965): pp. 123–29.

Pym, Denis. "The Politics and Ritual of Appraisal," *Occupational Psychology,* 47 (1973): pp. 231–35.

Zawacki, Robert, and Taylor, Robert. "A View of Performance Appraisal from Organizations Using It." *Personnel Journal,* June 1976, pp. 290–92; 299 ff.

8. EMPLOYEE TRAINING

Berger, Lance. "A Dew Line for Training and Development: The Needs Analysis Survey," *The Personnel Administrator,* November 1976, pp. 51–55.

Cullen, James, et al. "Training: What's It Worth?" *Training and Development Journal,* August 1976, pp. 12–20.

Goldstein, Irwin. *Training: Program Development and Evaluation.* Monterrey: Brooks/Cole, 1974.

Hinrichs, John. "Personnel Training," in Marvin Dunnette (ed.), *Handbook of Industrial and Organizational Psychology.* Chicago: Rand McNally, 1976.

Newell, Gale. "How to Plan a Training Program," *Personnel Journal,* May 1976, pp. 220–25.

Odiorne, George. "Training Director—Personnel Manager: "Who's in Charge Here?" *Training and Development Journal,* June 1976, pp. 3–6.

Otto, Calvin, and Glaser, Rollin. *The Management of Training.* Reading, Mass.: Addison Wesley, 1970, chaps. 2, 3, 4, 7, 9.

9. MANAGEMENT DEVELOPMENT

Byham, William, and Robinson, James. "Interaction Modeling: A New Concept in Supervisory Training," *Training and Development Journal,* February 1976, pp. 25–33.

Byham, William, et al. "Transfer of Modeling Training to the Job," *Personnel Psychology* 29 (1976): pp. 345–49.

Campbell, John P., et al. *Managerial Behavior, Performance, and Effectiveness.* New York: McGraw Hill, 1970.

Engel, Herbert. *Handbook of Creative Learning Exercises.* Houston: Gulf, 1973.

Glueck, William F. "Managers, Mobility, and Morale," *Business Horizons,* January-February 1975, pp. 65–70.

Goldstein, A. P., and Sorcher, M. *Changing Supervisory Behavior.* New York: Pergamon, 1974.

Goldstein, Arnold. *Training: Program Development and Evaluation.* Monterrey: Brooks/Cole, 1974, chaps. 4, 5.

James, Muriel. "The OK Boss," *Psychology Today,* February 1976, pp. 31–36; 80 ff.

Mahler, Walter, and Wrightnour, William. *Executive Continuity.* Homewood: Dow Jones—Irwin, 1973, chaps. 6, 7.

Moses, Joseph, and Ritchie, Richard. "Supervisory Relationships Training: A Behavioral Evaluation of a Behavior Modeling Program," *Personnel Psychology* 29 (1976): pp. 337–43.

Rettig, Jack, and Amano, Matt. "A Survey of ASPA Experience with Management by Objectives, Sensitivity Training, and Transactional Analysis," *Personnel Journal,* January 1976, pp. 26–29.

Strauss, George. "Organization Development," in Robert Dubin (ed.), *Handbook of Work, Organization, and Society.* Chicago: Rand McNally, 1976.

10. COMPENSATION

Avery, F. Elliott. "Using Information Derived from Surveys," in Milton Rock (ed.), *Handbook of Wage and Salary Administration.* New York: McGraw Hill, 1972.

Belcher, David, and Atchison, Thomas. "Compensation for Work," in Robert Dubin (ed.), *Handbook of Work, Organization, and Society.* Chicago: Rand McNally, 1976.

Cheek, James. *How to Compensate Executives.* Homewood: Dow Jones—Irwin, 1974.

Engelke, Glenn. "Conducting Surveys," chap. 14 in Milton Rock (ed.), *Handbook of Wage and Salary Administration.* New York: McGraw Hill, 1972.

Geare, A. J. "Productivity from Scanlon-Type Plans," *Academy of Management Review,* July 1976, pp. 99–108.

Henderson, Richard. "The Changing Role of the Wage and Salary Administration," *Personnel,* November-December 1976, pp. 53–63.

Lawler, E. E. *Pay and Organizational Effectiveness.* New York: McGraw Hill, 1971.

Lawler, E. E. "Reward Systems," In Richard Hackman and Lloyd Suttle (eds.), *Improving Life at Work.* Santa Monica: Goodyear, 1977.

Lawler, Edward. "New Approaches to Pay: Innovations That Work," *Personnel,* September-October 1976, pp. 11–23.

Meyer, Herbert. "The Pay for Performance Dilemma," *Organizational Dynamics,* Winter 1975, pp. 39–50.

Nash, Allen, and Carroll, Stephen. *The Management of Compensation.* Monterrey: Brooks/Cole 1975.

Patten, Thomas. *Pay.* Chicago: Glencoe Press, 1977.

Rock, Milton. "Management Executive Compensation," In John Glover and Gerland Simon (eds.), *Chief Executives Handbook.* Homewood: Dow Jones —Irwin, 1976.

Sherman, George. "The Scanlon Plan: Its Capabilities for Productivity Improvement," *The Personnel Administrator,* July 1976, pp. 17–20.

Thomsen, David. "Calculating the Score on ESOPs: Winners and Losers," *Compensation Review* 7, 4 (1975): pp. 47–53.

11. BENEFITS AND SERVICES

Annual Survey by Chamber of Commerce on Fringe Benefits in *Nations Business.* Yearly.

Ashall, Robert, and Child, John. "Employee Services: People, Profits, or Parkinson?" *Personnel Management,* Fall 1972, pp. 18–22.

Chapman, Brad, and Otteman, Robert. "Employee Preferences for Various Compensation and Benefit Options," *The Personnel Administrator,* 1975.

Erlenborn, John. "Problems in Pension Plan Regulation," *Labor Law Journal* 27, 4 (April 1976): pp. 195–200.

Goode, Robert V. "Complications at the Cafeteria Checkout Lines," *Personnel* 51, 6 (November-December 1974): pp. 45–49.

Hopkins, Mary, and Wood, Marcia. "Who Wants to Retire?" *The Personnel Administrator,* October 1976, pp. 38–41.

Jewett, Matthew W. "Employee Benefits: The Need to Know," *Personnel Journal* 55, 1 (January 1976): pp. 18–22.

LaBerge, Ray. "Canadian Retirement Policies." *The Labour Gazette,* June 1976, pp. 316–19.

Meyer, Mitchell, and Fox, Harland. *Profile of Employee Benefits.* New York: The Conference Board, 1974.

Pension Facts. *Pension and Retirement Plans: A Review,* 1975, pp. 1–12.

Shaw, W. R. "Benefit Communication: Problem and Opportunity," *Canadian Personnel and Industrial Relations Journal,* January 1976, pp. 32–39.

Tilove, Robert. "A Twentieth Century Fund Report," *Public Employee Pension Funds.* New York: Columbia University Press, 1976.

U.S. Bureau of Labor Statistics. *Employee Compensation in the Nonfarm Economy.* Washington, D.C.: U.S. Government Printing Office, 1976.

Wahrobe, Thomas. *Aggressive Benefits Management.* New York: Amacon, 1976.

Walker, James. "Will Early Retirement Retire Early?" *Personnel* 53, 1 (January-February 1976): pp. 33–39.

Werther, William. "Variable Benefits: A New Approach to Fringe Benefits," *Arizona Business* 22, 0 (November 1975): pp. 18–22.

12. HEALTH AND SAFETY

Anderson, C. Richard. *OSHA and Accident Control Through Training.* New York: Industrial Press, 1975.

Ashford, Nicholas. *Crisis in the Workplace: Occupational Disease and Injury: A Report to the Ford Foundation.* Cambridge: The MIT Press, 1976, chaps. 1, 3.

Barnum, Darold, and Gleason, John. "A Penalty System to Discourage OSHA Violations," *Monthly Labor Review,* April 1976, pp. 30–31.

Burton, John. "Workers' Compensation Reform," *Labor Law Journal,* July 1976, pp. 399–406.

Ellis, Lee. "A Review of Research on Efforts to Promote Occupational Safety," *Journal of Safety Research* 7, 4 (December 1975): pp. 180–89.

Ettkin, Lawrence, and Chapman, J. Brad. "Is OSHA Effective in Reducing Industrial Injuries?" *Labor Law Journal,* July 1975, pp. 236–49.

OSHA. *Annual Report to the President,* Yearly.

Paul, Robert. "Workers' Compensation: An Adequate Employee Benefit?" *Academy of Management Review* 2 (1977).

U.S. Department of Labor, Bureau of Labor Statistics. *Occupational Safety and Health Statistics: Concepts and Methods,* BLS Report 438. Washington, D.C.: Bureau of Labor Statistics, 1975.

U.S. Department of Labor. *Injury Rates by Industry, 1975.* Washington, D.C.: Bureau of Labor Statistics, 1976.

U.S. Department of Labor. *Occupational Safety and Health Statistics of the Federal Government.* Washington, D.C.: Occupational Safety and Health Administration, 1976.

13. EQUAL EMPLOYMENT OPPORTUNITY/HUMAN RIGHTS

Affirmative Action Book. Reading, Mass: Addison-Wesley, 1976.

Decker, Louis, and Reed, Daniel. "Affirmative Action for the Handicapped," *Personnel,* May-June 1976.

EEOC, 11th Annual Report, January 1976. Washington, D.C.: Superintendent of Documents, U.S. Government Printing Office, 1976.

Flanagan, Robert. "Actual versus Potential Impact of Government Antidiscrimination Programs," *Industrial and Labor Relations Review,* 75–76, pp. 486–507.

Glazer, Nathan. *Affirmative Discrimination.* New York: Basic Books, 1976.

Heckman, James, and Wolpin, Kenneth. "Does the Contract Compliance Program Work? An Analysis of Chicago Data," *Industrial and Labor Relations Review,* 1975–76, pp. 544–64.

Lockwood, Howard. "Equal Employment Opportunities," chap. 4.7 in Dale Yoder and Herbert Heneman, Jr. (eds.), *Personnel and Industrial Relations Handbook.* Berea, Ohio: American Society for Personnel Administration, 1976.

Nisberg, J. "A Response to Affirmative Action Planning," *The Personnel Administrator* 20 (January 1975): pp. 27–31.

Pié, Bette. "Affirmative Action: Can the Voluntary Approach Work?" *The Business Quarterly*, Spring 1976, pp. 15–19.

Purcell, Theodore. "How G.E. Measures Managers in Fair Employment," *Harvard Business Review*, November-December, 1974, pp. 99–104.

14. LABOR RELATIONS AND GROUP REPRESENTATION

Anthony, Richard. *"When There's a Union at the Gate,"* Personnel, November-December 1976, pp. 47–52.

Bok, Derek, and Dunlop, John. *Collective Bargaining in the United States: An Overview.* New York: Simon and Schuster, 1970.

Bureau of National Affairs. *Labor Relations.* Washington, D.C., 1976.

Davey, Harold. "How Arbitrators Decide Cases," *Labor Law Journal* 25, 4 (April 1974): pp. 200–209.

Estey, Martin. *The Unions.* New York: Harcourt Brace, 1976.

Getman, Juluis, et al. *Union Representation Elections: Law and Reality.* New York: Russell Sage Foundation, 1976.

Goodfellow, Matthew. "How to Lose an NLRB Election," *The Personnel Administrator*, September 1976, pp. 40–45.

Richardson, Reed. *Collective Bargaining by Objectives.* Englewood Cliffs, N.J.: Prentice Hall, 1977.

Sloane, Arthur, and Whitney, Fred. *Labor Relations.* 3d ed. Englewood Cliffs, N.J.: Prentice Hall, 1977).

Werther, William, and Lockhart, Carol. *Labor Relations in the Health Professions.* Boston: Little Brown, 1975.

15. DISCIPLINE AND THE DIFFICULT EMPLOYEE

Follmann, Joseph. *Alcoholics and Business.* New York: Amacon, 1976.

Hemphill, Charles, Jr. *Management's Role In Loss Prevention.* New York: Amacon, 1976.

Hemphill, Charles, and Hemphill, Thomas. *The Secure Company.* Homewood: Dow Jones—Irwin, 1975, chap. 3.

Mager, Robert, and Pipe, Peter. *Analyzing Performance Problems.* Palo Alto, Calif.: Fearon Publishers, 1970.

Steinmetz, Lawrence. *Managing the Marginal and Unsatisfactory Performer.* Reading, Mass.: Addison-Wesley, 1969.

16. EVALUATION OF THE PERSONNEL FUNCTION

Bureau of National Affairs. *"Labor Policy and Practice: Personnel Management.* Washington, D.C., 1975.

Employee Absenteeism and Turnover, Personnel Policies Forum 106. Washington, D.C., Bureau of National Affairs, May 1974.

Lahiff, James. "The Exit Interview: Antiquated or Underrated?" *The Personnel Administrator,* May 1976, pp. 55–60.

Locke, Edwin. "The Nature and Causes of Job Satisfaction," in Marvin Dunnette (ed.), *Handbook of Industrial and Organizational Psychology.* Chicago: Rand McNally, 1976.

Odiorne, George. "Evaluating the Personnel Program." In Joseph Famularo (ed.), *Handbook of Modern Personnel Administration,* chap. 8. New York: McGraw Hill, 1972.

Peterson, Donald, and Malone, Robert. "The Personnel Effectiveness Grid PEG," *Human Resource Management,* Winter 1975, pp. 10–21.

Index

INDEX OF CASES